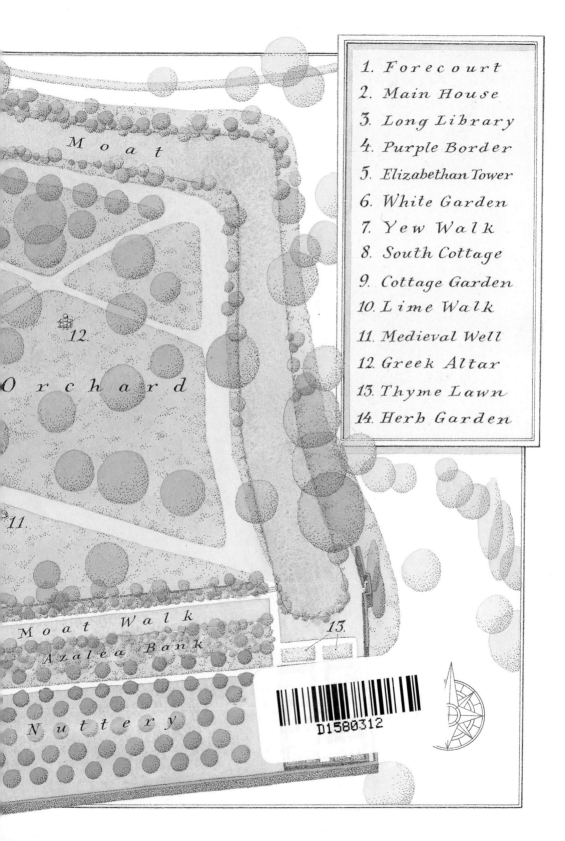

Moat

12.

Orchard

11.

Moat Walk

Azalea Bank

Nuttery

13.

D1580312

IN YOUR GARDEN

and

IN YOUR GARDEN AGAIN

Vita Sackville-West

IN YOUR GARDEN

and

IN YOUR GARDEN AGAIN

Introduced by

Victoria Glendinning

London

THE FOLIO SOCIETY

2010

In Your Garden and *In Your Garden Again* were first published
separately in 1951 and 1953 respectively by Michael Joseph Ltd.
This Folio Society edition is based on the text of the first editions,
with minor emendations.

This edition published by The Folio Society,
44 Eagle Street, London WC1R 4FS
www.foliosociety.com

This edition is published by arrangement
with Frances Lincoln Ltd.

Binding: Sissinghurst silhouette, based on a
photograph of the Elizabethan Tower at Sissinghurst
Castle garden (© *David Dixon/NTPL*)

Endpaper: Garden plan by Neil Gower, based
on a plan of Sissinghurst Castle garden
prepared by Christine and Stuart Page

Typeset in Baskerville at The Folio Society.
Printed on Abbey Wove paper at Martins the Printers Ltd,
Berwick-upon-Tweed and bound by Hunter & Foulis,
Edinburgh in blocked and printed cloth

CONTENTS

CONTENTS

IN YOUR GARDEN AGAIN

ILLUSTRATIONS

vii

The Elizabethan Tower at Sissinghurst Castle Garden, Kent. Photograph by David Dixon, December 2007. (© *David Dixon/NTPL*)

View through an arch to the Yew Walk, Sissinghurst Castle Garden, Kent. Photograph by Jonathan Buckley, May 2007. (© *Jonathan Buckley/NTPL*)

The Rose Garden at Sissinghurst Castle Garden, Kent. Photograph by Jonathan Buckley, June 2007. (© *Jonathan Buckley/NTPL*)

BETWEEN PAGES 258 AND 259

The Cottage Garden at Sissinghurst Castle Garden, Kent. Photograph by David Dixon, 2005. (© *David Dixon/NTPL*)

The Nuttery at Sissinghurst Castle Garden, Kent. Photograph by Jonathan Buckley, April 2007. (© *Jonathan Buckley/NTPL*)

View from the Old Garden at Hidcote Manor, Gloucestershire. Photograph by Stephen Robson, May 2003. (© *Stephen Robson/NTPL*)

The pond at Hidcote Manor, Gloucestershire. Photograph by Nick Meers, July 1994. (© *Nick Meers/NTPL*)

The White Garden at Hidcote Manor, Gloucestershire. Photograph (detail) by Nick Meers, June 1994. (© *Nick Meers/NTPL*)

INTRODUCTION

Reading this collection of Vita Sackville-West's gardening articles from the *Observer* is like having a conversation with her. 'Is that a good idea?' she asks, as she considers training an Abutilon as a standard. 'I have not tried it yet.' She is relaxed and confidential. 'What, I wonder, do you feel about rock gardens? Personally, I am against them.' She speaks directly and personally, inviting response, seeking advice as well as giving it. As a result, she received thousands of letters – more than five hundred in one week when she wrote about the strawberry grape. People told her that they changed from *The Sunday Times* to the *Observer* just because of her articles.

This book puts together two volumes of articles, selected by herself. *In Your Garden* was published in 1951 and *In Your Garden Again* in 1953. She began writing the weekly articles in 1946 and kept them up for fifteen years, so what is here represents only a tiny fraction of her output. But since the garden at Sissinghurst had reached its first peak of perfection – though no garden-owner ever feels perfection is reached – in the 1950s, it turned out to be a good moment to have captured the essence. The great interest for us, today, is to take a look at what that essence was, to pinpoint the differences between then and now, and to decide whether Vita Sackville-West still has something to teach us.

Like most children, she had her own garden-patch at Knole, where she grew up. But in childhood, it was the great and ancient house itself which caught her romantic imagination, rather than the garden. She began her gardening in her early twenties at Long Barn, the first country home she had with her husband Harold Nicolson, only a couple of miles from Knole. Writing and gardening were to be the occupations and preoccupations of her whole life, and the two merged and reinforced one another.

One difference between then and now is that even at Long Barn she had plenty of help, the wages paid by her mother – for not to employ gardeners, for a woman of her class and generation, would have been as strange as not having a cook. Before the war, at Sissinghurst, she had three full-time gardeners plus a part-timer. She began gardening at a propitious time, when the massed bedding of bright annuals beloved of the late Victorians was falling out of fashion in favour of naturalistic and imaginative designs, cottage-garden plantings, one-colour gardens, and garden 'rooms', all concepts that

ix

she was to adopt herself. She knew these new gardens and their creators, including Miss Jekyll at Munstead in Surrey, and went many times to see Lawrence Johnston and his influential garden, Hidcote, in Gloucestershire. (Her 1949 article about Hidcote, written for *The Journal of the Royal Horticultural Society*, is included in this volume.)

It was at Sissinghurst that Vita came into her own. Sissinghurst was really the love of her life – the place where she became more and more reclusive as she grew older, and where, after her two sons left home, she was mostly alone, or alone with one of her long sequence of women lovers. Her husband Harold Nicolson was a diplomat, and often overseas where she only rarely joined him; and, when he gave up diplomacy for writing and politics, he always spent the working week in London. Although the garden was very much 'her thing', Harold was deeply involved in its development. He was passionately concerned about its structure, planning and design, and she with plants and planting. It was an ideal partnership.

When they first saw Sissinghurst in April 1930, the land around the ruinous group of ancient buildings was a tangle of 'old bedsteads, ploughshares, old cabbage-stalks, old broken-down earth closets, old matted wire and mountains of sardine tins, all muddled up in a tangle of bindweed, nettles and ground elder' – but she and Harold had fallen in love with the place. The first thing she ever planted there was a lavender bush, and among the rubble they found an old, indestructible, dark-red gallica rose, 'the Sissinghurst Rose'.

By early 1931 there were massive plantings of daffodils and roses, and by the end of the following year the main layout of the gardens was completed, even though there were several expensive changes of landscaping and design. But the death of her mother released family money, and the profits from her bestseller *The Edwardians* meant that Vita could afford to be ambitious, ordering shrubs and trees in dozens. By 1938 the garden was good enough to be opened to the public for charity. Ten years later, it was open not only for charity; the shillings in the box went towards what Vita called her 'wages fund'. In spite of her need for seclusion and privacy, and her avoidance of social life, she never resented the garden visitors in the least, but made herself informally available for questions and discussion, informing readers in May 1948 that her garden would be open 'every day until the end of October'.

When she began writing these weekly pieces the year after the end of World War II, she was in her mid-fifties. Even though her long and lovely poem *The Garden* had just won the Heinemann prize, she was uncertain about her achievement as an author and had, during the war, got into the habit of drinking too much. She was, in fact, rather depressed. In the last year of the war she began to have trouble with her back. Arthritis was diagnosed, which later affected her hands. In the autumn of 1946, when her gardeners were planting 'thousands of narcissus' in the orchard, she was, for the first time, unable to work alongside them. She also had a heart condition, which she did her best to ignore. But her life as a practical, hands-on gardener was becoming problematic, which made her very sad. The success of the gardening articles did much for her self-esteem and, whether she liked it or not – for she was a bit ambivalent about this – they brought her more fame and popularity with the wider public than did any of her poems or novels.

There had been a great upsurge of vegetable-growing during the war, stimulated by national shortages and the government's 'Dig for Victory' campaign. Although the usual vegetables for the house were grown at Sissinghurst, Vita was only interested in the unusual – calabrese, petit pois, mange-tout, Hamburg parsley – and she urged vegetable gardeners to become more enterprising. But her articles are, overwhelmingly, about flowers and shrubs and how to deploy them, and about her own ideas and her own vision, based on her experience. Even though austerity, and rationing, went on for years in Britain after the end of the war, her approach struck a chord in the new and more optimistic post-war world.

The essence of her gardening lies in the sureness of her vision. She is passionate about what she likes and what she does not. 'I like generosity wherever I find it, whether in gardens or elsewhere.' She likes mass plantings, and all lavishness and 'exaggeration' – except when it comes to exaggerated, 'improved' blooms. She hates anything inflated, double varieties, and gaudy colours; she hates the ubiquitous roses American Pillar and Dorothy Perkins, she hates hybrid tea roses – 'neat little, hard little, tight little scrimpy dwarfs' – and loves old roses grown as shrubs, 'species roses, and the great wild shrubby roses flinging themselves about'. She loves low, small plants, and 'rugs and mats and pillows' of herbs and Alpines. She hates park-bench green, and advocates whitewashing terra-cotta flower-pots, and painting barrels the colour of milky coffee. Acknowledging that there is snobbery among gardeners as well as among 'other sections of the community', she defines it as a rejection of the 'trite', the lurid and the obvious. She discourages bad taste, advising one reader against plaster gnomes and toadstools, but tactfully. Even though she wrote elsewhere that the first virtue in gardening was 'ruthlessness', she approaches plants as she does people, both as she says benefiting from 'a little extra kindliness and understanding'.

And then, we have the tentative beginnings of the White Garden. 'It is amusing to make one-colour gardens,' she wrote in January 1950. 'For my

xi

own part, I am trying to make a grey, green, and white garden.' She goes on to expand the concept and list the plants that will fulfil it. 'It may be a terrible failure.' (She had actually thought of it ten years before, and described the planting plan to Harold; he had recently played it back to her as his own idea. That is how marriage works.) The White Garden became Sissinghurst's most famous feature, copied in lesser gardens all over the country.

She had written about gardening before; *Some Flowers*, part of which is included in this volume, dates from 1937, and in 1938 she had contributed 'Country Notes' to the *New Statesman*. ('Country Notes' were collected up into a book in 1939.) Nor was she altogether alone in pioneering gardening journalism. From 1946, the year in which she began at the *Observer*, C. H. Middleton had a regular column in the *Daily Express* (and on radio, *Gardeners' Question Time*, still with us, started in 1947). She is writing, in the *Observer*, for a middle-class audience, many of whom would have employed a gardener, but few of whom would have had her scope or resources. She tries hard to address those readers who only have small front gardens – although to her a 'small garden' really means 'anything from half an acre to two acres' – and responds imaginatively to those wanting to make special displays for the Festival of Britain in 1951 and the coronation of Queen Elizabeth in 1953. For the latter, she suggests planting a mulberry tree 'that will grow with her reign until, as we hope, she attains the eventual age of her great-great-grandmother towards the year 2008'. She draws the line at giving advice about hanging baskets and window-boxes – she is not a 'town gardener'.

The popularity of her articles added enormously to the number of garden visitors to Sissinghurst. Enthusiasts and personal friends of the owners had always visited great gardens, but this was something else. By the mid-1950s, there were sometimes traffic jams in the approach to the house, and she had to provide WCs. More than half a century on, garden-visiting is a national pastime, and facilities of all kinds are provided, and expected. In Vita's time all this was new.

Sissinghurst, largely through her articles, contributed to the concept of garden-visiting as a 'good day out' and, equally importantly, to the mushroom-growth of the gardening industry to cater for the enthusiasms of the hobby gardener and the informed amateur. Suppliers and garden centres today market year-round container-grown plants often obtained from elsewhere. But in the years when Vita was writing these articles, serious gardeners raised most of their own stock from seed. Nurseries raised their own plants and sold them on when sufficiently mature, and in dormancy. 'Catalogues arrive by every post' and, 'carried away and astray', she regularly over-orders.

She shares her 'bright ideas' and garden fantasies, visualising new plant combinations and imagining what one *might* do – which has a poignancy, given that her arthritis condemned her to a good deal of dream-gardening, even though she remained wholly in command of everything that was done outside, every day.

Gardening articles today often tell the reader of specialist growers for a particular plant, but not the cost. Then, it was the other way round. It was considered unacceptable, when Vita was writing, to advertise in a newspaper feature the names of nurseries and seedsmen (though it was all right to name them when the articles appeared in book form); but she often tells her readers the precise prices of plants she recommends, which would be unrealistic nowadays, since sources are so numerous and prices vary enormously depending on quality and the supplier.

Another difference is the attitude to wild flowers. Vita, when she was young, would cheerfully dig up wild flowers to replant in the garden. But around 1950 she becomes aware of the widespread use of selective weed-killers, endangering wild species in the fields and hedgerows, and changes her tune. One might collect seeds, 'but please do not dig them up'. She continues however to advocate digging up wild cherry seedlings from the woods – and tells how she gets into trouble for it.

So how useful, for today's gardener, is this volume? Is its interest merely antiquarian? I don't think so. For a start, it is compelling reading, hard to put down. And it is fascinating and a little uncanny to share in the evolution of a garden style that would dominate the second half of the twentieth century. Every reader will still find something in it that he or she has been looking for – in my own case, some shrewd words about pond-gardening, and about how to manage the mimosa *Acacia dealbata*.

This book also has literary value. Vita was a poet, and tosses in unusual words which send one to the dictionary: rathe, gridelin, foison. She invents a new between-seasons season, and calls it 'wint-pring'. She quotes from Marvell, Milton, Shakespeare. Every now and then there is a rashly lyrical phrase – a 'rabble incarnadine' of autumn foliage, for example. For readers of her novels, there is a queer echo from her *Seducers in Ecuador* (1924) in which her hero wore coloured spectacles which transformed the world and enabled him to inhabit other people's fantasies; in July 1951 she describes the 'magical effect' on her perceptions when she tries on the 'amber-coloured spectacles' of a man visiting her garden. And then there are her aphorisms, which stick in the mind. 'The good gardener is the gardener who makes experiments.' 'Whatever looks right *is* right.' 'Sow thinly and thin out remorselessly.'

She is beguilingly modest, sharing her failures. Pondering whether or not to divide *Iris pumila*, 'I have come to the conclusion, after many years of sometimes sad experience, that you cannot come to any conclusion at all.' Even though she believes that 'practical experience is worth more than many pages of print', she is aware that although she has the practical experience she has no formal training, and is not a 'scientific gardener'. (In 1956 this woman, who lectured at the Royal Horticultural Society and had already influenced a generation, actually signed up for a correspondence course in horticulture.) She does not pretend it was easy to churn out a piece every week: 'Not for the first time', she writes in January 1953, 'I find myself at a loss to know what to write about' – and turns again to the catalogues, and wish-lists of unusual plants. It is little wonder that when in 1961, after a bout of bronchitis, she finally gave up the articles it was with 'great relief', as she wrote in her diary. She died in June of the following year.

VICTORIA GLENDINNING

In Your Garden

Foreword

It was with some reluctance that I agreed to the publication of these snippets in book-form. They were all very well as they appeared, weekly or at longer intervals according to the space available in the columns of *The Observer*; but when it came to dressing them up into the solidity of a real book with stiff covers and the expectation of a place to itself on somebody's shelves, I quailed at their incompleteness, their repetitiveness, and also at the haphazard way they had been dotted about the years.

Two problems confronted me. Should I amplify them or leave them to stand just as they had appeared? And should I rearrange them, grouping them under months and seasons, although I had not always written them on the seasonal system? In the end I compromised, making a few additions where it seemed desirable and putting the articles into chronological order.

It will readily be understood that neither *The Observer* nor any other journal could have allowed the 'free advertisement' of publishing the names and addresses of nurserymen and seedsmen. This led to considerable exasperation on the part of my readers; 'What is the good of recommending these out-of-the-way things unless you tell us where to obtain them?' It led also to a formidable increase in my correspondence; I think two thousand inquiries arising out of one article was the record, but on several other occasions a thousand letters arrived, done up in bundles of fifty, tied round with string. I trust and believe that I answered them all. If anyone was overlooked, I take this opportunity of offering an apology.

Here in this book, where no such restrictions prevail, I have added most of the appropriate names and addresses, and have also supplied a short general list in an appendix. This does not mean that I have attempted to give a comprehensive list of all the nurserymen or seedsmen in our country. It merely means an indication of where you can get shrubs, trees, bulbs, roses, flower-seeds, and whatever you want.

I should like to express my thanks to *The Observer*, both for printing my articles in the first instance and for allowing me to reprint them here; to *The Spectator* for permission to include *A Little Flower Book*; and to the Editor of the Royal Horticultural Society's Journal, for permission to include a note on the garden at Hidcote Manor. I cannot, alas, extend my thanks to

Messrs Cobden Sanderson, the original publishers of *Some Flowers* in 1937, since that most estimable firm went out of business some years ago.

Some of the essays in that book are reprinted here, on pages 115–45.

V.S.-W.
Sissinghurst Castle,
Cranbrook, Kent.

January

Some generous friend may have given you a plant-token for Christmas, and you may be wondering, as I am now wondering, how best to expend it. A plant-token is a real gift from heaven; it represents an extravagance one might hesitate to commit for oneself; a luxury, an extra, a treat. One has no alternative, for, unlike a cheque, one cannot virtuously put it to the reduction of one's overdraft. There is nothing to be done with it except to buy a plant.

Could one do better than choose the autumn-flowering cherry, *Prunus subhirtella Autumnalis*? In England it might more properly be called winter-flowering, for it does not open until November, but in its native Japan it begins a month earlier; hence its autumnal name. Here, if you pick it in the bud and put it in a warm room or a greenhouse, you can have the white sprays in flower six weeks before Christmas, and it will go on intermittently, provided you do not allow the buds to be caught by too severe a frost, until March.

It is perhaps too ordinary to appeal to the real connoisseur – a form of snobbishness I always find hard to understand in gardeners – but its wands of white are of so delicate and graceful a growth, whether on the tree or in a vase, that it surely should not be condemned on that account. It is of the easiest cultivation, content with any reasonable soil, and it may be grown either as a standard or a bush; I think the bush is preferable, because then you get the flowers at eye-level instead of several feet above your head – though it can also look very frail and youthful, high up against the pale blue of a winter sky.

How precious are the flowers of mid-winter! Not the hot-house things, nor even the forced trusses of lilac, most of which, I understand, come from Holland, but the genuine toughs that for some strange reason elect to display themselves out of doors at this time of year. The Winter-sweet opens its yellow starfish against a wall, and the twisted ribbons of the Witch-hazel are disentangling themselves on their leafless branches. Both of these sweet-scented winter flowerers should qualify for a choice with the plant-token.

Garrya elliptica is not so often seen, though it has been known in this country since 1818; its nickname, the Tassel Bush, describes it best, for it hangs itself from December onwards with soft grey-green catkins eight or ten inches in length, like bunches of enormous caterpillars among the very dark leaves.

Some people think it dismal, but a large bush is an imposing sight if you have the patience to wait for it. It does require patience, for it dislikes being moved and, therefore, must be planted small; also you must insist upon getting a male plant, or there will not be any catkins. The female plant will give you only bunches of black fruits. As it will thrive against a north wall, however, where few other things will thrive, it may well be left there to take its time without occupying the space wanted for something else.

January 15, 1950

Someone has been pleading with me to put in a good word for Sweet-briar. I do so most willingly, for a hedge of Sweet-briar is one of the most desirable things in any garden.

It is thorny enough to keep out intruders, should it be needed as a boundary protection; in early summer it is as pretty as the dog-rose, with its pale pink single flowers; in autumn it turns itself into a sheer wall of scarlet hips; and on moist muggy evenings after rain the scent is really and truly strong in the ambient air. You do not need to crush a leaf between your fingers to provoke the scent: it swells out towards you of its own accord, as you walk past, like a great sail filling suddenly with a breeze off those Spice Islands which Columbus hoped to find.

These are many virtues to claim, but even so we may add to them. It is the Eglantine of the poets, if you like that touch of romance. True, Milton seems to have confused it with something else, probably the honeysuckle:

> . . . through the Sweet-briar or the Vine,
> Or the twisted Eglantine . . .

but what does that matter? it is pedantic to be so precise, and we should do better to take a hint from Milton and plant a *mixed* hedge of honeysuckle and Sweet-briar, with perhaps an ornamental vine twining amongst them – the purple-leafed vine, *Vitis vinifera purpurea*, would look sumptuous among the red hips in October.

I have never seen a hedge of this composition; but why not? Ideas come to one; and it remains only to put them into practice. The nearest that I have got is to grow the common *Clematis Jackmanii* into my Sweet-briar, planting the clematis on the north side of the hedge, where the roots are cool and shaded and the great purple flowers come wriggling through southwards into the sun. It looks fine, and the briar gives the clematis just the twiggy kind of support it needs.

Sweet-briar is a strong grower, but is often blamed for going thin and scraggy towards the roots. I find that you can correct this weakness by planting your hedge in the first instance against a system of post-and-wire, and subsequently tying-in the long shoots to the posts and wire instead of pruning them. Tie the shoots horizontally, or bend them downwards if need be, thus obtaining a thick, dense growth, which well compensates you for the initial trouble of setting up the posts and the wire. They will last for years, and so will the briar.

The common Sweet-briar will cost you 2s. 6d. to 3s. a plant, and the single plant will spread, horizontally, twenty feet or more. The Penzance hybrid briars are more expensive, 4s. 6d. to 5s. each. *Amy Robsart*, with deep rose flowers, and *Lady Penzance*, with coppery-yellow flowers, are particularly to be recommended.

January 22, 1950

It is amusing to make one-colour gardens. They need not necessarily be large, and they need not necessarily be enclosed, though the enclosure of a dark hedge is, of course, ideal. Failing this, any secluded corner will do, or even a strip of border running under a wall, perhaps the wall of the house. The site chosen must depend upon the general lay-out, the size of the garden, and the opportunities offered. And if you think that one colour would be monotonous, you can have a two- or even a three-colour, provided the colours are happily married, which is sometimes easier of achievement in the vegetable than in the human world. You can have, for instance, the blues and the purples, or the yellows and the bronzes, with their attendant mauves and orange, respectively. Personal taste alone will dictate what you choose.

For my own part, I am trying to make a grey, green, and white garden. This is an experiment which I ardently hope may be successful, though I doubt it. One's best ideas seldom play up in practice to one's expectations, especially in gardening, where everything looks so well on paper and in the catalogues, but fails so lamentably in fulfilment after you have tucked your plants into the soil. Still, one hopes.

My grey, green, and white garden will have the advantage of a high yew hedge behind it, a wall along one side, a strip of box edging along another side, and a path of old brick along the fourth side. It is, in fact, nothing more than a fairly large bed, which has now been divided into halves by a short path of grey flagstones terminating in a rough wooden seat. When you sit on this seat, you will be turning your backs to the yew hedge, and from there I hope you will survey a low sea of grey clumps of foliage, pierced here and there with

7

tall white flowers. I visualize the white trumpets of dozens of Regale lilies, grown three years ago from seed, coming up through the grey of southernwood and artemisia and cotton-lavender, with grey-and-white edging plants such as *Dianthus Mrs Sinkins* and the silvery mats of *Stachys lanata*, more familiar and so much nicer under its English names of Rabbit's Ears or Saviour's Flannel. There will be white pansies, and white peonies, and white irises with their grey leaves . . . at least, I hope there will be all these things. I don't want to boast in advance about my grey, green, and white garden. It may be a terrible failure. I wanted only to suggest that such experiments are worth trying, and that you can adapt them to your own taste and your own opportunities.

All the same, I cannot help hoping that the great ghostly barn-owl will sweep silently across a pale garden, next summer, in the twilight – the pale garden that I am now planting, under the first flakes of snow.

January 14, 1951

January seems the wrong time of year to think of planting bulbs, but there are some which should be planted in March or April, so this is the moment to order them. I would recommend the Kaffir Lily, officially called *Schizostylis coccinea*, with its pretty pink variety called *Mrs Hegarty*. It resembles a minia-ture gladiolus, and it has the advantage, from our point of view, of flowering in October and November, when it is difficult to find anything out of doors for indoor picking.

The Kaffir Lily will cost you anything from seven shillings to eight or nine shillings a dozen. One dozen will give you a good return, if you plant them in the right sort of place and look after them properly. Planting them in the right sort of place means giving them a light, well-drained soil in full sun. Looking after them properly means that you must give them plenty of water during their growing period, when their leaves are throwing up, rather as you would treat an amaryllis, the Belladonna lily. You should realize that they are not entirely hardy, especially in our colder counties; but they are reasonably hardy in most parts of England; a thin quilt of bracken or dry leaves next winter will keep them safe for years. It is remarkable what a little covering of bracken will do for bulbs. Speaking for myself, I cannot imagine anything less adequate than a draughty scatter of bracken on a frosty night; give me a thick eiderdown and blankets every time, and a hot-water bottle, too, but bulbs which are buried deep down in the earth will keep themselves warm and safe with the thinnest cover from frost above them.

Another bulb, or corm, you should order now and plant in March is *Tigridia*, the Mexican Tiger-flower. This is a wildly beautiful exotic-looking thing. It throws only one flower at a time, and that flower lasts only one day, but it is of such superlative beauty and is succeeded by so many other blooms, day after day, that it is well worth the 3s. 9d. you will have to pay for a dozen of mixed varieties. A sunny place is essential, and, like dahlias, they should be lifted and stored through the winter.

January 21, 1951

This is the time to think of ordering bulbs of the autumn-flowering crocus. If the nurseryman knows his job, they will not be sent to you until midsummer or even August, but it is advisable to order now in case the supply runs out, or, to put it in more familiar language, get in at the top of the queue.

We are so well accustomed to associating crocuses with spring that it may come as a surprise to some people to learn that some sorts of crocus will flower with as vernal an appearance from September onwards into November. *Crocus speciosus* is one that should be ordered now; it is cheap to buy, 2s. 6d. a dozen, 17s. 6d. a hundred; I bought a dozen last year and how lovely they were, chalices the colour of Parma violets rejoicing my autumnal heart, coming out in September so unexpectedly to turn autumn into spring. *C. speciosus Cassiopea* comes out later, October–November; *C. speciosus globosus* in November, the latest of all. These are both a little more expensive than the type, at 3s. 6d. a dozen; but do plant even a little patch of six or twelve, in a special corner.

Then there is *Crocus sativus*, the Saffron crocus, a pinkish-lilac colour. How difficult these colour descriptions are! This flowers in October, and costs from 2s. 6d. to 3s. a dozen. If you want something more unusual, there is *C. asturicus atropurpureus*, dark violet, which in a mild winter might go on flowering into December, 4s. a dozen. I am sorry these small things should have to suffer such gigantic names; but when you work it out, you find that *Crocus asturicus atropurpureus* merely means the very dark purple crocus, native to the Asturias province of northern Spain.

I have by no means exhausted the list, and have not even touched on the *Colchicum*, which many people are apt to confuse with the autumn-flowering crocus. The only point in common, for those who do not want to be bothered with botanical differences,* is that they should both be ordered now for August delivery. Owing to what we have been taught to call shortages of newsprint, I shall have to leave the *Colchicum* till next Sunday, when I can

---

* If you do want to be bothered with botanical differences, the crocus belongs to the family *Iridaceae* (irises) and the *Colchicum* to the family *Liliaceae* (lilies). Confusion is increased by the fact that *Colchicum autumnale* is popularly known as the Meadow Saffron, and *Crocus sativus* as the Saffron crocus.

devote my four hundred words to this most lovely and surprising race. Messrs Wallace, Messrs Barr, and Mr Ralph Cusack all have good lists of the crocus and the *Colchicum*. Their addresses will be found at the end of this book.

I have no means of thanking the anonymous sender of a registered packet addressed to me; but if he should happen to be a reader of these articles, will he please accept my unspeakable thanks? He (or she?) will understand.

January 28, 1951
The colchicums, as I said, should be ordered now for summer delivery. They are more expensive than the crocuses, ranging from 6s. 6d. to 10s. 6d. a dozen, but being larger they make more effect. A drift of them, especially in grass, is a brilliant sight in September and October; they should not be planted on a lawn, as the big leaves which appear in spring or early summer are unsightly; and do not plant them where sheep or cattle graze, as they are poisonous to animals. The ideal place is an orchard, where their pink or lilac cups will coincide with the apples hanging overhead, but if the grass is rough remember to cut it just before the flowers break through or they will be lost to sight. The end of August is a safe time for this operation.

They do not object to a little light shade, such as would be thrown by the fruit trees, but they are equally happy in full sun. It may surprise you that a bulb planted in July or August should leap into flower so soon afterwards, and it may surprise you even more to find that when the bulbs arrive in their paper bag they should already be showing a bleached-looking growth, rather like celery. Do not worry. Cut a hole in the turf, drop the bulbs in, two to three inches deep, stamp the turf down again, and leave them to do what nature intended.

Speciosum and *autumnale* are both good varieties, rosy in colour; there are white forms of these also. *Bornmulleri* and *byzantinus* are magnificent; and one of the finest is the hybrid *Lilac Wonder*, rather more expensive at 10s. 6d. a dozen. Other very fine hybrids are *Rosy Dawn*, bright pink; and *The Giant*, a softer pink; and you can also obtain a mixture of the new hybrids at 10s. 6d. a dozen. I do not care so much for the double-flowered kind, *autumnale roseum plenum*, since I think the beauty of a colchicum or of a crocus, apart from the colour, lies in the pure lines of the goblet-like shape; this, like many other things, is a matter of taste.*

A word of practical advice: put a ring of slug-bait round each clump as soon as the pale noses appear, and be quick about it, because the pale nose of today is the full flower of tomorrow. Otherwise you will wonder how anyone could ever recommend a thing of such rags and tatters.

* Messrs Wallace, and Messrs Barr and R. Cusack all have good lists of colchicum.

February

In response to many requests, I pursue the subject of plants that will flower out of doors during the winter months. *Chimonanthus fragrans*, in English the Winter-sweet, should have a place of honour. Although it was introduced from China so long ago as 1766, it is not often seen now except in the older gardens, and in honesty I should warn purchasers of young plants that it will not begin to flower until it is five or six years old. But it is worth waiting for. Extremely sweet-scented, even in the cold open air, long sprigs loaded with the strange maroon-and-yellow flowers can be cut all through January and February; it lasts for two or three weeks in water, especially if you smash the stems with a hammer, a hint which applies to all hard-wooded growth. The Winter-sweet will eventually reach to a height of ten feet or more; it is happiest grown against a wall for protection, but I have seen it growing into a big bush in the open in a garden in Kent – not my garden, alas!

The text-books instruct us to prune it hard back to the old wood immediately after it has finished flowering; I obediently followed these instructions for years, and got nothing but some truncated little miseries in consequence; then I rebelled, as all good gardeners should rebel when they find their own experience going against the text-book, and left my Winter-sweet unpruned one year, with the rich reward of longer sprays to cut for indoors. I fancy that this extravagant cutting will provide all the pruning that is necessary.

If you are the sort of gardener that likes raising your own nursery stock, leave a couple of sprays to develop their gourd-shaped fruit, and sow the seed when ripe in a pot or pan. It germinates very obligingly.

I hesitate to insult readers of *The Observer* by recommending the merits of so well known a plant as the winter-flowering jasmine, *Jasminum nudiflorum*, introduced from China in 1844. We all grow it now. I picked long sprays of it on December 4th and all the buds opened indoors in water, lasting for several weeks. The flowers and buds are not very frost-resistant out of doors; so here is a hint: grow a plant of it in a large pot; leave the pot standing out of doors all summer and autumn; bring the pot indoors in November; train the shoots round some bamboo canes; stand the pot on the floor in a corner of your room; don't forget to water it; put a large plate or bowl under the pot or your carpet will suffer; and having done all this you may confidently expect a golden fountain for two or three months unaffected by the weather outside.

In a mild season the Algerian Iris, generally called *Iris stylosa*, but, more correctly, *Iris unguicularis*, should start flowering in November and continue until March. They vary in colour from a lavender blue to a deep purple (there is also a white form) and are from six to eight inches high.

The clumps should be planted at the foot of a south wall, full sun, in the most gritty soil imaginable; they love old mortar rubble, gravel, ashes, broken bricks; they flourish on a starvation diet; hate being transplanted or otherwise disturbed; are loved by slugs and snails, so be sure to put down some Meta-and-bran, and pick them while still as closely furled as an unbroken flag round its flag-staff. They will then unfurl in the warmth of your room; you can watch them doing it.*

February 1948

It is agreeable sometimes to turn for a change from the dutifully practical aspects of gardening to the consideration of something strange, whether we can hope to grow it for ourselves or not. A wet January evening seemed just the time for such an indulgence of dreams, and in an instant I found my room (which hitherto had boasted only a few modest bulbs in bowls) filling up with flowers of the queerest colours, shapes, and habits. The first batch to appear, thus miraculously conjured out of the air, were all of that peculiar blue-green which one observes in verdigris on an old copper, in a peacock's feather, on the back of a beetle, or in the sea where the shallows meet the deep.

First came a slender South African, *Ixia viridiflora*, with green flowers shot with cobalt blue and a purple splotch: this I had once grown in a very gritty pan in a cold greenhouse, and was pleased to see again. Then came the tiny sea-green Persian iris, only three inches high, which I had seen piercing its native desert but had never persuaded into producing a single flower here. Then came *Delphinium macrocentrum*, an East African, which I had never seen at all, but which is said to rival the Chilean *Puya alpestris* in colouring.

Puya alpestris I knew. A ferocious-looking plant, and reluctant. Seven years had I cherished that thing in a pot, before it finally decided to flower. Then it threw up a spike and astonished everybody with its wicked-looking peacock trumpets and orange anthers, and side-shoots on which, apparently, hummingbirds were supposed to perch and pollinate the flower.

And now here it was again, in my room, this time accompanied by the

* See pp. 16–17.

humming-birds which had been lamentably absent when I had flowered it after seven years. There were quite a lot of birds in my room by now, as well as flowers. For *Strelitzia reginae* had also arrived, escorted by the little African sun-birds which perch and powder their breast-feathers with its pollen. It is rare for plants to choose birds as pollinators instead of insects; and here were two of them. *Strelitzia reginae* itself looked like a bird, a wild, crested, pointed bird, floating on an orange boat under spiky sails of blue and orange. Although it had been called regina after Queen Charlotte the consort of George III, I preferred it under its other name, the Bird of Paradise Flower.

Then, as a change to homeliness, came clumps of the old primroses I had tried so hard to grow in careful mixtures of leaf-mould and loam, but here they were, flourishing happily between the cracks of the floorboards. Jack-in-the-Green, Prince Silverwings, Galligaskins, Tortoiseshell, Cloth of Gold; and as I saw them there in a wealth I had never been able to achieve, I remembered that the whole primula family was gregarious in its tastes and hated the loneliness of being one solitary, expensive little plant. They like huddling together, unlike the Lichens, which demand so little company that they will grow (in South America at any rate) strung out along the high isolation of telegraph wires.

There seemed indeed no end to the peculiarities of plants, whether they provided special perches for the convenience of their visitors, or turned carnivorous like the Pitcher-plants. Why was it that the Vine grew from left to right in the Northern hemisphere, but refused to grow otherwise than from right to left in the Southern? Why was the poppy called *Macounii* found only on one tiny Arctic island in the Behring Sea and nowhere else in the world? How had it come there in the first place? In a room now overcrowded with blooms of the imagination such speculations flowed easily, to the exclusion of similar speculations on the equally curious behaviour of men.

The walls of the room melted away, giving place to a garden such as the Emperors of China once enjoyed, vast in extent, varied in landscape, a garden in which everything throve and the treasures of the earth were collected in beauty and brotherhood. But a log fell in the fire: a voice said: 'This is the BBC Home Service; here is the news,' and I awoke.

February 5, 1950

The hardy border carnation has long been popular, and with the introduction of the Chabaud carnation its popularity has increased. M. Chabaud was a botanist from Toulon who, in about 1870, raised this hybrid between the old perennial carnation and the annual kind. The seeds of the original Chabaud carnation are now on sale in this country, and certainly ought to be grown by every gardener who has half-a-dozen seed-boxes to spare.

There are two sorts, the annual and the perennial. The annuals are divided into the *Giant Chabaud*, the *Enfant de Nice*, and the *Compact Dwarf*. They should be sown in February or March in boxes of well-mixed leaf-mould, soil and sharp sand. They require no heat; but in frosty weather the seedlings should be protected. Do not over-water. Keep them on the dry side. Plant them out when they are large enough, in a sunny place with good drainage. (I think myself that they look best in a bed by themselves, not mixed in with other plants.) Their colour range is wide: yellow, white, red, purple, pink, and striped. They are extremely prolific, and if sown in February should be in flower from July onwards. If you care to take the trouble, they can be lifted in October and potted, to continue flowering under glass or indoors on a window-sill, i.e. safely away from frost, well into the winter.

The perennial sort, which is perfectly hardy, should be sown March–June and planted out this summer to flower during many summers to come. Those gardeners who appreciate a touch of historical tradition will be gratified to know that in the variety called *Flamand* they are getting a seventeenth-century strain and may expect the flaked and mottled flower so often seen in those enchanting muddles crammed into an urn in Dutch flower-paintings. Indeed, the catalogue of these seeds is full of romance, not only historical but geographical, if you agree with me that there is something romantic in the thought of Provence, from which your seeds will come. Have you been to St Remy, that Roman settlement in what was once south-eastern Gaul, where a Roman triumphal arch still stands, and where flowers are now grown in mile-wide stretches for the seed market? It must be a wonderful sight, when all the carnations and zinnias and petunias are in flower, staining the bistred landscape of Van Gogh's Provence in acres of colour.

This is perhaps neither here nor there in an article on practical gardening, but I always get led away in excitement over the plants I recommend. I was led away also by a note in the same catalogue about petunias, a special strain grown by the nuns in a convent near Toulon. I have not tried these yet, but I mean to. I like thinking about those Sisters in Toulon, pottering about their convent garden, saving their petunia seeds, and sending them to us in England for our delight.*

The agent from whom the carnation and petunia may be obtained is George Roberts, Davington Priory, Faversham, Kent.

* Alas, in all honesty I must add that the petunias were a disappointment. They were supplied under separate-named colours, but I fear the good nuns must have been too much preoccupied with their devotions to take sufficient care of their seed-crop.

February 12, 1950

Not everybody, these days, can be bothered with sowing annuals, not even the hardy penny-packet kinds such as clarkia and godetia, which will grow anywhere and make so bright a show throughout the summer. Most people are going in for the permanent things, such as the flowering shrubs, giving less trouble for more reward. I have myself eliminated nearly all annuals from my garden; but there are two which I obstinately retain: the zinnia and the Morning Glory.

These are both half-hardy, which means that you must not risk a spring frost catching them. If you have glass, you can sow them in seed-boxes in March or April, but if no glass, then they can be sown out of doors towards the end of May, on the place where they are to flower. Honestly, I don't think you lose much time by adopting this method, and you certainly save yourself a mort of trouble.

I have long since abandoned the practice of sowing zinnias in seed-boxes, and I do believe that you get sturdier plants in the long run, when the seedlings have suffered no disturbance. Sow the seeds in little parties of three or four, and thin them remorselessly out when they are about two inches high, till only one lonely seedling remains. It will do all the better for being lonely, twelve inches away from its nearest neighbour. It will branch and bulge side-ways if you give it plenty of room to develop, and by August or September will have developed a spread more desirable in plants than in human beings.

Some people do not like zinnias: they think them stiff and artificial-looking. But they are surely no more artificial-looking than dahlias, which they some-what resemble, and their colours are even more subtle than the colours of the dahlia. In zinnias, you get a mixture of colours seldom seen in any other flower: straw-colour, greenish-white, a particular saffron-yellow, a dusky rose-pink, a coral-pink. The only nasty colour produced by the zinnia is a magenta, and this, alas, is produced only too often. When magenta threatens, I pull it up and throw it on the compost-heap, and allow the better colours to have their way.*

The Morning Glory is a joy every year. Those enormous sky-blue trum-pets that open every morning before breakfast and shut themselves up again between luncheon and tea . . . You must make sure to get the right kind: it is called *Ipomea rubro-coerulea, Heavenly Blue*. Messrs Sutton have it.

Here I should like to add a note which did not appear in *The Observer*, because it is really no use telling the readers of a short article in a weekly

* See also pp. 138–9.

15

journal about things they cannot obtain. It leads only to frustration, indignant letters, and irritability all round.

The seed of a very special form of *Ipomea* was given to me by my friend, Mr Noel Sutton. What a gift! He had got it from India, and it was called *Ipomea bona-nox*. It flowered only at night; so you had to sit up with it if you wanted to catch it in flower. It might have been carved out of the thinnest flakes of ivory.

February 19, 1950

A correspondent writes to suggest that I should supply 'a few extra tips' on growing the Algerian iris. It seems a good idea. They are most obliging plants, even if maltreated, but a little extra kindliness and understanding will bring forth an even better response. As is true of most of us, whether plants or humans.

Kindliness, so far as the Algerian iris is concerned, consists in starving it. Rich cultivation makes it run to leaf rather than to flower. What it really enjoys is being grown in a miserably poor soil, mostly composed of old lime and mortar rubble and even gravel: a gritty mixture at the foot of a sunny wall, the grittier and the sunnier the better. Sun and poverty are the two things it likes. To give it the maximum of sun to ripen itself off during the summer, you should chop down its leaves in May or early June and let the sun get at it for so long as our climate allows. There is no more that you can do for it except to guard it against snails and slugs. It is vital to do this if the flower is not to be nibbled and tattered by these creatures, which hibernate so happily within the leaves and in the cracks of the wall. Any proprietary slug-bait will do the job for you, or you can make your own mixture, which is far cheaper and just as efficacious, with Meta tablets, smashed into a fine powder and mixed with bran, tea-leaves, or even sawdust. It may be unkind to the snails, but one has to make one's choice.

The Algerian iris is known to most of us as *Iris stylosa*. It should, in fact, be called *Iris unguicularis*, because this is the older botanical name for it, *unguiculus* meaning a small or narrow claw. Do we have to bother about that? Let us, rather, record that it is the native of stony ground in Algeria, Greece, Crete, Syria, and Asia Minor, and that it accommodates itself very willingly to our island, flowering before Christmas sometimes, especially after a hot, dry summer, and continuing to flower in mild weather right into March.* You should search your clumps of the grass-like leaves every day for possible buds, and

* Someone told me that the deep purple form originated on one of the Greek islands, but they couldn't remember which.

pull the promising bud while it still looks like a tiny, tightly rolled umbrella, and then bring it indoors and watch it open under a lamp. If you have the patience to watch for long enough, you will see this miracle happen.

If you have not yet got this iris in your garden and want to acquire it, you can plant it in March or April; but September is the best time for transplanting. It does not much like being split up and moved, so, whenever you acquire it, do make sure that it does not get too dry until it has had time to establish itself. After that, it will give you no trouble.

February 26, 1950

A dear near neighbour brought me a tussie-mussie this week. The dictionary defines tuzzy-muzzy, or tussie-mussie, as *a bunch or posy of flowers, a nosegay*, and then disobligingly adds that the word is obsolete. I refuse to regard it as obsolete. It is a charming word; I have always used it and shall continue to use it, whatever the great *Oxford Dictionary* may say; and shall now take my neighbour's tussie-mussie as a theme to show what ingenuity, taste, and knowledge can produce from a small garden even in February.

My neighbour has many difficulties to contend with. She is not young, she is into her seventh decade. She has no help in her house. Her garden is windswept, and the soil is a stiff Weald of Kent clay. (Only those who have tried to garden on Wealden clay can appreciate what that means.) A jobbing gardener from time to time is all that she commands. She does most of the work herself. Yet she manages to produce a bunch such as I will now describe to you.

It is composed of at least five different flowers, all perfectly chosen. She goes always for the best, which I am sure is the secret of good gardening: choose always the best of any variety you want to grow. Thus, in the bunch she brought me, the violets were *pink* violets, the sort called *Cœur d'Alsace*, and the one *Iris reticulata* she put in was the sort called *Hercules*, which is redder than the familiar purple and gold. The grape-hyacinths were the small sky-blue *azureus*, which flowers earlier and is prettier than the dark blue later sort. The crocus in her bunch was not the common yellow, but had brown markings on its outside; I think it may be *C. susianus* or it may be Moonlight, but I forgot to ask her. The anemone that she put in must be a freakishly early bloom of *Anemone St Bavo*, amethyst petals with an electric-blue centre. How wise she is to grow *Anemone St Bavo* instead of the coarser *Anemone St Brigid*.

The moral of this article, if any newspaper article may have a moral, is that it just shows what you can do if you put your mind to it. I have received many letters saying: 'Do tell us what we can do in a small garden.' My neighbour's tussie-mussie is the answer. She grows those exquisite things in a small, quarter-of-an-acre grassy space under apple trees, and somehow produces a jewelled effect rather like the foreground of Botticelli's *Primavera*. They are all low and brilliant and tiny; and no more difficult to grow than their more ordinary relations.

Some day I must write an article describing the way my neighbour has designed her garden; and also, perhaps, what she manages to do with her small, unheated greenhouse. You would be surprised.

February 4, 1951

I notice that people become enraged over the names of plants, and I don't wonder. I wish only that they would not blame it on me. 'Why,' they write indignantly, 'why can't you give us a good honest English name instead of all this Latin?' Well, whenever there is an English name, I do give it; I prefer it myself; I would much rather call a thing Bouncing Bet than *Saponaria officinalis*; but when there is no name in the vernacular, our common speech, what am I to do?

Instead of getting cross about it, we should do better to take an intelligent interest in discovering what lies behind these apparently appalling names. There is always a reason, and the best reason is that by using an international idiom, such as Latin, botanists and gardeners can understand one another all the world over. If I see that a plant is described as *azureus* I know instantly that it is blue, and so does my opposite number in Brazil, France, or Pakistan. If it is described as *azureus vernus*, I know that it is not only blue, but that it flowers in the spring. Then if you want to indicate what explorer first found it, you tack on, say, *Farreri*, or *Fortunei*, which we can all manage, or *Mlokosewitchii*, which perhaps we can't.

There appear to be two principal grievances. I hope I have disposed of the first one, but I do suggest that some society such as the Royal Horticultural Society might supply an inexpensive alphabetical glossary for easy reference. If such a thing exists, I do not know of it. It would be a great convenience; we should all rush to look up *strobiliformis* or *quintuplinervius*, only to discover that it meant *shaped like a fir-cone*, and *five-veined* in the description of a leaf.

The second grievance concerns changes of botanical name. I admit that it is very puzzling to be brought up in our childhood to call lilac *lilac*, and syringa *syringa*, and now suddenly to be told in our middle-age that we must call lilac *syringa* and syringa *philadelphus*; but here again there is a good respectworthy reason, in the attempt either to get back to the first names given by earlier botanists, or to define a new botanical classification, in the interest of accuracy and in the avoidance of confusion.

All the same, sentimentally, Bet may bounce as happily as she likes over my garden, and all her friends, too.

February 11, 1951

With the Festival of Britain approaching, many people will be thinking how to make their front gardens as attractive as possible for the passing motorist. An English village street, gay with flowers, can be as pretty a sight as anyone could wish to see; and, moreover, is not to be found elsewhere in just that way, thanks to our climate and to the Englishman's passion for gardening. Most of these small front gardens are already well furnished with beds, but it would be pleasant to feel that something more permanent was also being planted, to commemorate the Festival year, as things were planted to commemorate the Coronation in 1937.

Such permanent planting inevitably means trees or shrubs, both of which unfortunately have a habit of growing until they begin to obscure the light from the windows. Then the occupant of the house quite understandably prunes the poor thing back into a sort of mop head, when all its beauty is lost. A mop on top of a stick is very different from the loose, natural development of the mature plant smothered in flower or blossom. An ingenious way of getting out of this difficulty is to train the branches along post and wire, like an espalier apple or pear in an old kitchen garden. The flowering trees, by which I here mean the prunus, the pyrus, the Japanese cherries, the almonds, and all the other members of those lovely families, lend themselves very obligingly to such treatment, and I am sure prefer it to being hacked about and thwarted from what they want to do, which is to give as generously as they can of their load.

Have I made myself clear? No, I don't think I have. I often long to draw a little explanatory diagram, but I can't draw. So, without the aid of a diagram, may I suggest that you might run a row of flowering trees from your front gate to your front door, training them horizontally so that they will not obscure the light from your windows and yet will make a path of blossom from gate to door along our village streets.

It is not too late to plant now. You can plant anything between now and March.

Next Sunday I will write something about hedges of roses, fronting the road; another blandishment for our guests, and a pleasure for ourselves in the years after our guests have gone.

March

There are several kinds of Hellebore, but the two varieties usually seen in English gardens are more familiar under their prettier names of Christmas rose and Lenten rose, *Helleborus niger* and *Helleborus orientalis* respectively. Why the Christmas rose, which is white, should be called black in Latin I could not imagine until I discovered that the adjective referred to the root; but I still cannot imagine why people do not grow both these varieties more freely. They will fill up many an odd corner; their demands are few; and they will give flowers at a time of year when flowers are scarce.

As for their demands, they like a cool place, say a west aspect or a niche shaded by shrubs; a fairly heavy soil, and if it is moist so much the better; the one thing they will not stand is a poor sandy soil which gets dried out in the summer. They do not like being disturbed either, so plant them where you intend them to remain. If you buy plants you will have to wait a couple of years before they do anything very much about flowering, but once established they will improve steadily, especially if you give them an occasional mulch of compost, leaf-mould, or rotted manure.

It is, of course, cheaper to grow them from seed than to buy plants, and the seed germinates very readily if it is freshly harvested, say from the garden of a friend, in May or June.

Both the Christmas and the Lenten roses are true to their association with the calendar, which means that from December to April the clumps of one or the other are in flower. The Christmas rose is ideal for picking, lasting for weeks indoors if you split the stems. Cover the clump with a hand-light, to avoid splashing with mud from heavy rain. The Lenten rose, alas, is unreliable as a cut flower; sometimes, by splitting the stems, it can be induced to hold up its lovely wine-coloured head for a few days, but at other times under the same treatment it flops mournfully after a few hours; I have never made out why.*

Those who share my taste for greenish flowers may like to grow the Corsican hellebore (*H. corsicus*), a tough and handsome plant whose tightly packed head of strangely livid blossoms will last either out of doors or in a bowl of water from early March to May. Before the flower buds open they look not unlike a bunch of Muscat grapes, but presently they open out flat, when they

* Subsequent information: plunge the tips of the stalks into nearly boiling water.

look like a miniature pale green water lily, if you can imagine a water lily about the size of a penny.

March 9, 1947

A pot of cyclamen is a favourite Christmas present, and very nice, too, but by this time (March) some recipients may be wondering what to do with it. Don't throw it away. It will repeat its beauty for you year after year if you treat it right. Treating it right means (1) keeping it moist so long as it continues to flower and to carry leaves; (2) letting it dry off by degrees after the last buds have opened and faded away; (3) keeping it, still in its pot, *unwatered*, in a frost-proof place during the remaining cold weeks, and then standing it out of doors, still unwatered, still in its pot, throughout the spring and early summer in a shady place; (4) starting it into life again in July or August. Starting it into life again merely means giving it water again – very simple. It will then begin, quite quickly, to show new buds all over the corm; but to get the best out of it you ought then to re-pot it. It likes a rather loose soil, made up of fibrous loam, some gritty sand, and a handful of bone-meal, all mixed well together. *Do not bury the corm*; it should sit on top, three-quarters visible. Do not water too much at first, water more generously when autumn comes and you bring your pots into the shelter of a warm greenhouse if you have one; or on to a warm window-sill if you have not.

Do not ever, at any time, give too much water. If you do, your plant will very quickly notify you by turning its leaves yellow and by developing a soft rot in the stems of the flowers. There seem to be two schools of thought about the best way to water. Some growers say it is better to avoid overhead watering which may cause the corm to rot, and that it is better to stand the pot in a saucer or bowl with an inch or so of water, thus absorbing the moisture through the porous pot up into the roots, remembering to empty the water away when you think the plant has had enough. Other growers condemn the saucer idea.

A cottage friend of mine who grows some superb cyclamen on her kitchen window-sill tells me that her grandmother advised her to water them with weak tea. This may sound like an old wives' tale, but the tales of some old wives sometimes turn out to be right.

There are two kinds of cyclamen: the Persian, which is the one your friends give you, and which is not hardy, and the small, outdoor one, a tiny edition of the big Persian, as hardy as a snowdrop. These little cyclamen are among the longest-lived of garden plants. A cyclamen corm will keep itself going for more years than its owner is likely to live. They have other advantages: (1) they will grow under trees, for they tolerate, and indeed enjoy, shade;

(2) they do not object to a limy soil; (3) they will seed themselves and (4) they will take you round the calendar by a judicious planting of different sorts. *C. neapolitanum*, for instance, will precede its ivy-like leaves by its little pink flower in late autumn, white flowers if you get the variety *album*; *C. coum*, pink, white, or lilac, will flower from December to March; *C. ibericum* from February to the end of March; *C. balearicum* will then carry on, followed by *C. repandum*, which takes you into the summer; and, finally, *C. europaeum* for the late summer and early autumn. Some botanists believe this to be a native; it was certainly recorded here in the reign of Queen Elizabeth, when, if beaten into little flat cakes, it was considered 'a good amorous medicine to make one in love'.

Anyone who grows the little cyclamen will have observed that they employ an unusual method of twiddling a kind of corkscrew, or coil, to project the seeds from the capsule when ready. One would imagine that the coil would go off with a ping, rather like the mainspring of a clock when one over-winds it, thus flinging the seeds far and wide, and this indeed was the theory put forward by many botanists. It would appear, however, that nothing of the kind happens, and that the seeds are gently deposited on the parent corm. Why, then, this elaborate apparatus of the coil, if it serves only to drop the seed on to a hard corm and not on to the soft receptive soil? It has been suggested, notably by Mr A. T. Johnson, that this concentration of the seeds may be Nature's idea of providing a convenient little heap for some distributing agent to carry away, and he points out that ants may be seen, in later summer, hurrying off with the seeds until not one is left. I confess that I have never sat up with a cyclamen long enough to watch this curious phenomenon of the exploding capsule; and I still wonder how and why seedlings so obligingly appear in odd corners of the garden – never, I must add, very far away from the parent patch.

You may find some of them a little difficult to obtain now, but *C. europaeum*, *coum*, and *neapolitanum* are still listed by nurserymen, and are the three varieties I would recommend for a start. So accommodating are they that you can plant them at almost any time, though ideally they should be planted when dormant, i.e. in June or July. Messrs Barr & Sons, King Street, Covent Garden, London, wc2, have a good list.

March 5, 1950

Successful gardening is not necessarily a question of wealth. It is a question of love, taste, and knowledge. The neighbour about whom I was writing on page 17 possesses all these virtues, added to fingers so green that the water must surely turn emerald in the basin every time she washes her hands. There are two things I should like to describe to you in connection with my neighbour: one is the way she has designed her garden, and the other is the way she makes use of her small greenhouse.

Which shall I take first? The greenhouse, perhaps, since this is the time of the year when one can make the best use of a greenhouse for growing seeds and for producing a display of flowers. My neighbour does both, and does it in the most unconventional fashion. It would make any professional gardener laugh, and would send him away scratching his head with a lot to think over. She does the oddest things. She digs up clumps of violets from her outdoor garden and has them blooming exuberantly in pots, the small pink violet and the little almost-blue one; and as she takes the trouble to whitewash her pots, instead of leaving them to their normal hideous terra-cotta colour, you may imagine how the flowers gain in beauty as they pour over those blanched containers, white and clean as blancoed tennis-shoes. She digs up clumps of snowdrops and cro- cuses, and packs them into an ordinary pudding basin. One end of the house is all flowers and colour; the side-stagings are devoted to seed-boxes.

She has not many real wooden seed-boxes. There are cardboard dress- boxes tied round with string to prevent them from disintegrating, and old Golden Syrup tins, and even some of those tall tins that once contained Slug- death, and some of those little square chip-baskets called punnets. I verily believe that she would use an old shoe if it came handy. In this curious assortment of receptacles an equally curious assortment of seedlings are com- ing up, green as a lawn, prolific as mustard-and-cress on a child's bit of flan- nel. There are cabbages and lettuces in some of them; rare lilies in others; and I noted a terrified little crop of auriculas scurrying up, as though afraid that they might be late for a pricking-out into the warm earth of May.

It all goes to show what you can do if you try, in gardening. There are such possibilities, not necessarily expensive.

I was half mistaken, by the way, in describing this greenhouse as unheated. It *is* unheated as a rule, but on a chilly evening when a threat of frost is in the air an electric tube underneath the staging can be turned on by means of a switch located in the kitchen. What could be simpler? No need to bother with a stoke-hole or paraffin radiators; no need to go out into the cold night. It is rather an extravagant method, but that it is clean and labour-saving cannot be denied.

March 12, 1950

This is going to be about designing a small garden. By a small garden I mean anything from half an acre to two acres. It is a big subject to tackle in so short an article. I can hope only to give a few general ideas.

The small garden may be a bungalow garden, or a council-house garden, or the garden round an old cottage, or the garden round a new house on a main bus route. Whichever it is, the true gardener will wish to make the most of the patch of the planet Earth at his personal and particular command. In most cases his design will be dictated by the shape of his patch, and by the position of his dwelling-house in it: thus, he may feel compelled to have a straight path running from the front gate to the front door, and to arrange his flower-beds, his borders, and his bit of lawn accordingly, in which case his garden will look exactly like his next-door-neighbour's garden. What I would like to suggest is that a little ingenuity can vary the pattern.

I have three gardens in mind. One of them has been constructed in front of a small house facing the road. It has been turned into a landscape garden on a miniature scale. The path does not run straight from the front gate to the front door but wanders round sideways, and the middle part of the front garden is occupied by a deep pool surrounded by weeping willows and *Iris sibirica*, reflecting their pale mauve and their deep purple into the water. Some Irish yews have also been planted; and they now reflect their images into the pool, duplicating themselves in the watery mirror and making this tiny garden look twice the size it is.

My next garden also faces a road, a main road. It would have been easy, and obvious, to turn this into a conventional sort of garden. But the owners have designed it cleverly: they have put it sideways to the house, so that the flower-beds, which ought, in the conventional way, to be geometrically set along the house, are put in a surprising way alongside.

My third garden is the sort of garden I like best. It is a cottage garden of the best sort, kept by a true gardener. This is a garden that slopes rather vaguely downhill towards Romney Marsh, with views of the Marsh beyond it. It is packed with flowers at all times of the year, so exquisitely arranged that they gain their full value wherever they are. I remember specially a planting of the blue primrose mixed with the blue scilla round the base of a grey stone well-head, a perfectly chosen combination.

March 19, 1950

Several correspondents have asked me to say something about that strangely coloured black and green flower commonly called *Iris tuberosa*, or the Snakeshead iris, which is to be found in florists' shops during March and April, sold in bunches, rather cheap. I like being asked these questions, because they come as a challenge to my own many failures in gardening and make me examine my conscience to see where I have gone wrong. I have certainly gone wrong over my *Iris tuberosa*. I planted it in rather too shady a place, under an apple tree, in a rich old soil, and I now see that it ought to be given the maximum of sun, in a gritty, well-drained soil, exposed to as much baking as our English summer will afford.

It should not be difficult to grow. The tuber will cost you from 4s. 6d. to 5s. 6d. a dozen, and it should increase itself if you put it in the right sort of place, dry, hot, and sunny. An Italian by origin, it grows wild in other parts of southern Europe, all indicating that it would enjoy conditions as near as we can get to the Mediterranean coast.

A wise precaution: mark its position in the garden by a stick or a ring of stones, because it disappears altogether during the summer, and thus is liable to get dug up by mistake.

This may sound rather dull, perhaps: but my researches into the history of *Iris tuberosa* did not prove dull in the least. It is an interesting plant, in both botanical and mythological terms. Botanically it is not a true iris at all. Its real name is *Hermodactylus tuberosus*, which being interpreted, means finger of Hermes (Mercury), and *tuberosus*, of course, refers to the tuberous rootstock, which does indeed bear some resemblance to the fingers of the human hand. Having got thus far, I began to reflect on its familiar sobriquet, the Snakeshead, and to wonder whether the current explanation was correct in attributing the name to a fanciful likeness to the head of a snake. Perhaps, I thought, there may be a double meaning, for although the sombre sinister colouring and spiteful shape do suggest the spitting head of a reptile, it is also true that Mercury's winged wand, the *caduceus*, that swift and elegant symbol of the most roguish of all the minor gods, was twirled round by two interlaced serpents. Would it be possible, and even probable, I wondered, that the name might have a classical origin we never suspected? I like to think so. I like to think that the messenger of the gods, Hermes in Greece, Mercury in Rome, gave his symbol as the name to one of our messengers of spring.

March 26, 1950

We now approach the time of year when the thoughts of Man turn towards the pruning of his roses. Knives and secateurs are now at their sharpest. Brandishing these objects of destruction, battalions of professional and amateur gardeners advance, prepared to do their worst, as they have immemorially been taught. The word of command has gone out: 'Cut almost to the ground; cut down to the second or third bud; cut till nothing is left except a couple of inches sticking up. Be pitiless, be ruthless; prune for fine blooms, exhibition blooms, even if you don't intend to exhibit. Never mind about the appearance of your garden, or the natural alacrity of your roses. Snub them as hard as you can, even as Victorian parents snubbed their children.'

It rejoices me to see that different ideas are creeping in. The rose, even the hybrid Teas and the hybrid Perpetuals, is no longer to be regarded as a stunted dwarf, but as a wildly blossoming shrub. Let her grow up, even to three or four feet in height, and throw her head about as I believe that she was meant to. This truth first dawned upon me during the war, when as a Land Army representative I had occasion to visit many small gardens in pursuit of owners who had been called away. Their gardens were turning into a sad disorder of weeds, but the roses reared themselves up, superb and proud, just because they had not been interfered with for two, three, four, five years. Then in the well-kept garden of a friend I saw similar rose-bushes which, she assured me, had scarcely been touched since she planted them thirty years ago. She had merely snipped the tips; had taken out the dead wood and the weak growth; and for the rest had left them to their will. The result was lavish and surprising.

My liking for gardens to be lavish is an inherent part of my garden philosophy. I like generosity wherever I find it, whether in gardens or elsewhere. I hate to see things scrimp and scrubby. Even the smallest garden can be prodigal within its own limitations, and I would now suggest that you should try the experiment of NOT slaughtering your roses down to almost ground level, at least for this year; and see what happens.

I know that I have touched only the outskirts of this controversial subject. There is so much to be said, and so many different types of rose to deal with, that it all becomes confused and confusing. Everyone agrees that the hybrid Musk and the species roses are better without the knife, but no doubt the new unorthodoxy about the hybrid Teas will evoke screams of protest. I am prepared to admit that it might not suit them all. The only thing is to be bold; try the experiment; and find out.

April

April 6, 1947

I must start with a warning not to despair about plants apparently killed by the frosts, ice-rain, east winds, and other afflictions they have had to suffer. (Written in April 1947.) They may look dead now, but their powers of revival are astonishing. You may have to cut some shrubs down to ground level, but my recommendation would be not to dig anything up rashly until you are quite, quite certain that it has no intention of putting out green shoots again. This certitude may not come until the summer is well advanced. I remember the agreeable surprises we got after the cruel winter of 1940.

All garden work has been so much delayed that many people will have to rely on generous sowings of annuals this year for extra colour. If you have not time to spare for the ideal method of growing them in boxes and then planting them out, you still have a large choice of those which may be sown straight into the ground. A finely broken soil; sow thinly, not too deep; thin out remorselessly, for most annuals will fill a space from a foot to two feet wide if given the chance, looking sturdy and bushy instead of drawn and spindly; and remember that it is far more effective to sow large patches of a few varieties than small patches of many. What you sow must depend upon your personal taste and the colouring you want. As a change from the usual jumble, pretty and gay though that may be, you might find it more original to concentrate on one colour. A combination of *Phacelia*, *Nigella* (love-in-the-mist), *Nemophila*, *Asperula azurea*, would give a brilliant blue effect, especially if massed in front of delphiniums. Coreopsis, Eschscholtzia, Calendula Orange King and Lemon Queen, Nemesia yellow and orange (not quite hardy) would lie like a pool of sunlight. Mauve and purple stocks, Alyssum Lilac Queen, mauve Candytuft, mauve Godetia, Clarkia Purple Prince, Petunias (not quite hardy), make a sumptuous association. These are only a few suggestions, just enough, I hope, to indicate what scope there is for ingenuity.

April 2, 1950

A very pleasing little shrub or small tree, not often seen in gardens, has been in flower since the middle of March. It is not at all showy, and most people would pass it by without noticing, unless they happened to catch a whiff of the scent. It is pure vanilla.

This is *Azara microphylla*.

I would hesitate to recommend it except to gardeners who want something their neighbour probably hasn't got; but, after all, it is for those gardeners that I write these articles. Gardeners who want something different from the usual, and yet something easy to grow. *Azara microphylla* is quite easy to grow. It is an evergreen; it has neat little shiny leaves that look as though they had been varnished; and it has this tiny yellow flower which is now spreading its scent over my writing table and into the whole of my room. I sit and sniff. Wafts of vanilla come to me as I write.

Azara microphylla is a native of Chile, in South America. Some authorities say that it is not hardy here in Britain except in the favoured climate of Devon or Cornwall. I don't believe this. I have got it thriving where I live in Kent, and I have seen a twenty-foot-high tree of it in the rather colder climate of Gloucestershire. So I would say: plant it and risk it.

It likes to be planted in leaf-mould. It would do well trained on to a wall with a north, or east, or west aspect; by which I mean that the early morning sun would not get at it after a frosty night. This is always an important point to remember when you are planting things affected by frost and by the warm morning sun which comes as too great a shock after the chill of the night. Plants must be let down gently. The transition must not be too quick.

Another shrub I would like to recommend is *Osmanthus delavayi*. This, also, like the *Azara microphylla*, has dark green box-like leaves and a scented flower, white, not yellow. It flowers in March and April, and you can cut it and cut it, and the more you cut it the better it grows. It is well worth the attention of gardeners who want something away from the ordinary.

How charming they are, and how subtle, these early spring-flowering shrubs! We are all well accustomed to watching the daffodils come up year by year in the orchards; but how few of us think of fanning our English air with vanilla from *Azara microphylla* or with the scent of the *Osmanthus* which Father Delavay found in Yunnan some sixty years ago.

April 9, 1950

For once, instead of giving advice, may I ask for it? How does one protect the choicer sorts of primroses from the attack of sparrows? Has any reader of these articles a sovereign remedy against this naughty, wanton, wild destruction? Short of putting automatic cartridges amongst my primroses, I have done everything I can think of. I have made a sort of cat's cradle of strong black thread, pegged down in the hope that the birds would catch their nasty little claws in it as they alighted and thus be frightened and discouraged. It doesn't work. The sparrows don't seem to mind. I can suppose only that they crawl underneath the threads and nip the flowers off, scattering the buds and the heads all over the ground at dawn before I have got up in the morning.

This is a real SOS. I have quite a collection of uncommon primroses, Jack-in-the-Green, Madame Pompadour, Cloth of Gold, and so on, but what is the good of that if the sparrows take them all? I would try not to grudge them their fun if it was of any benefit to them, but it isn't. They are mischievous hooligans who destroy for the sake of destruction.

Some of these old primroses are very charming and there are signs that, like several other old-fashionable flowers, they are coming back into favour. Unfortunately they are neither easy to obtain nor to grow. Sometimes one sees a happy clump of the double white or the double purple in a cottage garden, but then it is a truism that things will flourish without any attention at all in a cottage garden, when all the skill and science of the professional well-instructed gardener leads only to the petering-out of the last miserable sickly survivor. Still, the doubles do not appear to be so choosy, and a half-shady corner with plenty of leaf-mould should suit them. They associate very gladly with their relations the Auriculas, or with the Hepaticas (a kind of anemone), and they are all, I think, plants for an intimate recess where their low beauty may be studied apart from the flauntings of their spring contemporaries such as the daffodils. They need to be observed in the small secret of their chosen shade.

This is all very well, but what am I to do about the sparrows?

The Pasque-flower, *Anemone pulsatilla*, is blooming just now, for Easter as its name indicates. This is a native of our Downs, getting rare in its wild state, but still cultivated in gardens. It is a soft and lovely thing, pale lilac in colour with a silvery floss-silk surround: and it can now be obtained also in a rosy-pink colouring, which mixes and merges most exquisitely with the original mauve of the native. Maurice Prichard & Sons, Riverslea Nurseries, Christchurch, Hampshire, specialize in these. There is also a white form. It is easy to grow anywhere, though as a native of the chalk hills it appreciates a bed of limy rubble in the sun.

The sparrows so far, touch wood, have left it alone.

April 16, 1950
When I was small I had a book called *Flowers that do not disappoint*. They nearly all did, but that was probably my fault so far as the annuals were concerned. Hardy annuals should not disappoint, and there is still time to sow them in

April, so useful for filling bare patches or for making a display in the window-boxes of town houses.

The charm of annuals is their light gaiety, as though they must make the most of their brief lives to be frivolous and pleasure-giving. They have no time to be austere or glum. They must always be youthful, because they have no time to grow old. And so their colours are bright, and their foliage airy, and their only morality is to be as cheerful as possible, and to leave as much seed as they can behind them for their progeny to continue in the same tradition. This, of course, is the one thing you must not let them do: all seeding heads must ruthlessly be snipped off if you want to prolong the exuberance of flowers.

So much advice has been given about sowing annuals that it is perhaps unnecessary to repeat it in too much detail. The ground should be well dug, but, generally speaking, not over-enriched, unless it is very poor. It should be broken down into a fine surface tilth. The piece of advice that people never take is: sow thinly and thin out remorselessly; but if ever you have noticed a solitary plant growing with ample space all round it you will be better disposed to listen. The smaller the seed the shallower it should be sown, and it is better to sprinkle some fine soil over your sowings than to attempt to rake them in, a method which usually results in an uneven distribution. Look out for slugs. Put twiggy sticks among those seedlings that will eventually grow tall enough to need staking.

In a short article like this it is impossible to give an exhaustive list, but I might single out a few annuals that are less commonly grown than the usual clarkias, godetias, and so on. To take one of the tiniest first, I am very fond of *Leptosiphon*; only three inches in height, but very varied in colour, it is charming as an edging, or among stones, or in paving. It likes full sun. *Linaria* associates well with it, being several inches taller, but of the same delicate character, as the name *Fairy Bouquet* will suggest. *Phacelia campanularia*, nine inches, sown in large patches, will quickly make a mat of gentian-blue.

Among the stronger colours, *Coreopsis Crimson King* is a brilliant bronze dwarf. *Dimorphotheca aurantiaca*, the orange South African daisy, looks like a patch of sunlight on the ground (but shuts itself up when the sun goes in); and among the calendulas there is a strain called by the repulsive name of *Art Shades*, which throws a variety of pretty colours in apricot, buff, and straw, less violent than the old *Orange King*. A study of a seedsman's catalogue will give many suggestions, and there is also a very useful book, *Annuals* by Roy Hay, published by the Bodley Head at 12s. 6d.

April 23, 1950

A very pretty, clean little tree which has been in flower since the middle of this month (April) is the golden-barked Manchurian cherry, *Prunus maackii*. With its pale green leaves and masses of tiny white flowers, it makes a change from the innumerable pinks and reds of the flowering trees one now sees in most gardens. I called it a little tree, because mine is not very old yet, but I believe that eventually it will grow to a height of forty feet. It must then be a lovely sight.

My thanks to all those who have written about remedies against the attack of sparrows on primroses. For the benefit of other sufferers, of whom there appear to be many, I append a list of recommendations, which of course would apply equally to attacks on other flowers, such as the yellow crocus, a particular victim. Pepper seems to be the favourite deterrent, though rather an expensive one; but dry mustard, flowers of sulphur, Keating's powder, soot, powdered naphthalene, quassia, soft soap, paraffin-and-water, saffron, Jeyes' fluid, Izal, and basic slag are all mentioned. Earthenware saucers sunk into the ground and filled with water find great favour. Wire pea-guards (to be removed daily after breakfast), wire netting to be bent into the shape of a mobcap over each plant, fish-netting, the old nursery fireguard, old hair-nets, sprigs of holly, and 'an ordinary dark glass bottle on the ground', have all been found helpful. Some handfuls of confetti have also been found to do the trick.

Among things to dangle, I am advised to use Glitter-bangs, tin foil, potatoes stuck with pheasants' feathers, pieces of bright blue paper, a bell, and the coloured tops of TT milk bottles. I am most grateful to the gentleman who sent me a regular necklace of these. Among the unkinder remedies I find mouse-traps, bright unbreakable beads for the sparrows to chip their beaks upon, 'the body of a sparrow on a little gibbet', and 'a masterful young cat'. It seems, however, that an old fur among the plants will take the place of real cats, and that a pair of white china dogs has proved very efficacious. A palisade of wooden pipe-lighters is advised, also of bits of looking-glass or of old gramophone records, splintered, 'preferably Bing Crosby'. One humanitarian advocates a Sparrow Corner where the offenders may disport themselves in sand-boxes and bird-baths, and may amuse themselves with the sorrel, spinach and Sweet William, that you will have provided for them; but not all the sufferers are humanitarians, and in cases of great exasperation a shot-gun or a catapult may be brought into action.

Kindest of all, perhaps, is the recommendation to try Christian Science, to which it would appear that our feathered enemies are most susceptible.

I have left to the last the question of cotton. Apparently I went wrong in using strong black thread. I ought to have used thin cotton, of the 50 variety, and not thread at all. Even *blue* cotton would have been better. I apologize. And now you can take your choice.

April 30, 1950

The season for flower-shows is now in full swing, and soon the Chelsea Show will open for four days. But beware. On that first day it will be open to Fellows only, so if you are not a Fellow of the Royal Horticultural Society you will not be able to get in. It is no use hoping to borrow a Fellow's ticket, because on this occasion they are not transferable. On the second day the entrance will cost you 10s., and on the subsequent days, which are cheaper, the crowd will be greater and many of the exhibits will begin to look sorry for themselves after all that time in a hot tent.

You will by now have perceived the moral of these remarks, which is to join the RHS without delay. The RHS has not asked me to say this, and will probably be surprised by so gratuitous an advertisement, should ever it come to its attention, but I truly feel that the advantages of Fellowship are wide enough to justify me in pointing them out. Some readers of *The Observer*, which, as I well know from my correspondence, finds its way all over the British Isles and elsewhere, may protest that flower-shows held in London are not of much interest to them. I sympathize. It is irritating to be told about things you cannot yourself enjoy, unless you have a very altruistic nature indeed. So let me give a list of other advantages.

You receive a free copy of the monthly RHS journal, which in itself is worth the whole subscription. You have the right of free entrance to the RHS gardens at Wisley, Surrey, and also to the fortnightly shows at the Society's halls in Vincent Square, London, sw1. If you cannot avail yourself of this privilege you can lend your ticket to a friend. You have the right to exhibit any plant or plants of interest at these shows, including Chelsea. And, finally, you have a share, free, in the annual distribution of seeds from the Wisley gardens, a share which is doubled if you live more than thirty miles from London. A list will be sent you from which to make your choice.

All particulars can be obtained from the Secretary, RHS, Vincent Square, London, sw1.

The Balsam poplar has now unfolded its very sticky leaf-buds and is scenting the air. It surprises me that this deliciously scented tree should not be more widely grown. It is not too large for even a small garden, and if only our road planners and village beautifiers would plant it in avenues along our new roads, or in clumps round our old village greens, every motorist would surely stop with an inquiring sniff. Smells are as difficult to describe as colours, but I should describe this one as a sweet, strong resin, powerful enough to reach for yards around in the open air and almost too strong to put in a vase in your room.

Do not allow yourself to be fobbed off, as I foolishly was, by anyone telling you that *Populus candicans* is as good as *Populus balsamifera*. It isn't. You must insist on getting *P. balsamifera*, alternately known as *tacamahac*, which I take to be a Red Indian name, for the tree is a native of the United States and Canada.

P. trichocarpa is also said to be very powerfully scented. If you can get cuttings from a friend's garden it will save your pocket, for all poplars root very readily from cuttings and will even throw out white worm-like roots in a glass of water. Like all poplars, the balsam-scented tribe grows very rapidly.

May

By the time this article appears the lilac should be in flower. It is not called lilac now by the experts: it is called syringa; and what we used to call syringa is now called philadelphus. All very confusing, so let us incorrectly retain the old names for the moment, when everyone will know what I mean.

Lilac (or laylock, if you prefer) is one of the few old favourites which has been definitely improved in recent years. Frankly, the pale mauve type was a washy thing. The newer sorts have gained in colour, size, and scent. I suppose that everyone is by now familiar with the earlier improvements: *Souvenir de Louis Späth*, and *Charles Joly*, both dark red; or *Charles X*, deep purple; or *Madame Lemoine*, double white; none of which is easy to beat. But not everyone, I find, is familiar with the more recent hybrids, carrying truly noble plumes of immense weight: *Réaumur*, dark red; *President Poincaré* and *Pasteur*, both claret; *Congo*, very dark reddish-purple; *Jeanne d'Arc*, double white; *Mme F. Morel*, mauvish pink; *Maréchal Foch*, red.

Any lilac is 'easy': they do not object to lime, in fact they like it; they need no pruning, though it is most advantageous to cut off the faded flowers, *this is really important*; they are perfectly hardy; and very long-lived unless they suddenly die back, which sometimes happens. Few plants could give you more for 8s. 6d. or half a guinea. Of course they repay rich cultivation; most plants do. And they like the sun.

The old syringa, or Mock Orange, is another easy-going shrub, too often forgotten. Personally I like the early, very sweet-scented species, called *coronarius*, found in most old gardens; but *Virginal*, with double flowers, is a lovely cool green-and-white sight in midsummer; and so are *Belle Etoile* and *purpureomaculatus*, both blotched with maroon in the centre. *Grandiflorus* is the one with big single white flowers, very decorative but entirely scentless, which may be a recommendation for people who do not like heavily scented flowers in their rooms. By the way, if you strip all the leaves from cut branches of syringa they will last far longer, besides gaining in beauty. Try. And smash the woody stems with a hammer.

I end with a counsel and with a warning. *Counsel*: try to see plants in bloom during the coming months, either in private gardens open to the public – and there are many, my own garden, for instance, is open every day until the end of October – or at shows, or in nursery gardens, or in gardens such as Kew and the Royal Horticultural Society's place at Wisley. There is no better way of judging what plants really look like and what really appeals to you. *Warning*: this applies to slug-bait. Whatever you use, keep it away from dogs and cats, either by mixing it with tea-leaves or by tilting something like a tile or a piece of glass over it. It is wise to be on the safe side.

May 9, 1948

Agreeable incidents do continue to occur from time to time, even in 1948; and there still seem to be days when things marvellously go right instead of wrong, rarities to be recorded with gratitude before they can be forgotten.

Such a day, culminating in such an incident, was given to me recently. I had had occasion to drive across ten miles of Kent, through the orchard country. The apple-blossom was not yet fully out; and it was still in that fugitive precious stage of being more of a promise than a fulfilment. Apple-blossom too quickly becomes overblown, whereas its true character is to be as tightly youthful as an eighteen-year-old poet. There they were, the closed buds just flushing pink, making a faintly roseate haze over the old trees grey with age; closed buds of youth graciously blushing as youth must blush in the presence of age, knowing very well that within a few months they themselves would turn into the apples of autumnal fruit.

But if the apple-blossom was no more than a pink veil thrown over the orchards, the cherry was at its most magnificent. Never had it looked more lavish than this year (1948), nor so white, so candidly white. This heavy whiteness of the cherry, always enhanced by the contrasting blackness of the branches, was on this particular afternoon deepened – if white may be said to deepen – by a pewter-grey sky of storm as a backcloth; and I thought, not for the first time, how perfectly married were these two effects of April: the dazzling blossom and the peculiarly lurid heaven which is only half a menace. Only half, for however wrathful it may pretend to be overhead, there are gleams of light round the edges, with lances of sun striking a church tower somewhere in the landscape. It is not a true threat; it is a temporary threat, put on for its theatrical effect – Nature's original of that most strange and beautiful of man's new inventions, flood-lighting.

Enriched by these experiences I came home, expecting no further delight that day; but on arrival I saw a closed van at the front door. Having long awaited some spare parts to repair the boiler, dreary, yet necessary, I walked round to the back of the van, thinking how quickly utilitarian life returned to

35

oust beauty, and with a sigh prepared to investigate some graceless assortment of ironmongery whose function would be incomprehensible to me. But there was no such thing. Instead, a smiling young man confronted me, saying he did not know if I would be interested, but he had brought these . . . and opened the van as he spoke.

'These' were giant pansies, thousands and thousands of them. The van's dark interior was a cavern of colour. Some royal hand had flung rugs of velvet over the stacks of wooden trays. Purples were there; and subtler colours than purple: bronze and greenish-yellow and claret and rose-red, all in their queer cat-faces of crumpled velvet. I stood amazed. What an imaginative young man, I thought, to hawk this giant strain round the countryside, selling his plants to any buyer. When I questioned him, he said, modestly, that he hoped people would not be able to resist them.

He was probably right, and I wish him good luck in his enterprise. As for those whose houses do not lie on his road, a packet of seed should serve the purpose, and by next spring the ground should appear as though spread with the most sumptuous carpet from Isfahan.

May 15, 1949

An unusual way of treating clematis is to grow it horizontally instead of vertically. For this, you need a kind of oblong trellis of bamboo sticks, supported at each of the four corners on four stout little posts, about two feet high from the ground; or a rectangle of rabbit wire or sheep wire will do equally well, besides proving more durable. The effect to be aimed at is a low, flat, open-work table top, under which you plant your plant, and allow it to grow up through. Every few days in the growing season, you will have to go round and weave the strands in and out of the wire or trellis, for clematis grows at an amazing rate, once it starts, and its instinct is to grow perpendicularly, not flatly: but do this as gingerly as you can, for clematis seems to resent the touch of the human hand.

Does all this sound too complicated? It isn't really, and the reward is great. For one thing you will be able to gaze right down into the upturned face of the flower instead of having to crane your neck to observe the tangle of colour hanging perhaps ten or twenty feet above your head. The full beauty of the flower is thus exposed to you, in a way that it never is when you see it only from underneath. And for another thing, the clematis itself will get the benefit of shade on its roots, in this case its own shade, with its head in the sun, which is what all clematis enjoy.

The big-flowered Jackmanii type is the most suitable for growing like this, or the Patens group, because both these kinds have flat flowers. The

36

well-known dark purple Jackmanii looks splendid, or its variety *rubra*. *Nelly Moser* is a pale mauve, with a pink stripe; *Gipsy Queen* a very deep purple.

The same idea could be extended to many other climbers, say Honeysuckle, or the annual Morning Glory, and even to the strong-growing kinds of rose. The hybrid perpetuals, such as *Frau Karl Druschki*, white, or *Ulrich Brunner*, cherry-red, or *Hugh Dickson*, dark red, or the old pink thornless rose, *Zéphyrine Drouhin* (hybrid Bourbon) will break out from every joint if bent over in this way or merely pegged down to the ground at the tip of the shoots. The extra crop of flowers you will thus obtain imposes rather a strain on the plant, so leave only three or four shoots and give a little encouragement with manure or compost.

May 29, 1949

In these somewhat scrappy notes I go, rightly or wrongly, on the assumption that my readers welcome suggestions for something which, though not difficult to grow, is a little out of the ordinary. This week I would therefore like to put in a plea for some tulips less usually seen than our old friends the Cottage or the Darwin. I know full well that tulips will be over by the time these words appear in print, but as all good gardeners keep a note-book for their autumn orders months ahead, I put forward these hints for your autumn list.

The Parrot or Dragon tulips are well named, for some of them really do suggest the more gaudy macaws in their colouring, and the jagged edges of their petals always remind me of the wyvern, that winged heraldic cousin of the dragon. I tried this comparison on a gardening friend, who stared at me blankly and said she couldn't think what I meant, and what was a wyvern anyhow? But still I think that one should look at flowers in an imaginative way, to squeeze the fullest enjoyment from them.

The pink *Fantasy*, with its apple-green feathering, is fairly common; *Red Champion* is a deeper version of *Fantasy*, a real cherry-red, opening to an enormous size, and heavily fringed; *Orange Favourite*, smudged with buttercup yellow and green, not quite so large; the *Blue Parrot*, which is not blue at all but a deep mauve, really the colour of blackberry fool (horticulturists sometimes have very queer ideas about naming colours); *Sunshine*, a golden yellow – all these are fun to grow, and no more expensive to buy than the ordinary tulip.

But there are other far more frenzied variations. *Gadelan* was the maddest-looking tulip I ever had in my garden. It was smeared with as many colours as a painter's palette after a good day's work – dark blue, dark red, purple, green, white – and as to size, it must have measured eight inches across when fully opened. This costs 1s. 3d. a bulb, so I got only three as an experiment, and abstained altogether from the *Black Parrot* at a guinea. *Gadelan* was enough, for the moment, to keep me satisfied and startled.

'Parroting', as it is called, is due to genetic change, i.e. a kind of sporting. It is not a disease.

May 7, 1950

Perhaps I should entitle this article 'In Your House', or 'Your Garden in Your House', because I want to write something about cut flowers, inspired by an interesting letter from a gentleman describing himself as a botanist and horticulturist who has carried out researches on this very subject. This is the time of the year when owners of gardens begin to pick more recklessly, with less dread of spoiling their outdoor show, but this pleasurable occupation does take a long time, and the busy woman wants to make her flowers last as long as possible.

'The cause of difficulties with cut flowers', says my correspondent, 'lies in the entry of air into the water-tubes of the flower stems during the period between cutting the flowers and placing them in water.' To prevent such disappointment, he recommends that you should place your newly cut flowers in recently boiled water while it is still just above tepid, i.e. not hot enough to sting your hand but warm enough to give your fingers an agreeable sensation of warmth. Cut your flowers, he says, during dull, sunless hours; a recommendation that we have all found out for ourselves; but I wonder how many readers of this article are going to go wandering round with a kettle of recently boiled water? These things take time, and one has other things to do. Still, I shall try it.

My correspondent condemns as an old wives' tale the placing of aspirin tablets or copper coins in the water. He gives a slight approval to lumps of charcoal, in so far as they absorb air from the water. I suppose that we all have our theories, but this idea of air entering the stems is worth consideration. I pass it on to you.

I now return to the garden proper. Have you got *Viburnum carlcephalum*? If not, please get it at once. It is a hybrid of *Viburnum carlesii*, which we all know and grow, and it is a far better thing. Its head of flower is tighter and denser; its scent is stronger; and its habit is vigorous. My own plant is young and small; but I am told by people who have seen it growing fully developed that it makes a huge bush in course of time. It is one of the most exciting things I have grown for years past; not very exciting as to its colour, which is white flushed with pink in the bud, but most exciting as to its powerful scent.

It is flowering now, April–May, and is obtainable from Messrs John Scott, The Royal Nurseries, Merriott, Somerset.

Halesia carolina, the snowdrop tree, is also just coming into flower. This is a very pretty flowering tree, seldom seen; it is hung with white, bell-shaped blossoms, among pale green leaves, all along the branches. It can be grown as a bush in the open, or trained against a wall. There is a better version of it called *Halesia monticola*, but if you cannot obtain this from your nurseryman *Halesia carolina* will do as well. Messrs Hillier, of Winchester, however, list them both.

May 14, 1950

Some proverbs are piercingly true; some are not true at all; some are half true. One of the half-true ones is the one that says familiarity breeds contempt.

Contempt is the wrong word. What we really mean is that we take certain virtues for granted when we live with them day by day. Our appreciation becomes blunted, even as the beautifully sharp blade of the pruning-knife someone gave us as a Christmas present has become blunted by Easter. There are things we grow in our gardens and forget about, and then remember suddenly, as I have just remembered the Sweet Woodruff, that meek, lowly, bright green native of Britain, so easy to grow, so rapid in propagation – every little bit of root will grow and extend itself – keeping weeds down and making a bright green strip or patch wherever you want it.

Sweet Woodruff is its pretty English name. *Asperula odorata* is its Latin name. It is obtainable from The Herb Farm, Seal, Sevenoaks.

You can use it in many ways. You can grow it where other plants would not grow, in shade and even under the drip of trees. You can grow it as a covering plant to keep weeds away. Then, in the autumn, you can cut the leaves and dry them and make them into sachets which smell like new-mown grass and have the faculty of retaining their scent for years.

It is not showy. Its little white flowers make no display, but it is a useful carpeter for blank spaces, and it certainly makes 'sweet bags' for hanging in the linen cupboard to discourage the moth or to put under your pillow at night. Take note that it has no scent until it is cut and dried, so do not be disappointed if you walk beside it in the garden and catch no puff of scent as you stroll. Which reminds me that this month of May is the time to sow that small, dim-coloured thing, *Matthiola bicornis*, the night-scented stock. I have just sown half an ounce of it, which cost me no more than 1s. 3d., all along the pathway at the foot of a yew hedge, and now look forward to some warm evening when the pale barn-owl is ranging over the orchard and the strong scent of the little stock surprises me as I go. This is anticipating the summer, when only recently snow lay upon the ground, but this modest little annual is so easily forgotten that a prod of reminder should not come amiss. If you mix the seed with the seed of Virginian stock, you will get a little colour in the day-time as well as the scent after dusk.

May 21, 1950

Snobbishness exists among gardeners, even as it exists among other sections of the community. The gardener's special brand consists in a refusal to grow plants which, of startling beauty in themselves, have become too trite to seem worthy of a place in any self-respecting gardener's garden.

Trite is a sharp, unkind little word. In the dictionary definition it means 'worn out by constant use; devoid of freshness or novelty; hackneyed, commonplace, stale'. I must agree that we all get tired of seeing certain plants all over the place – aubrietia, for instance, being allowed to blanket every so-called rock garden; and the Virginia creeper, *Ampelopsis veitchii*, glued to red-brick houses, where its colour swears horribly with the brick when it turns to flame in autumn. Yet, could we but behold either of these for the first time, we should shout in amazement.

It is too late to hope for such an experience, but I do suggest that much can be achieved by using these poor vulgarized plants in a different way and in the right place. There is, for instance, a big silver birch of my acquaintance into which a Virginia creeper has loosely clambered. When I first saw it I couldn't think what it was. Great swags and festoons of scarlet hung in the sunlight amongst the black and silver branches of the tree, gracefully and gloriously looping from bough to bough, like something (I imagine, perhaps incorrectly) in a tropical forest, or at any rate like a stained-glass window or like glasses of wine held up to the light. It convinced me once and for all that *Ampelopsis veitchii* should be grown *transparently*, not plastered against a wall. Any tall old tree would serve the purpose, an ancient pear or apple, or a poplar, if you cannot command a silver birch; and I think the same advice would apply to many of the ornamental vines, such as *Vitis coignetiae*, with its great shield-shaped leaves of pink and gold, or *Vitis purpurea*, whose name explains itself.

Aubrietia has certainly been overdone, but I still maintain that this Rock-cress can be used with tact and advantage. Tact means that it should not be allowed to ramp too freely. Advantage means that it should be set against the background that suits it best. A grey wall or a whitewashed wall, or grey paving-stones, all make a good background, especially if you avoid the insipid old pale mauve and choose only the best strains, such as *Cambria*, red;

40

Crimson Queen; *Godstone*, deep purple; *Kelmscott Beauty*, a double red; *Vindictive*, violet-red. These can all be supplied by Robinson Gardens Ltd, Eltham, Kent.

Aubrietia will not always come true from seed, but cuttings will come true, and on the whole I find that they do not revert. Even if they do hybridize amongst themselves, you may get an interesting novelty peculiar to your own garden, which is the ambition of every true gardener.

May 28, 1950

The roses are coming out, and I hope everybody will take the opportunity of seeing as many of the *old* roses as possible. They may roughly be described as roses which should be grown as shrubs; that is, allowed to ramp away into big bushes, and allowed also to travel about underground if they are on their own roots and come up in fine carelessness some yards from the parent plant. It is impossible in so short an article to give an adequate list, and even more impossible to indicate their charm, usefulness, and beauty, but there are gardens in which they may be seen and nurserymen from whom they may be obtained. (One garden where a large collection may be seen is Hidcote Manor, in Gloucestershire, near Broadway and Chipping Campden; for times of opening, which are several days a week, consult the National Trust, 42 Queen Anne's Gate, London, SW1. I put this in for the benefit of readers who live in that part of the country; and must add that, apart from its old roses, it is, perhaps, the loveliest garden in the west of England.*

The old roses are a wide subject to embark on. You have to consider the Gallicas, the Damasks, the Centifolias or Cabbage, the Musks, the China, the Rose of Provins . . . all more romantic the one than the other. Take this phrase alone: 'In the twelfth century the dark red Gallic rose was cultivated by the Arabs in Spain with the tradition that it was brought from Persia in the seventh century.' That is pure poetry, surely, although it comes from a serious article in a serious journal and was not intended as anything but a mere statement of fact. It should send us with a new zest in pursuit of these once neglected beauties.

They are not neglected now; their virtues are recognized by professional gardeners and amateur gardeners alike. True, I have heard conventionally minded people remark that they like a rose to be a rose, by which they apparently mean an overblown pink, scarlet, or yellow object, desirable enough in itself, but lacking the subtlety to be found in some of these traditional roses which might well be picked off a medieval tapestry or a piece of Stuart needlework. Indeed, I think you should approach them as though they were textiles

* See also a note on Hidcote Manor, reprinted on pages 149–55 of this book.

rather than flowers. The velvet vermilion of petals, the stamens of quivering gold, the slaty purple of *Cardinal Richelieu*, the loose dark red and gold of *Alain Blanchard*; I could go on for ever, but always I should come back to the idea of embroidery and of velvet and of the damask with which some of them share their name. They have a quality of their own; and from the gardener's point of view they give little trouble. No pruning to speak of, only a yearly removal of dead wood, and some strong stakes which seldom need renewing.

Have I pleaded in vain?

June

In a recent article I referred briefly to the fact that many privately owned gardens are now regularly thrown open to the public, and as this remark appears to have aroused some interest, I thought I might take this opportunity of amplifying it. I made it in a desire to urge keen gardeners to see as many gardens as possible, for the sake of the practical hints they might pick up there, apart from the pleasure they might gain. Nothing could be more useful to the amateur gardener than to observe other people's ideas, other people's successes, and other people's failures. At flower-shows, such as the Chelsea Show, one knows that every plant has been specially grown, richly fed, and luxuriously prepared for the great moment, thus arousing our suspicion that its grower has sat up with it night after night, holding an umbrella over it when too heavy a thunder-shower threatened its petals; ready with a hot-water bottle lest a late frost should come with a cold breath; and in many ways cosseting it for the supreme peak of its life when it must be exposed to the gaze of the King and Queen and all the Royal Family at a morning preview, and then to the expert criticism of Fellows of the Royal Horticultural Society during the afternoon. A plant in a garden is different from this: it has had to take its chance. It has been ordinarily grown. It has suffered from our common climate even as we all have to suffer. Seeing it grow in somebody else's garden, we can assess its normal performance; we can then decide whether we ourselves like it and whether we dare to attempt it or not.

These gardens now open to our wandering inspection are widespread and various. They range over all the counties of England, Scotland, and Wales. I have been looking through the England and Wales list, which runs so generously into seventy pages.* What enticements are therein offered! Who could resist the desire to penetrate without delay into precincts with such romantic names as Hutton John, Heronden Eastry, Nether Lypiatt, Bevington Lordship, St John Jerusalem, Castle Drogo, The House in the Wood, or Flower Lilies? All poetry is there, suggestive and evocative. One could go and sit in those gardens on a summer evening, and imagine what one's own garden (and one's life) might be. And again, who could fail to respond to the magic of an invitation to 'Magna Carta Island, until dusk', or to a garden mysteriously named The Isle of Thorns?

* Ninety-three pages in the 1951 list.

43

Nor is this all. At Tinker's Corner, for instance, you are offered tea *and music*; Bickleigh Castle provides flood-lighting and a moated Saxon chapel, modestly adding '*romantic interest*', which one can well believe. Little Whyley Hall somewhat startlingly tenders not only cups of tea but big-game herds. You can see Shelley's birthplace and Rudyard Kipling's house. You will be given 'strawberries if ripe' at Kempsons in June. At Old Westwell you can see fur rabbits; peach blossom, topiary and rare shrubs are elsewhere suggested for your enjoyment. And if you like to see how Royalty lives, you can go to Sandringham on any Wednesday during June, July, and September.

These are no more than random pickings out of an immense bran-pie. Anyone who wants the complete list can get it from the Organizing Secretary, National Gardens Scheme, 57 Lower Belgrave Street, sw1, telephone Sloane 9948. You pay a shilling entrance fee, and all benefit goes to the Queen's Institute of District Nursing. (*Note*: I should add that since this article appeared, the Queen's Institute has come to an arrangement with the National Trust, by which a percentage of the takings is given to the National Trust towards the cost of such gardens as are the property of the Trust.)

June 12, 1949

The rheumatic, the sufferers from lumbago, and the merely elderly, would all be well advised to try a little experiment in sink or trough gardening. By sink or trough we mean either those old-fashioned stone sinks now rejected in favour of glazed porcelain or aluminium; or the stone drinking-troughs with which pigs and cattle were once content before they had heard of concrete. Repudiated now by man and beast, they can be picked up in a house-breaker's yard for a few shillings; and, raised to hand-level on four little piers of brick or stone, may provide in this their second life a constant pleasure and interest to those keen gardeners who for one reason or another can no longer stoop or dig, but who still wish to fidget happily with their favourite occupation.

Fidget is perhaps the right word, for this is indeed a miniature form of gardening. The sink-gardener is like a jeweller working in precious stones. He makes his designs, trying experiments which he can alter when they fail to satisfy him, if he had the wisdom to keep a few pots in reserve. Out comes the offending colour, and in goes the befitting colour, neatly dropped in without any root disturbance.

Choose as deep a trough as possible, to get the maximum depth of soil. It must have a hole for drainage; and crocks spread over the whole bottom for the same purpose. The soil should be a mixture of fibrous loam, leaf-mould, sharp silver sand, and very finely broken up bits of old flower-pots. On top of this gritty bed you then arrange rocks or even flat stones. No one can dictate to you how to dispose your rocks, for this will be according to each person's fancy, but one can at least make some suggestions about what to plant. It is very important to keep everything to the right scale. Here is a short list of things which should do well: *Thymus serpyllum* for carpeting; *saxifrages* of the Kabschia or the encrusted kind; the tiny Alpine forget-me-not, *Myosotis rupicola*; the tiny Alpine poppy; *Bellis Dresden China*, a very bright pink little daisy; *Erinus alpinus*, pink; *Veronica allionii*, violet spikes; *Allium cyaneum*, a five-inch-high blue garlic; and even the midget roses, *Roulettii* and *Oakington Ruby*; and the innumerable bulbs such as the early species crocuses (*Sieberi*, *Tommasinianus*), and the early species tulips such as *linifolia*, bright red, or *dasystemon*, green and grey; or *orphanidea*, bronze; and scillas and chionodoxas and grape-hyacinths . . . the list would be endless, had I the space. Not having the space, I must leave readers to their imagination. There is plenty of scope.

June 26, 1949

I am no blind believer in the 'improved' modern flower: I don't like delphiniums with stalks like tree-trunks; I don't like roses with no scent and a miserable constitution; but for the Russell lupins and the bearded irises one must make an exception. Everyone knows, and grows, the lupins; not everyone, I think, has yet realized the extreme beauty of the irises. So as June is just the moment to see them in flower I thought I would remind you of their beauty and their many advantages.

Their beauty is beyond dispute. No velvet can rival the richness of their falls; or, let us say, it is to velvet only that we may compare them. That is surely enough to claim for any flower? They suggest velvet, pansies, wine – anything you like, that possesses texture as well as colour. (Wine, to a connoisseur, does possess texture.) Then, as to their advantages, they are the easiest plants to grow. All they ask is a well-drained, sunny place so that their rhizomes may get the best possible baking; a scatter of lime in autumn or in spring; and division every third year.

It may sound tiresome and laborious to dig up and divide plants every third year, but in the case of the iris it is a positive pleasure. It means that they increase so rapidly. Relatively expensive to buy in the first instance, by the end of the second or third year you have so large a clump from a single rhizome that you can break them up, spread them out, and even give them away. The best time to do this is immediately after they have finished flowering – in other words, at the end of June or beginning of July. Do not bury the rhizome, but leave it showing above the ground; this, again, is in order to let the sun reach it. The plant knows this, however, and will push itself up even if you do cover it over; but why give it that extra bit of trouble, when it already has a great deal to do?

Colours must, of course, be left to the individual taste. Those which we may roughly call reddish include *Cresset, Senlac, Mrs Valerie West, Maréchal Ney, Red Rover* and *Cheerio*, which has nothing wrong with it except its name. The wine-coloured ones include the magnificent *Betelgeuse, Melchior* and *Ambassador. Cinnabar* is a rich pansy-purple, very tall. All of these range in price from 1s. 6d. to 3s. 6d. There are also many fine yellows; but the best thing is to obtain a catalogue from a nursery that specializes in irises, say Messrs Wallace, Tunbridge Wells; or the Orpington Nurseries, Orpington, Kent. The descriptions are not misleading, for no adjective could be too extravagant. It is only you that will be.

June 4, 1950

I have a gardening dodge which I find very useful. It concerns colour-schemes and plant-groupings. You know how quickly one forgets what one's garden has looked like during different weeks progressively throughout the year? One makes a mental note, or even a written note, and then the season changes and one forgets what one meant at the time. One has written 'Plant something yellow near the yellow tulips,' or 'Plant something tall behind the lupins,' and then autumn comes and plants have died down, and one scratches one's head trying to remember what on earth one intended by that.

My system is more practical. I observe, for instance, a great pink, lacy crinoline of the May-flowering tamarisk, of which I put in two snippets years ago, and which now spreads the exuberance of its petticoats twenty feet wide over a neglected corner of the garden. What could I plant near it to enhance its colour? It must, of course, be something which will flower at the same time. So I try effects, picking flowers elsewhere, rather in the way that one makes a flower arrangement in the house, sticking them into the ground and then standing back to observe the harmony. The dusky, rosy *Iris Senlac* is just the right colour: I must split up my clumps as soon as they have finished flowering and make a group of those near the tamarisk for next May. The common pink columbine, almost a weed, would do well for under-planting, or some pink pansies, *Crimson Queen*, or the wine-red shades, as a carpet; and, for something really noble, the giant fox-tail lily, *Eremurus robustus*, eight to ten feet high. I cut, with reluctance, one precious spike from a distant group, and stick it in; it looks fine, like a cathedral spire flushed warm in the sunset. Undoubtedly I should have some *eremuri* next year with the plumy curtains of

46

the tamarisk behind them, but the *eremuri* are too expensive and one cannot afford many of them.

This is just one example. One has the illusion of being an artist painting a picture – putting in a dash of colour here, taking out another dash of colour there, until the whole composition is to one's liking, and at least one knows exactly what effect will be produced twelve months hence.

To conclude, may I recommend planting tamarisk? It is graceful, hardy, and no bother. You can control its size by hard pruning, if necessary, though for my own part I like to see it growing free. *T. pentandra*, sometimes called *T. hispidi aestivalis*, flowers in August and September; *T. tetrandra* is the one I have been writing about, and flowers in May. *T. anglica* flowers in late summer and does particularly well by the sea, where it can be used as a windbreak. They all strike easily from cuttings in autumn.

June 11, 1950
There is an evergreen argument about growing roses from cuttings. Nurserymen deprecate the method, for several obvious reasons preferring to bud their young scions on the various stocks of briar, e.g. a plant of saleable size is obtained in a shorter time; secondly, where a large supply of one variety is required the number of buds provided by the parent plant is probably larger than the number of cuttings which could be taken from it; thirdly, they contend (and they may be right) that the vigour of the wild stock improves the constitution of its fosterling.

Not being a nurseryman, I find it both cheap and amusing to raise a supply of roses for myself. Either I increase a variety which I have already got, or beg from a friend a cutting of something desirable which I lack. Thus, in a couple of years' time I have a sturdy little party growing away *on their own roots*; they have cost me nothing; and I know that every fresh growth they throw up from the base is not one of those wicked suckers which, if overlooked, will eventually swamp the rose back to the stock of *Rosa canina* or *Rosa rugosa*. It will be a growth of the true rose, and can either be left where it is, or transplanted, or given away.

The procedure is simple. You take cuttings of well-ripened wood, with a heel at the base, and plant them *very firmly* in rows in some spare bit of ground, not where the sun will scorch them, and leave them there for a year, by which time they should be rooted and ready to move to their permanent quarters. The end of September or the beginning of October is the best time, I find, though some people advocate July as an alternative. The most important points to remember are that the wood must be well matured, i.e. not too soft, and that the cuttings must be trodden in so firmly that no wind can wobble them loose and no thaw after frost can heave them up. It is advisable to look them over whenever such dangers have occurred, and if necessary to tread them in again.

Do not expect one hundred per cent success; some of them are bound to fail. It is a wise precaution to insert twice as many cuttings as you really need. It must also be remembered that some roses refuse to strike, for instance some of the Centifolias; but experience is the best guide, and, generally speaking, you should be rewarded with the smuggest self-satisfaction. A healthy rose-bush which you have yourself created is far more gratifying than one which arrives, ready-made, in return for a postal order. The experiment grows upon one after the first triumphs, and before long you may find yourself raising your own stock of flowering shrubs by the same method. Perhaps I should add that a hormone preparation such as Seradix A, obtainable from any sun-driesman, is a great help in stimulating the formation of roots. Instructions are sent with the bottle.

June 18, 1950

Two years ago I had what I thought might be a bright idea. It has turned out so bright, in both senses of the word, that I must pass it on.

I had two small windswept beds (the size was eight yards long by five yards wide each), divided by a path of paving-stones down the middle. I tried every sort of thing in them, including a mad venture of hollyhocks, which, of course, got flattened by the prevailing south-west wind, however strongly we staked them. So then I decided I must have something very low growing, which would not suffer from the wind, and scrapped the hollyhocks, and dibbled in lots and lots of thyme, and now have a sort of lawn which, while it is densely flower-ing in purple and red, looks like a Persian carpet laid flat on the ground out of doors. The bees think that I have laid it for their especial benefit. It really is a lovely sight; I do not want to boast, but I cannot help being pleased with it; it is so seldom that one's experiments in gardening are wholly successful.

The thyme we used was the cultivated or garden form of the wild thyme, *Thymus serpyllum*, the form you see creeping about between paving-stones on paths and terraces. *Serpyllum* comes from the Latin *serpere*, to creep; think of ser-pent; and in fact two old English names for the wild thyme were serpille and serpolet. My serpolet lawn . . . The Romans believed its fragrance to be a rem-edy for melancholia; and in later years, our own Elizabethan times, it was thought to cure sciatica and whooping cough, headache, phrenzy, and lethargy.

48

We had the common purple sort, and the sort called *coccineus* to give the redder patches, and also a little of the white, which varied the pattern.

I have planted a few bulbs of small things in amongst the thyme, to give some interest in the spring, when the thyme is merely green. A patch of crocuses; a patch of the miniature narcissus; a patch of the little pink cyclamen. It occurs to me also that if you have not a flat bed to devote to a thyme lawn you could fill a sunny bank with it. Steep grass banks are always awkward to mow, but the thyme would not need any mowing, and it should revel in a sunny exposure with the good drainage of a slope. You might plant some of the rock-roses, or sun-roses, hybrids of *Helianthemum vulgare*, amongst the thyme on a bank, though I would not do so in a thyme lawn, where it would spoil the effect of flatness. These sun-roses can be obtained in a variety of brilliant colours, ranging from pale buff and yellow to tomato-pink and deep red, and they flower for at least six weeks during May and June.

I know I get too easily carried away by some new enthusiasm and by the ideas it suggests; but that is half the fun of gardening. I will not apologize too humbly; so, instead of boasting, I will make two practical recommendations as an end to this article. First, do plant *Abelia triflora*. It flowers in June, grows to the size of what we used to call Syringa, and is smothered in white, funnel-shaped flowers with the strongest scent of Jasmine. Second, do plant *Cytisus battandieri*. This is a broom; and when it has grown into a large tree it is hung with gold-yellow tassels in June, with a peculiar scent. I could not think what the scent was, till my kind host who had it growing in his garden fixed it for me: 'It is the scent of pineapple mixed with fruit salad.' He was right.

Cytisus battandieri is supposed to be hardy, but I suspect that in cold districts it would be safer to train it against a wall.

June 25, 1950

Spring and summer are well provided with flowering shrubs, but it is a puzzle to know what to grow of a shrubby nature for colour in the later months of July, August, and September. There are the *hibiscus (Althea frutex)*, some of which are attractive with their hollyhock-like flowers, blue, pink, red, blush-pink, lavender, or white; and they have the advantage of living to a great age, for I remember seeing one in south-western France with a trunk the size of a young oak. Its owner assured me that it had been in her garden for over a hundred years. '*Mais bien sûr, madame, c'est mon arrière-grand-père qui l'a planté.*' It had been trained as a standard, with a great rounded head smothered in creamy flowers blotched with purple, giving the effect of an old-fashionable chintz; but, charming as the hibiscus can be, I suspect that it needs more sun than it usually gets here, if it is to flower as we should like. Perhaps I have been unlucky, although I did plant my hibiscuses – or should it be hibisci? – in the warmest, sunniest place.

Far more satisfactory, I find, are the hardy fuchsias. It is quite unnecessary to associate them only with Cornwall, Devon and the west coast of Scotland. Several varieties will flourish in any reasonably favourable county, and although they will probably be cut to the ground by frost in winter, there is no cause for alarm, for they will spring up again from the base in time to flower generously in midsummer. As an extra precaution, the central clump or crown can be covered with dry leaves, bracken, or soil drawn up to a depth of three or four inches; and in case of extremely hard weather an old sack can temporarily be thrown over them. Their arching sprays are graceful; I like the ecclesiastical effect of their red and purple amongst the dark green of their foliage; and, of course, when you have nothing else to do you can go round popping the buds.

The most familiar is probably *Fuchsia magellanica Riccartoni*, which will flower from July to October. *F. gracilis* I like less; it is a spindly-looking thing, and *F. magellanica Thomsoni* is a better version of it. *F. Mrs Popple*, cherry-red and violet; *Mme Cornelissen*, red and white; and *Margaret*, red and violet, are all to be recommended. They will cost you about 3s. 6d. a plant, and they like a sunny place in rather rich soil with good drainage. You can increase them by cuttings inserted under a hand-light or a frame in spring.

Other pretty and useful things for the late summer are the *Indigoferas*. They have pinkish, pea-like flowers dangling all along the tall, curving sprays. Like the fuchsias, they will probably get cut down in frosty weather, but this does not matter, because in any case you should prune them to the ground in April, when, like the fuchsias, they will shoot up again. They thrive at the foot of a south wall. There are several varieties, all desirable: *Gerardiana*, *Potaninii*, and *Pendula*.

Lespedeza sieboldii (sometimes called *Desmodium penduliflorum*) resembles the indigoferas, and is a most graceful plant. Messrs Hillier, of Winchester, list them.

July

This is a good moment to think of your future stock. Plants, and even seeds, are expensive to buy, but by raising your own nursery you can get plants by the thousand if you wish, for no cost beyond your own time and labour. It is well worth saving the seeds of annuals, biennials, and even perennials, either from your own garden or the gardens of friends who may have better varieties than you have. They must be quite ripe, and can be stored in little air-tight tins, such as the tins that typewriter ribbons come in, and sown in September when they will have time to make sturdy growth before the winter. Pansies, Indian pinks, columbines, foxglove, forget-me-not, primrose, polyanthus, anemones, lupins, and many other garden flowers can be thus harvested. Sow them thinly in drills on a finely pulverized seed-bed, and move them to their flowering quarters in the spring.

Remember that home-saved seeds will not necessarily come true, as the insects will have interfered with them. All the same, it is worth trying, and you might even get an interesting hybrid.

If you feel more ambitious you will be well advised to buy some packets of the improved varieties from a regular seedsman. Messrs Sutton, of Reading, have some fine columbines. *Crimson Star, Scarlet and Gold, Longissima,* a magnificently long-spurred yellow, and *Azure Fairy*, a really lovely pale blue, will all surprise you if you have hitherto grown only the old-fashioned kinds. The results of a pinch of seed from the grand new delphiniums (obtainable from Messrs Blackmore and Langdon of Bath), if you can't cadge some from a friend, will put you out of conceit with the sorts that have hitherto contented you. Seeds of the hybrid *Alstroemeria*, or Peruvian lily, will germinate freely, but as they are rather tricky to transplant, I should advise you to sow them direct where you want them eventually to grow; they like good drainage and full sun, and the *Ligtu* hybrids, pink or buff-coloured, are the sort to ask for; or *Alstroemeria haemantha* if you want a flaming orange one. Cover the seedlings with bracken, or with the twiggy tops of old pea-sticks if you haven't any bracken, for the first winter of their young life.

Lilies may also be raised from seed, instead of paying half a crown or more for a single bulb. *Lilium regale* will come up as thick as mustard and cress by this method; you will have to wait two or possibly three years before the bulbs come to flowering size, but think of the economy and of the staggered crop that you can raise, if you sow even one little row of seed every year.

Clematis will grow from seed, and so will broom; but as both these hate being disturbed it is advisable to grow them single in small pots, when they can be tipped out without noticing that anything has happened.

Cuttings of many flowering shrubs such as ceanothus, can be taken in July. Set them very firmly in a drill filled with sharp sand, in the open in the shade. As with rose cuttings, you should put in more than you need. A closed frame or even a hand-light put over cuttings for the first ten days or so will help them to strike, but they will give quite good results without this. Remember the hormone preparation recommended for rose cuttings on p. 48; it will very greatly help any cutting to strike: simple instructions are supplied with the bottle.

July 10, 1949

One learns a lot from visiting other people's gardens. One gets ideas. I got a lot of ideas from a famous garden I visited recently; so many, that I feel like a wine-glass spilling over; so many, that I cannot compress them all into this short article. So in this article I will concentrate only on the hedges I saw in that famous garden.

Hedges are always an important feature in any garden, however small, however large. Hedges are the things that cut off one section of the garden from another; they play an essential part in the general design. The only question is: What shall we plant for our hedges?

In this article I shall disregard the question of the flowering hedges; that is another subject, to which I hope to revert later on. I am here concerned only with the solid, useful hedge, deciduous or evergreen. We don't show nearly enough imagination about these. We still stick to such dull things as privet or *Lonicera nitida*, not realizing that we can make a muddle-of-a-hedge, which has a solidity and a character of its own.

In that famous garden I saw many different kinds of hedge, all planted in an imaginative mixture. There was yew mixed with box, and yew mixed with holly, and holly mixed with copper beech, and hornbeam mixed with ordinary beech, and one hedge mixed with five different sorts of plants in it – beech, holly, yew, box, and hornbeam, I think they were – but the most surprisingly sumptuous hedge, to my mind, was one made entirely of the copper beech.

We all know the copper beech as a tree; but few of us have thought of growing it as a hedge. Grown as a tree it has now acquired suburban associations. It works in with such things as *Prunus pissardii*, very pretty in their way, but with which we are now only too familiar. Grown as a hedge, the copper beech acquires a completely different character. You would not believe the richness of its colouring. It has purple tinges in the depths of it, a sort of mulberry purple, and then Venetian red; and then the tips of the young shoots so bright a ruby as they catch the sunlight – oh, why, I cried to myself, don't we all plant even a short length of copper beech hedge? For my own part, I am certainly going to.*

July 24, 1949

There comes an awkward moment between June and September. Unless we go in for herbaceous borders, for which few of us can now afford the space or the time, if indeed we still had the taste for them, the garden is apt to go blank and green and colourless in these months of high summer. Annuals are our best hope, but annuals mean a good deal of trouble, especially in a dry season. So we turn to our faithful friends the flowering shrubs; and find very little.

Still, there are some. The misty blue ceanothus, *Gloire de Versailles*, which can be grown either as a bush or against a wall, is at its best in July. The deeper blue plumbago, *Ceratostigma willmottiana*, flowers a little later, but sometimes coincides with the ceanothus, when they make a lovely sight planted in conjunction; and *Caryopteris mastacanthus* (or its variety *Clandonensis*), a low-growing shrub with grey leaves and powdery blue spikes, might join the group, with *Perowskia atriplicifolia* mixed in the foreground. A blue and silver corner, where only the names are vile.

Then there are the lavenders, so satisfactory at all seasons, but especially in this barren time of July and August. The old English lavender, *Lavandula spica*, is always a stand-by, whether you grow it as a hedge on either side of a path, or as a single bush. A particularly fine form is called *Twickle Purple*, and *spica gigantea* is the tallest of all, but there are other forms of lavender which one doesn't see so often. There is the very dark purple, *atro-purpurea nana compacta*, and there are white lavenders and pink lavenders, in fact a great range of lavenders which are all very valuable in the garden at this time of the year. They are no more difficult to grow than our old friend the ordinary English lavender. Try them. The good gardener is the gardener who makes experiments.

They should all be cut back to the old wood after flowering to prevent them from getting straggly.

Then, if you like white flowers, as you should – for what can be more romantic than white flowers in the moon-drenched summer nights? – grow *Romneya coulteri*, the big shrubby Californian poppy, and *Hoheria*

* See also pp. 152–3.

53

*lanceolata.** Not absolutely hardy, it resembles a syringa, which we are now taught to call *philadelphus*, but which we always knew as syringa in our youth. These syringas, or philadelphus, are also very useful shrubs for the late summer garden. You have *Virginal*, with big white flowers, and *P. purpureo-maculatus*, white with a purple blotch in the centre; both scentless, alas, unlike the spring-flowering *P. coronarius*. Then there are the tree hollyhocks, or *Hibiscus syriacus*, sometimes listed as *Althea frutex*, which you can get with blue flowers, or claret-coloured, or white, or mauve. They flower in August.

July 2, 1950

There are some moments when I feel pleased with my garden, and other moments when I despair. The pleased moments usually happen in spring, and last up to the middle of June. By that time all the freshness has gone off; everything has become heavy; everything has lost that adolescent look, that look of astonishment at its own youth. The middle-aged spread has begun.

It is then that the *Alstroemerias* come into their own. Lumps of colour . . . I have mentioned them before, I know, but a reminder will do no harm. They are in flower now, so this is the opportunity to go and see them, either in a local nurseryman's plot, or in a private garden, or at a flower-show. The yellow Peruvian lily, *A. aurantiaca*, was and is a common sight in cottage gardens and old herbaceous borders, where it was regarded almost as a weed, but it has been superseded by the far more beautiful *Ligtu* hybrids, in varied colours of coral and buff, and by *A. haemantha*, a brilliant orange. (Keep the orange away from the coral, for they do not mix well together, and whoever it was who said Nature made no mistakes in colour-harmony was either colour-blind or a sentimentalist. Nature sometimes makes the most hideous mistakes; and it is up to us gardeners to control and correct them.)

The *Ligtu* hybrids of *Alstroemeria*, and also the orange *A. haemantha*, can and should be grown from seed. You sow the seed in February or March, where you intend the plant to grow and flower. I am sure I am right in recommending this method. One reason is that the seed germinates very freely; another reason is that the roots of *Alstroemeria* are extremely brittle, and thus are difficult to transplant; and the third reason is that plants are expensive to buy and may fail owing to the difficulty of transplantation. Therefore I say sow your own seed and wait for two years before your clumps come to their fulfilment.

You could also sow one or two seeds in a pot, in those cardboard pots which dissolve after they have been dropped into the ground – this is perhaps the ideal method.

* See also pp. 56–7.

They demand full sun and good drainage, by which I mean that they would not like any shade or a water-logged soil. They are sun-lovers. They also demand staking, not stiff staking, but a support of twiggy branches to hold them up; otherwise they flop and snap and lose their beauty, lying flat after a thunderstorm of rain or a sudden gale, such as we get from time to time in our usually temperate country. This is a counsel of caution. Prop up your *Alstroemerias*, if you take my advice to grow them, by twiggy pea-sticks.

They are the perfect flower for cutting, lasting weeks in water in the house.

The seedlings would like a little protection in winter if there is a hard frost. Some bracken will do, scattered over them. Once established, they are hardy enough to withstand anything but a particularly bad winter. It is only the young that are tender, needing a little love and care.

July 9, 1950

A plant which I find always arouses a good deal of interest in the summer here is *Humea elegans*. Visitors walk round sniffing and saying: 'What is that curious smell of incense? One might imagine oneself in an Italian cathedral instead of an English garden.' They are quite right, for its other name is the Incense Plant.

Eventually they track it down to a six- to eight-foot-tall plant, with large, pointed dark green leaves and a branching spike of feathery cedarwood-coloured flowers. It is neither showy nor conspicuous, and nothing but the scent would lead you to it among its more garish companions, such as the delphiniums; yet it is graceful in its growth and well deserves its adjective *elegans*. It makes its influence felt in more subtle ways than by a great splash of colour. It steals across the air as potently and pervasively as the Sweet-briar on a damp evening. I stick it into odd corners, where people pass, or sit on benches, and pause for a moment before going on their way.

A native of Australia, it is not hardy here, and must be treated as a half-hardy biennial sown under glass in early summer, kept away from frost, and planted out in the late half of May or beginning of June. For this reason I cannot advise anyone to grow it who has not the advantage of a frost-proof greenhouse in which to raise it; but those fortunate gardeners who have even a tiny warmed greenhouse might well experiment with a few seeds in a pot: six seeds will give six plants, and six plants will be enough to scent the garden, especially if planted under the windows. It will tolerate half-shade, but the flower develops a richer colour in the sun; in the shade it dims off into exactly the same dingy tan as an old flower-pot. It likes a rich soil; it would love to be fed with liquid manure, and will grow all the better if you have time to give

it this extra diet or a handful of Clay's fertilizer; but if you have not the time
– and who has the time to attend to all these extra and special requirements?
– it will do adequately well in ordinary garden soil, and will give you all the
reward you can reasonably demand.

An additional attraction is that the flowering spike will last for at least a
year indoors if you cut it off in autumn before the rain has come to sodden
it. I kept some sprays of it in a vase for so long that I began to loathe the sight
of the thing; it turned dusty long before it started to fade and die; it reminded
me of those Everlasting Flowers, the *Helichrysums*, which are only too everlasting indeed.

You can save and ripen your own seed of it by cutting a spray or two and
laying it out on sheets of paper in a sunny place. Do this before it has the
chance to become blackened and sodden by autumnal rains.

I think I should add a word of caution. Some people appear to be aller-
gic to *Humea elegans*, which brings them out in a rash which is anything but elegant. (Some primulas have this effect on some people.) It is a chancy danger
which I would not wish any reader to incur owing to any fault of mine.

A visitor to my garden went off with a plant of it in a pot in his motor-car
and not only did he arrive home scratching, but also his dog.

July 16, 1950

A beautiful thing in flower just now (July) is the Californian tree-poppy. It is
not exactly a herbaceous plant; you can call it a sub-shrub if you like; whatever you call it will make no difference to its beauty.

With grey-green glaucous leaves, it produces its wide, loose, white-and-
gold flowers on slender stems five or six feet in height. The petals are like
crumpled tissue paper; the anthers quiver in a golden swarm at the centre. It
is very lovely and delicate.

I don't mean delicate as to its constitution, except perhaps in very bleak
districts. Once you get it established it will run about all over the place, being
what is known as a root-runner, and may even come up in such unlikely and
undesirable positions as the middle of a path. I know one which has wrig-
gled its way under a brick wall and come up manfully on the other side. The
initial difficulty is to get it established, because it hates being disturbed and
transplanted, and the best way to cheat it of this reluctance is to grow it from
root cuttings in pots. This will entail begging a root-cutting from a friend or
an obliging nurseryman. You can then tip it out of its pot into a complaisant
hole in the place where you want it to grow, and hope that it will not notice
what has happened to it. Plants, poor innocents, are easily deceived.

56

The Latin name of the tree-poppy is *Romneya*. There are two named sorts, *Romneya coulteri* and *Romneya trichocalyx*. They are both much the same, except for a few botanical differences. *Coulteri* is perhaps the better.

It likes a sunny place and not too rich a soil. It will get cut down in winter most likely, but this does not matter, because it will spring up again, and in any case it does not appear to flower on the old wood, so the previous season's growth is no loss. In fact, you will probably find it advisable to cut it down yourself in the spring, if the winter frosts have not already done it for you.

A good companion to the tree-poppy is the tall, twelve-foot shrub which keeps on changing its name. When I first knew and grew it, it called itself *Plagianthus lyalli*. Now it prefers to call itself *Hoheria lanceolata*. Let it, for all I care. So far as I am concerned, it is the thing to grow behind the tree-poppy, which it will out-top and will complement with the same colouring of the pale green leaves and the smaller white flowers, in a candid white and green and gold bridal effect more suitable, one would think, to April than to July. Doubts have been cast upon its hardiness, but I have one here (in Kent) which has weathered a particularly draughty corner where, in optimistic ignorance, I planted it years ago. There is no denying, however, that it is happier with some shelter by a wall or a hedge.

July 23, 1950

The flowers of *Magnolia grandiflora* look like great white pigeons settling among dark leaves. This is an excellent plant for covering an ugly wall-space, being ever-green and fairly rapid of growth. It is not always easy to know what to put against a new red-brick wall; pinks and reds are apt to swear, and to intensify the already-too-hot colour; but the cool green of the magnolia's glossy leaves and the utter purity of its bloom make it a safe thing to put against any background, however trying. Besides, the flower in itself is of such splendid beauty. I have just been looking into the heart of one. The texture of the petals is of a dense cream; they should not be called white; they are ivory, if you can imagine ivory and cream stirred into a thick paste, with all the softness and smoothness of youth-ful human flesh; and the scent, reminiscent of lemon, was overpowering.

There is a theory that magnolias do best under the protection of a north or west wall, and this is true of the spring-flowering kinds, which are only too liable to damage from morning sunshine after a frosty night, when you may come out after breakfast to find nothing but a lamentable tatter of brown suède; but *grandiflora*, flowering in July and August, needs no such considera-tion. In fact, it seems to do better on a sunny exposure, judging by the two plants I have in my garden. I tried an experiment, as usual. One of them is against a shady west wall, and never carries more than half a dozen buds; the other, on a glaring south-east wall, normally carries twenty to thirty. The reason, clearly, is that the summer sun is necessary to ripen the wood on which the flowers will be borne. What they don't like is drought when they are young, i.e. before their roots have had time to go far in search of moisture; but as they will quickly indicate their disapproval by beginning to drop their yellowing leaves, you can be on your guard with a can of water, or several cans, from the rain-water butt.

Goliath is the best variety. Wires should be stretched along the wall on vine-eyes for convenience of future tying. This will save a lot of trouble in the long run, for the magnolia should eventually fill a space at least twenty feet wide by twenty feet high or more, reaching right up to the eaves of the house. The time may come when you reach out of your bedroom window to pick a great ghostly flower in the summer moonlight, and then you will be sorry if you find it has broken away from the wall and is fluttering on a loose branch, a half-captive pigeon trying desperately to escape.

July 30, 1950

Most of the *Verbascums* (mulleins) are useful in the summer garden. The Cotswold hybrids are by now well known, *Cotswold Beauty*, *Cotswold Queen*, *Cotswold Gem*, and other members of their family, variously named but all looking as though clouds of small tawny or blushing moths had alighted all the way up the stalk, to remain poised there during the month of June. These hybrids are perennials, and, moreover, will sow themselves generously, so that once you have got them into your garden you need never be without them. Their only disadvantage, so far as I can see, is that they sometimes attract their own favourite brand of caterpillar, which eats the leaves into a semblance of lace-work; but he is very easily controlled, poor thing, by a dusting of derris powder.

The *Verbascum* which has excited me this summer, however, is not one of the Cotswold family, but something quite new to me in my ignorance, called *Verbascum Brusa*. Huge grey-green leaves, heavily dusted with flour, throwing up a spike six to seven feet tall, even more grey and woolly than the leaves. It fascinated me to watch this spike growing so rapidly, and to observe its pentagonal buds exploding one by one into the yellow flowers. They came gradually: a woolly grey bud one day, with a blunt yellow nose in the middle of it, and a flat yellow flower the next. They went on flowering for at least two months, through June and July.

I had planted my *Verbascum Brusa* against the dark background of a yew hedge. They looked very handsome there and they had the peculiar gift of inspiring all beholders to attempt a definition of what they looked like. For my own part, I had compared them to giant Roman candles, fireworks, tethered to the ground, but somebody came along and said they were like some strange sub-marine growth, waving about; and somebody else said they ought to be growing in a primeval landscape with a pterodactyl browsing amongst them. Anyway, they had the art of arranging themselves into grand curves, sweeping upwards, so that there was no upright monotony about them, nor did they demand any staking. I am assured by the nurseryman who introduced *V. Brusa* into this country from Brusa in Anatolia that it is a perennial, which I take leave to doubt. I think it is a biennial, but I fancy that it will ripen its own seed so that one should be able to harvest one's own supply for increase.*

Near them I had a group of *Onopordon arabicum*, grown from seed. It was too young this summer to throw up its noble spikes of blue thistle-like flowers, but its large grey leaves looked fine, with the same architectural quality as the leaves of acanthus, and the background of the yew hedge should be ideal for them.

* The verbascum proved itself very definitely to be a biennial.

59

August

I write this note far from home, on a not unenviable expedition which involves wandering round other people's gardens. Most of them are still suffering from the neglect of the war years, from shortage of labour, and probably also shortage of funds, and only in a few cases the prosperity of herbaceous borders still flaunted under the long old walls. Such luxuries are not for the majority, so I turned to consider the flowering shrubs, those permanent mainstays which increase in value with every year, and demand less attention than any other plant in the garden.

It is generally recognized that the late summer shrubs are far less numerous than those of spring; nevertheless, some were prominent.

In some gardens the hydrangeas were making a great display, but they look their best in large clumps, I think, not as the single specimens for which a small garden has only room; and in any case they always remind me of coloured wigs, so I really prefer the looser kinds called *paniculata*, which have a flat central head fringed by open sterile flowers; a particularly pleasing variety is called *Sargentii*.

Among the brilliant climbers, *Bignonia grandiflora* with red-orange trumpets was as startling as the humble nasturtium in colour, but far more graceful and much taller in habit. It should never be planted against red brick, but against grey stone or against a whitewashed cottage it looks both gay and splendid. (Nurserymen sometimes sell it under the name *Tecoma* or *Campsis radicans*.) The best variety is *Campsis Mme Galen*. Another orange climber, not quite so showy, goes by the unfortunate name of *Eccremocarpus scaber*; if I knew the English name for it, I would tell you. Perhaps it hasn't one. Not always considered quite hardy, it came through last winter unharmed. I notice also that that very lovely small flowering tree of white and gold, *Eucryphia intermedia*, has survived the winter; it is rather slow of growth, but all patient gardeners should plant at least one or two. It has the advantage of flowering while still quite young, in August just when such a stop-gap is most needed.

A reminder: bulbs for flowering in bowls next winter should now be planted in fibre, and kept in the dark till their little bleached noses show a couple of inches high. If a dark cupboard is not available, take the hint of a friend of mine who grew them most successfully under the sitting-room sofa.

August 7, 1949

It is not often that I mention vegetables, but I should like to put in a good word for the Globe artichoke. It appears to be almost unknown in this country. An enterprising greengrocer told me that he bought some in the market but had been obliged to throw them out, unsold, on to the rubbish heap. Yet there must surely be something to be said for a vegetable which is grown by the acre in such gastronomic countries as France and Italy.

There are three different kinds of artichoke: the Jerusalem, the Chinese, and the Globe. The Jerusalem, probably the best-known in England, is a tuber and is a most insipid vegetable on which no epicure should waste time or space. (It has no connection with Jerusalem, by the way: the name is a corruption of *girasole*, turning-with-the-sun, the Italian for sunflower, to which the Jerusalem artichoke is botanically related.) The Chinese, also a tuber, is seldom met with but highly to be recommended. It is like a little whorled sea-shell to look at, and is very useful in winter when vegetables are scarce. Plant the tubers in rows in March; do not allow the plants to get too dry in summer; lift the tubers in November, and store in sand, using them as you require. Boil them first, and then fry them in a little butter.

But it is the Globe artichoke I really want to plead for. This is not a tuber, but a tall and extremely handsome plant with deeply indented grey-green leaves which are most decorative in the garden and splendid in a big vase of summer flowers; they have a sculptural, architectural quality, like the leaves of acanthus, which gives dignity to the gay, mixed bunch. It thus serves a double purpose, for even if you decide not to use it as a vegetable it can still be grown for its foliage and for the thistle-like purple heads which it will produce if allowed to flower. These, however, are the heads you ought to eat before they reach the flowering stage; and do eat them *young*, I beseech you, before they have had time to grow old and tough. There are many ways in which they can be cooked; you can either boil them, whole, in salted water for twenty to thirty minutes and then eat them hot or cold, with melted butter or oil and vinegar respectively; or divest them of their leaves, using only the bottom – what the French call *fonds d'artichaut* – in a variety of dishes, as an entrée with half a tomato sitting on top, or as a savoury with cheese sauce, or stuffed *à la Barigoule* . . . but this is not a cookery book, and any good recipe book will give you ideas. An old tradition, on which I was brought up, says that after eating an artichoke you should drink a glass of cold water to bring out the flavour.

The Globe artichoke admittedly takes up a good deal of room: at least three feet wide and six feet tall, it may seem out of proportion in a small kitchen garden, but, as I have suggested, it may be given a place in the flower garden for its decorative value alone. It likes full sun, and it should be planted in April. It is reasonably hardy, but to be on the safe side you might cover it with some litter, or bracken, or ashes, during the winter months or especially if you foresee late frosts in May when the young shoots are coming up. I have never bothered to do this, and my artichokes have come safely through some very hard winters, but I pass on the advice for what it is worth. The gardening books, also, will tell you to renew your plants every three years. They may be right. All I can say is that my own plants have been in my garden for over twelve years and show no sign of going off; they crop as well as ever and have received little attention, so on this point I must disagree with the gardening books. Practical experience is worth more than many pages of print.

For the comfort of northern readers, I find that an old book printed in 1832 records that 'Nowhere does the artichoke arrive at greater perfection than in the Orkney Islands.'

August 21, 1949

I wrote of flowering shrubs for July and August recently, but there were many that I had no space to mention. I omitted, for example, the Etna broom, *Genista aetnensis*, which always seems to astonish people and earns me a reputation that I do not at all deserve. It is no more difficult to obtain or to grow than any other broom; and if you plant it in the right place, by which I mean, in an angle against a dark background, it will display itself for several weeks in July rather like that firework known as Golden Rain, familiar to us all on village greens on the 5th of November. It is indeed a lovely thing, as light and frail as spume, pouring its mist of golden flowers from an eventual height of fifteen to twenty feet, so brilliant as to startle you when you come upon it round the corner. Do plant at least one; but insist on getting it *in a pot* from your nurseryman: it dislikes being dug up by its roots out of the ground.

I have planted hypericums under the Etna broom; they are young as yet, but will eventually flower at the same time, and I think their richer, heavier yellow will go well with the airy golden fountain overhead. These hypericums are the shrubby kind, not the ordinary low-growing St John's Wort. They are *Hypericum patulum Henryii* and *Forrestii* for the most part, mixed with some treasured cuttings of better varieties, e.g. *H. Rowallane*, but if you just ask your nurseryman for the shrubby hypericum you cannot go far wrong. You will find that they will tolerate almost any ill-treatment; they will grow in shade or sun; they are most obliging, though on the whole they prefer a light soil; and for the housewife I may add that they are useful for cutting, every bud opening in water, day after day, which is a real consideration for one who has to 'do the flowers' in the house, and hasn't much time to renew fading blooms as they die.

The hydrangeas must be remembered for August; and there is *Buddleia alternifolia*, with long wands of purple, much more graceful than the common buddleia so attractive to all insects. *Clethra alnifolia*, the Sweet Pepperbush, has a tassel of white flowers with a good scent in August; not for northern gardeners but quite happy in the south.

Clerodendron fargesii and *Clerodendron trichotomum* are stocky little trees not often seen in our gardens. Their flower is insignificant, but they are worth growing for the berries which succeed the flower. Turquoise-blue and scarlet, these clusters of berries look more like an artificial hat decoration. They are shiny, brilliantly coloured, and look as though they had been varnished. Try at least one sample in your garden. *Fargesii* is the better of the two.

August 6, 1950

This is not the first time I have written about herbs, and no doubt it will not be the last. My own small herb garden is always encouragingly popular, with men as well as with the sentimentalists who I know fatally in advance are going to say that it is full of old-world charm. Thus I make no apology for recording an excellent idea sent to me by an American correspondent. It is not arty-crafty, but severely practical, many herbs being great spreaders, whose invasion must be kept in check; and it seems to me just the thing for anybody who wants a herb garden on a small scale, in a limited space.

You procure an old cart-wheel, the larger in diameter the better; you paint it white, with the outer rim green (where the iron tyre is), and sink the hub into a hole in the ground, so that the wheel will lie flush and level. This will give you a number of divisions in between the spokes in which to plant your herbs, plus the central hub, which you pierce through and fill with soil to grow one special, bushy little plant. (I suggest the dwarf dark purple lavender, Munstead variety.) My correspondent had fourteen divisions in which she planted chives, rue, sage, marjoram, basil, borage, balm, tansy, parsley, tarragon, rosemary, thyme, pennyroyal, and sage. Personally I should have included lovage, garlic, and caraway, but obviously the choice must be left to the grower.

She sent me a coloured photograph, and the effect of the flat white wheel, white spokes, and white hub was certainly very pretty, set in grass. Set in paving-stones it might be even prettier. All round the edge of the wheel, between the spokes, she had painted the appropriate names of the herbs in red. Then she had had another bright idea: behind her wheel she had sunk a semicircle of large tins with the bottoms knocked out, and in these she grew the real spreaders, such as the mints, which were thus kept under control.

Of course one always tries to improve on other people's ideas, and I thought to myself that it would be better to grow nothing but low herbs between the spokes. Tall things, such as tansy, tarragon, and melilot, would quickly rise to destroy the flat, clock-face effect of the wheel. And then I thought how pretty it would be to grow not only herbs but small treasures of bulbs and Alpine plants in the same way, in pockets of specially made-up soil between the spokes: saxifrages, and Lewisias, and the tiny narcissi, and the specie irises, and *Anemone hepatica*, and all the miniature things that come out in the spring.

August 13, 1950
I revert to the subject of hedges, since they are so important in a garden, large or small; and, moreover, now that many people are moving into new houses with a plot of land demanding enclosure, the question of hedges becomes urgent: what to plant and when to plant it. Generally speaking, early autumn is the best time, and let us remember always that money spent on a good hedge is money well invested, for year by year it gives an increasingly good return.

Our American friends do not like hedges. They do not share our love of privacy, and maintain that if you plant a hedge round your garden you are doing something undemocratic and may even have 'something to hide'. Fortunately for us and for the beauty of our country we suffer from no such notions. We might well, however, display a little more imagination in our choice of hedging plants, instead of sticking with such depressing fidelity to privet, quick, *Lonicera nitida*, and *Cupressus macrocarpa*.

There are two kinds of hedge, the useful and the ornamental. The useful hedge has the job of keeping animals out, and thus offers less scope for decorative informality, but life even in the country is not invariably a battle against cows or goats, and there are many plants which will afford charm and colour as well as providing the necessary line of demarcation. Rose hedges, for example, promise to become increasingly popular, and what could be lovelier than, say, a long stretch of some Hybrid Musk or sweet-scented Rugosa? Again, I can imagine such evergreen flowering shrubs as *Osmanthus delavayi* or *Choisya ternata*, or the silver-leaved *Elaeagnus macrophylla*, or the many-coloured cydonias – incorrectly called japonicas – or the many varieties of escallonia, especially valuable near the sea. It would be impossible to give anything approaching a complete list of suggestions here; but a most practical little book has just come out, at the moderate price of 1s. 6d.: *Better Hedges*, by Roy Hay, obtainable from Roy Hay Publications, Dolphin Cottage, Grayswood, Haslemere. Illustrated by photographs, it tells you how to plant; how to cultivate; how to cut; how to renovate; and, most valuable of all, ends up with eleven pages of special lists. These include hedge plants for small gardens; plants for formal or informal hedges; plants for the seaside, for semi-shade, for light soils, for heavy soils, for chalky soils; and some good hedge plants for various situations and purposes, with brief descriptions and instructions how to prune, trim and clip. There is also a note on hedge-cutting with labour-saving machinery.

August 20, 1950

At this time of the year, this dull time, this heavy August time, when everything has lost its youth and is overgrown and mature, the Japanese anemones come into flower with a queer reminder of spring. They manage, in late summer, to suggest the lightness of spring flowers. Tall, bold, stiff, they come up every year, and may indeed be regarded as a weed in the garden, so luxuriantly do they grow and increase.

The common white anemone *Japonica alba* is the one best known to us all. It is a most accommodating plant in many ways, because it does not resent being grown in half shade and is not particular as to soil. Neither does it require staking. It has a stiff resistant stalk. The only thing it resents is being moved. It takes at least two seasons to recover from removal; but when those two seasons have gone by, it will give you a rich return in white flowers with golden centres and a very long flowering period as bud after bud comes out. This alone makes it a satisfactory plant to grow in a shady or neglected corner where few other herbaceous plants would consent to flourish; but there are other varieties besides the common white, and it is to these that I would like to draw your attention.

The pale mauve one is, I suppose, almost as well known as the common white. It is very pretty, a lilac-mauve; but there are others, such as the variety called *Prince Henry*, a really deep mauve-pink, growing to a height of three to four feet and flowering from August to September. This will cost you 1s. 6d. a plant and is well worth it. There are also shorter ones, growing only to one or two feet, such as *Mont Rose*, which is described as old rose in colour, and *Profusion*, purplish-red, two feet high. I must confess that I have not grown *Mont Rose* or *Profusion* and know them only by repute; but *Prince Henry* grows in my garden, in a fortunate accidental association under the wine-coloured clematis *Kermesina*. This late-flowering clematis, belonging to the Viticella group of clematis, should be more often planted. It produces a mass of its small wine-coloured flowers, like a Burgundy wine held up to the light, at the very same time as the Japanese anemone *Prince Henry* comes to its best. They match one another to perfection.

My only grievance against the Japanese anemone is that it tires and droops once cut, and thus is no good for picking. But in the garden, however, it comes as a salvation in this dreary, uninteresting time of the year.

August 27, 1950

A lady asks me if she could make a miniature indoor garden on a large plate, 'if possible something bright for Christmas'. Well, it would have to be a very deep plate, almost a bowl, to give sufficient root-run if she wants her plants to be actually growing; and she would have to pierce holes at the bottom for drainage (which would not be easy, as the china would probably split in the process). This problem she could overcome by using the peat fibre supplied by sundriesmen for forcing bulbs in unpierced bowls, which for some mysterious reason does not require any outlet. I see no insuperable difficulty there. The only thing that worries me is the 'something bright for Christmas'.

There are few small bulbous plants which can be coaxed into flower by Christmas Day, at least not without a lot of forcing. There is the Paper-white narcissus, but this grows rather too tall for the sort of miniature garden my correspondent evidently has in mind; and there is the Roman hyacinth; but neither of these can accurately be described as bright. Some of the species crocuses might serve her purpose, and I have sent her an address (Messrs Wallace, The Old Gardens, Tunbridge Wells), where she can procure these. But on the whole I think that for her Christmas plate she had better adopt another method, patiently leaving her miniature garden for a few weeks later. The Christmas-plate method I would suggest is to fill her plate with damp sand, covering it over with moss, and sticking into it any berried twig or coloured leaf or freakishly out-of-season flower such as a primrose or violet or a belated rose-bud or Christmas rose (hellebore). It is surprising what one can find, poking about, especially in a mild season, and a plateful of odds and ends can be extremely pretty and amusing.

After the New Year matters become much easier. If she plants up her plate in September with small bulbs, and keeps it in a dark cupboard until the growth is an inch or two high, then brings it out into the light (not too strong a light until the growth has turned quite green), she may expect a gay little picture in January or February. Whether she mixes her bulbs or keeps to one sort in each plate must depend on her personal taste. Scillas, grape-hyacinths, chionodoxa (Glory of the snow), crocus, *Iris reticulata*, are all suitable for such treatment. A clump of snowdrops, lifted from the garden when its green noses begin to push through the soil, will come into flower in a surprisingly short time in a warm room. I have also dug up wild violets and primroses, and had them blooming very early.

I hope my correspondent will not introduce miniature gnomes or toadstools into her plate. She could, however, put a piece of looking-glass in the middle, not so much pretending to be a pool of water as to reflect and duplicate the heads of the little flowers growing around it.

September

September 29, 1946

The two great planting months, October and November, are close upon us, and those gardeners who desire the maximum of reward with the minimum of labour would be well advised to concentrate upon the flowering shrubs and flowering trees. How deeply I regret that fifteen years ago, when I was forming my own garden, I did not plant these desirable objects in sufficient quantity. They would by now be large adults instead of the scrubby, spindly infants I contemplate with impatience as the seasons come round.

That error is one from which I would wish to save my fellow-gardeners, so, taking this opportunity, I implore them to secure trees and bushes from whatever nurseryman can supply them: they will give far less trouble than the orthodox herbaceous flower, they will demand no annual division, many of them will require no pruning; in fact, all that many of them will ask of you is to watch them grow yearly into a greater splendour, and what more could be exacted of any plant?

Your choice will naturally depend upon the extent of your garden, but it should be observed that any garden, however small, has a house in it, and that that house has walls. This is a very important fact to be remembered. Often I hear people say, 'How lucky you are to have these old walls; you can grow anything against them,' and then, when I point out that every house means at least four walls – north, south, east, and west – they say, 'I never thought of that.' Against the north and west sides you can grow magnolias or camellias; on the east side, which catches the morning sun, you can grow practically any of the hardy shrubs or climbers, from the beautiful ornamental quinces, commonly, though incorrectly, called Japonicas (the right name is Cydonia, or even more correctly, Chaenomeles), to the more robust varieties of *Ceanothus*, powdery-blue, or a blue fringing on purple. On the south side the choice is even larger – a vine, for instance, will soon cover a wide, high space, and in a reasonable summer will ripen its bunches of small, sweet grapes (I recommend Royal Muscadine, if you can get it); or, if you want a purely decorative effect, the fast-growing *Solanum crispum*, which is a potato though you might not think it, will reach to the eaves of the house and will flower in deep mauve for at least two months in early summer.

And apart from these wall-plants, many small trees may be set in convenient places. The flowering cherries and crabs have fortunately become a feature of most gardens, and how gaily they contribute to the aspect of English villages and cottages during the spring. Many of them, however, tend towards a rather crude pink; and those who would wish to avoid this colour may be better advised to plant the subtler greenish-white cherry called Ukon (*Cerasus lannesiana grandiflora*) or the white-blossomed crab *Dartmouth*, with purplish-red fruits of remarkable beauty in the autumn; or that other crab, *Niedzwetzkyana*, with even more beautiful purple fruits. The almond, of course, will always be a favourite, partly because it flowers so early in the year; but if you are thinking of planting almonds now I would strongly recommend the variety called *Pollardii*, with a finer and deeper flower than the common kind usually seen.

The advantage of trees and shrubs is that they may be under-planted with bulbs – another activity which should not be neglected at this time of year. Daffodils, narcissi, and hyacinths should be got into the ground without delay. Bulbs are always a good investment, as they increase underground and may be lifted yearly, and the little offsets or bulbils planted out in a spare corner to develop. Such raising of one's own stock is much more satisfying than writing a cheque or buying a postal order.

September 4, 1949

The autumn catalogues are beginning to arrive, and have reminded me of the peonies. There are few more repaying plants. Rabbits dislike them; their flowering season extends through May and June; they last for a week or more as picked flowers for the house; they will flourish in sun or semi-shade; they will tolerate almost any kind of soil, lime-free or otherwise; they will even put up with clay; they never need dividing or transplanting; in fact, they hate it; and they are so long-lived that once you have established a clump (which is not difficult) they will probably outlive you. Add to all this that they will endure neglect. Mine struggled through the weeds of war and seem none the worse for it.

Of course, if you want to do them well, they will respond as any plant will respond to good treatment. If you have a little bone-meal to spare, fork it in during the autumn. But it is not really necessary. The only thing which is really necessary is careful planting in the first instance, and by this I mean that you should dig the hole eighteen inches deep; put in some rotted manure or compost at the bottom; fill it in with ordinary soil and *plant shallow*, i.e. don't bury the crown more than a couple of inches underground. This is important.

There are, roughly speaking, two different kinds of peony: the herbaceous, in which we may include the species, and the Tree peony (*Paeonia suffruticosa*, or *Moutan*). The Tree peony is not very easy to get nowadays, and you would have to pay anything from 10s. 6d. to 30s. for it. Still, it is worth the investment, especially as it will start to flower young and will flower more and more copiously as it advances in age. *Never cut it down.* Mine were destroyed for ever by a jobbing gardener, who also happened (unbeknownst to me) to be a Jehovah's Witness, when he cut them to the ground one autumn.

The herbaceous peony is the one we are accustomed to see in some not very attractive shades of red or pink in cottage gardens. Do not condemn it on that account. There are now many varieties, either single or double, ranging from pure white through white-and-yellow to shell-pink, deep pink, and the sunset colour you find in *P. peregrina*. This really flames; and its companion, *P. lobata Sunbeam*, is as good, if not better. As a yellow I would recommend *P. mlokosewitchii*, did it not cost 30s. a plant; I grew it from a sixpenny packet of seed myself, but you have to be very patient to do that. Apart from this, *P. Laura Dessert* is probably the best yellow at the more reasonable price of 7s. 6d. *Sarah Bernhardt*, at 6s., has enormous pale pink flowers, double; *Kelway's Glorious*, at 12s. 6d., is a fine white; *Duchesse de Nemours*, at 5s., is white with a slightly yellowish tinge and smaller flowers; *Martin Cahuzac* at 6s., a dark red, has leaves which colour well in autumn.

Messrs Kelway, Langport, Somerset, are large growers; and Mr J. Russell, Sunningdale Nurseries, Windlesham, has a remarkable collection of the tree peonies.

September 18, 1949

This article is going to be concerned with two very different things: a tree and a lily. The tree, which is called *Koelreuteria apiculata*, is of astonishing beauty in August when it is fully grown to its eventual height of fifteen to forty feet. For a tree to attain that height means waiting for some years, and therefore this recommendation must be addressed only to those who are responsible for the planting of trees in any public park or garden or to those who intend to stay put on their own plot of land: the owners of a freehold country cottage, for instance. Vagrant tenants cannot afford to wait so long.

I collected the seed of *Koelreuteria* in the abandoned garden of an old abbey in France, having no idea what it was. I could see only that it was of graceful growth, and was dangling with seed-pods like little Chinese lanterns, or like the pods of that plant we call the Cape gooseberry (*Physalis capensis*), and grow for winter decoration. Sown in a pan when I got them home, my seeds sprouted as generously as grass; I soon had a potential forest. I planted some seedlings out, and I did notice that the leaves turned a very pretty pink colour, but it was not until I saw a full-grown specimen in a neighbour's garden that I realized what a treasure I had got hold of. This specimen was in full flower;

70

bright yellow flowers borne on erect spikes about a foot tall, something like Golden Rod if you can imagine Golden Rod growing out of a tree right above your head, standing up boldly above tasselled masses of coral-pink seed-pods, and the leaves of a light feathery green. I do not exaggerate. The effect, against the blue sky, was amazing.

The lily I want to write about is *L. regale*, that sweet-scented trumpet which is perhaps the easiest of that tricky family to grow. There is no connection between it and the *Koelreuteria* except that they both come so easily from seed. Now the current price for flowering bulbs ranges from 16s. to 20s. a dozen, so if you want them in any quantity it will pay you to raise them from seed, and this is the moment to look out for seeding heads in your own or a friend's garden. You can also buy seed for 6d. to 1s. a packet, but it is more fun to crack open a seed-pod and shake out those marvellously packed, paper-thin seeds for yourself. Every one of them should germinate, and one pod alone should give you more lilies than you will ever have space for. Choose the seeds from the strongest plant; sow them in a seed-box and plant out the little bulbs next year in rows in a nursery bed where you can keep an eye on them; by the end of the second year you ought to be picking a few single flowers; by the end of the third year they ought to be fully developed. If you repeat the process yearly, thus staggering your supply of bulbs, you should never be without *L. regale* in your garden, at no cost.

You realize, of course, that you can do the same with those little black boot-buttons that appear on the stems of the old tiger-lily?

I cannot resist adding a note at a later date (1950) to pass on an amusing hint for growing lilies from seed. You need a screw-top jar, such as housewives bottle fruit in; a mixture of leaf-mould, peat, and loam, enough to fill the jar; and half a handful of seed. You make the mixture wet, and then squeeze it in your hand till it stops dripping and becomes a damp sponge. You then introduce it into the jar, sowing the seed in layers as you go, until the mixture and the seed have both reached the rim. You then screw on the top; put the jar on the window-sill in a warm room, and watch for the seeds which have come to the edge, where you can see them, to develop into little tadpole-like bodies which, you hope, will eventually become bulbs.

September 3, 1950

Reproachful letters reach me: how *can* I say that the August garden is dull and heavy? These letters are all courteous and kindly, but it is evident that their writers are pained. Several of them paint a picture of such gaiety that I remain abashed. It is, of course, perfectly true that if you have time for the annuals (and not too large a space to fill) you can have a blaze of colour lasting well into September. It was not difficult to visualize the swagger patches that my correspondents were looking at: petunias, ageratum, snapdragons, portulaca, cosmea, arctotis, larkspur, stocks, verbena, zinnias . . . the very thought of them made me blink. And to these must be added such perennials as the heleniums, the flat-headed yellow achillea, the rudbeckias, the gaillardias (there are two particularly fine ones, called *Tangerine* and *Wirral Flame*). And dahlias. And gladioli. And montbretia. Yes, perhaps I was wrong. I was probably thinking more of the sluggish trees, the overgrown hedges, the brambles bringing their first hint of autumn; and thus must acknowledge that my aversion to the August garden may be psychological rather than factual. I just cannot bear feeling that summer is petering out to its end, and spring so far behind.

As I have indicated, I don't grow many annuals except the zinnias, to which I am always faithful. There is, however, one which proved very decorative this year and remained in flower for a very long time; in fact, it is flowering still. This was *Venidium fastuosum*, a half-hardy South African daisy of enormous size, three inches wide at least, of the most brilliant, varnished-looking orange petals and a central ring of darkness round the base. Why, I wondered, looking into the heart of this garish thing, should Nature take so much trouble and display such inventiveness? Why such superfluous ingenuity? Why this eternal, inexplicable miracle of variation? Was it intended to appeal to us as human beings or to some insect in search of nectar?

There are hybrids of *Venidium* which should be worth trying, though *V. fastuosum* is probably the best. The hybrids are described in catalogues as ranging in colour from white to lemon and straw; there is also a dwarf strain, about a foot high, in yellow and orange. If one has facilities for starting them early, in boxes under glass, as is the usual practice with half-hardy annuals, they would, of course, come earlier into flower; but otherwise a sowing made out of doors towards the end of May, where they are intended to remain, would start flowering at the beginning of July and should continue right through August.

September 10, 1950

I wrote once in this column about a little lawn I had made of the cultivated or garden sorts of the common creeping thyme, but this article is going to be about the other sorts, too bushy or too wiry to be suitable for such a purpose. A narrow bed in a sunny place, say under a shed or a house wall, filled with a collection of various thymes, could be very charming and sweet-scented, and a great pleasure to the bees. It has the advantage of preferring a poor, stony soil, such as you often find against a construction where the builders have left their rubbish of rubble, mortar, and grit; places where greedier plants will refuse to grow without the enormous trouble of first redeeming the waste.

This consideration will doubtless appeal to the practical gardener quite as much as the more romantic associations with thyme. We have perhaps now forgotten that 'to smell of thyme' was a phrase used by the Greeks to express a literary elegance of style; or that medieval ladies embroidered a sprig of thyme surmounted by a bee, to denote courage as supplied by a decoction of thyme, and activity as demonstrated by the insect; or that an elaborate preparation of thyme enabled you to see fairies; or that it was 'very good to be given in either phrenzy or lethargy'; or that it cured you of the nightmare, and also of the melancholy.

There are said to be twenty-four different kinds of thyme, but few people will aspire to a complete assemblage. In a narrow bed such as I have imagined, say a couple of feet wide, I should be satisfied with half-a-dozen varieties. In the front I should plant low-growing kinds: *Thymus lanuginosus*, the grey woolly thyme, and *Thymus herbabarona*, which is also known as the Caraway thyme because of its peculiar scent, but which gets its official name because it was used to flavour that massive lump, the Baron of Beef.

Behind these low-growers I should plant the shrubby kinds. The golden thyme, *T. citriodorus aureus*, and the silvery thyme, *T. citriodorus argenteus*, both lemon-scented, as their name implies; and *T. ericafolius*, which is a heather-like shrublet, green tinged with yellow; and *T. nitidus*, about a foot high, with purple flowers.

It is possible to buy plants of all these, and seed of some of them, to be sown in March or early April; though it is said that the lemon-scented kinds will smell sweeter if raised from cuttings or little rooted bits, taken any time from May to September. It is thus not too late to beg for scraps, or to order from a nurseryman (a list of addresses is given on p. 271), for planting out this autumn. May I also suggest that a planting of small spring-flowering bulbs amongst them would give interest and colour in the early months of the year?

September 17, 1950

For two or three years past I have been trying to run to earth a plant called *Tropaeolum polyphyllum*, a native of Chile. 'Run to earth' is indeed the right phrase, for it buries itself so deep in the ground that it is impossible to dig up. All efforts to obtain a tuber from the garden of a friend, where it grows like a weed, proved vain; it simply snapped off, and for all I know the essential tuber was half-way down between Kent and the Antipodes. Now, however, in one week, I have found it advertised by two separate nurserymen, one of whom remarks that 'for some reason it has become rather rare'.

It should not be allowed to become rare, for it is a very showy, decorative thing, flowering in June, in long creeping trails of bright yellow nasturtium-like trumpets extending nearly a yard long from its grey-green leaves. I cannot improve upon the description given by one of the nurserymen listing it: 'It makes a wonderful effect with its glaucous foliage and garlands of blossom.' It certainly does. It looks like golden serpents writhing out of a sea-green base. The ideal place to plant it, I imagine, would be in a dry wall, say in some Cotswold garden, when it could tuck its roots into cool crevices and could allow its garlands of blossom to pour in golden waterfalls down some small vertical cliff of that lovely stone. Alternately it would look well in a rock garden, for it seems to demand stone to set it off, and thus is not so suitable for a bed or border.

The moral of its preference for deep rooting is to plant it deep at the outset, at least a foot to eighteen inches. I imagine that like its relation *Tropaeolum speciosum*, the flame-coloured nasturtium which does so brilliantly in Scotland and so poorly in England, it would not object to partial shade. Do not be alarmed when it disappears entirely during the winter: it will reappear in spring. It also has the pleasant habit of rambling about through anything which may be planted near it, and of coming up in unexpected places.*

A useful clematis flowering in September is *Clematis flammula*. I would not advocate it for an important or prominent place, as its masses of small white flowers are not in the least showy, but for scrambling over a rough shed or out-house, where its peculiarly musty scent may be caught by the passer-by. Its great virtue is that it will flourish in places which never get any sun, the picture of contentment on a cruelly dark north wall. There is a pale pink variety, which might be more pleasing, but I cannot speak from experience.

September 24, 1950

Catalogues arrive by every post, and are as bewildering in their diversity as in their monotony. What shall we order this autumn? Bulbs, shrubs, flowering trees, herbaceous plants, or what? How tempting the lists are! And how easy they make gardening sound! If you believed half they say you would look forward next year to a garden something between Kew and the tropical estate of some legendary millionaire in Guatemala. It is difficult to keep one's head. I always lose mine. Year after year I am decoyed into experiments which

* Messrs Pennell, Lincoln, and Mr Cusack, whose address is on p. 75, both list it.

I know are almost certainly doomed to failure. I cannot resist. Experience tells me that I ought to resist, but, like the poor mutt who falls to the card-sharper in the train, I fall to every list offering plants I cannot afford to buy and could not cultivate successfully even if I could afford them.

I have, however, received from Ireland a catalogue of such enchantment that it makes me revoke all my cautious mean resolutions. This Irish nursery-man is a man after my own heart. He writes of his wares in a lively, unstereo-typed style, starting off grandly with 'I like them all, or I would not have them in my list.' He is meticulous as to colour: 'I call mauve mauve,' he says, 'not blue.' He likes species, 'as nature made them, unhybridized by man, undis-torted by his whim'. Then I like his vigour. Writing of *Eremurus robustus* he says: 'Robust it is, by Jove! – with lovely strong pink spires rocketing up to ten feet,' and describes the roots of *eremurus* as apocryphal spiders. And he ends up with a plea that only a very disillusioned heart could disregard, 'Please do try some of those plants you may never have heard of' – which, after all, is the philos-ophy I myself have been preaching ever since I took to writing these articles.

Admittedly, many of his plants are for the connoisseur, but we can all find a special corner for treasures, and on the whole his claims for the ease with which they may be grown are not too madly exaggerated. I cannot go all the way with him over the blue Chilean, *Tecophilea cyanocrocus*, for instance, that in-credibly lovely thing which, as he rightly remarks, must be seen to be believed; or over *Ixia viridiflora*, which I have always found less reliable than the other ixias. Where I find myself in complete agreement is over his insistence on good drainage, for I am convinced that the enemy in these islands is damp rather than frost, and this, I suppose, must be his worry in Ireland even more than it is ours in England. I might add that his prices are low, even in com-parison with those of some Dutch bulb-growers.

His address is: Ralph Cusack, Uplands, Roundwood, Co. Wicklow.

October

Strawberries at the end of October, at negligible expense and negligible trouble. This does not mean that they will fruit *only* by October; it means that having fruited generously throughout the summer, from June onwards, they will continue to carry their crop until the first frost; I have, in fact, picked them so late as November.

This exemplary plant is the Alpine strawberry. The new garden varieties carry a much larger berry than the *fraises des bois*, which provide so frequent and delicious a feature of meals in Continental restaurants, and they certainly equal them in flavour. To enumerate their virtues deserves a whole paragraph. First, they require no straw, since the fruit is well up among the leaves, and only a berry here and there will rest upon the ground to become a prey for slugs. Then, for some extraordinary reason, the birds take no interest in them; consequently, no netting is necessary. Then, if a late frost should spoil the blossom, new blossom soon appears, which is more than can be said for the ordinary strawberry. Finally, they are neat little plants, and make a charming edging along a path, taking up very little room and being indeed quite decorative with their bright red berries and soft green leaves.

The best variety to grow as an edging is the runnerless *Baron Solemacher*, the sort called *Cresta*, which makes many runners, is rather untidy and is better in a bed to itself. There is also a runnerless *Strawberry Delight*, which can be had with a pale yellow as well as a red berry, but of this I cannot speak from personal acquaintance.

Their demands? Farmyard manure or compost will of course increase their luxuriance, but I have found them doing quite well without it in a reasonably good soil. They seem to prefer a little shade, where they become juicier and more luscious; and they must be picked very ripe, over-ripe if anything. One important point concerns the actual eating: they should be picked two or three hours in advance, then pricked with a fork or even slightly crushed, powdered with sugar, and left to stand in a bowl. If you can add a spoonful of red wine, or sherry or Madeira, so much the better; but perhaps that is a counsel of perfection.

To this hint for epicures, I should like to add a plea for greater enterprise in next year's kitchen garden. A grey monotony attends our English vegetables . . . and not only in their cooking. *Calabrese* as a change from cabbage; *Hamburg Parsley* instead of parsnips, or grated raw into a salad; *celeriac*, so useful in winter; Chinese artichokes instead of Jerusalem; the Globe artichoke, too, seldom seen in English gardens, though it is ornamental as well as useful; sorrel, which may be used like spinach, or to make soup. Potatoes, too, need not always be huge, floury, and somewhat insipid; try *Belle de Juillet*, or *Rosa* or *Kipfler*, if you can get them. Messrs Harrison, Maidstone, usually have them.

Herbs would require an article to themselves. I suppose that every cook has by now discovered the virtues of chives, but how many insist upon a plant of lovage, which, with shredded leaves, makes all the difference to sandwiches and salads? And how many gardeners bother to grow caraway, which is as easy as mustard-and-cress, sows itself everywhere, and yet produces plenty of seed?

Dill, associated in most people's minds with dill-water for babies, is almost indistinguishable from caraway in taste, and, moreover, is very pretty in a mixed bunch of summer flowers, with its flat greenish-yellow heads and upright carriage.

All very well if you live in the country, with a herb garden just outside the kitchen door, not necessarily larger than the top of the kitchen table, but what about the town dwellers? For their consolation, it is surprising how many herbs will flourish in a window-box, chives not the most despicable amongst them.

October 12, 1947
A new pleasure has abruptly entered my life, and I should like to pass it on to others: the Strawberry grape. It is perfectly hardy here in Kent, where an outdoor specimen, twenty years old, covers a cottage, and is now heavy with ruby-pink bunches this autumn even after the cruel winter of 1946–7. My own little vine is only in its second year, but is already fruiting so generously that a number of bunches had to be suppressed; it would have been unwise as well as unkind to let so young a thing carry more than eight. But I foresee that it will go on in strength and wealth.

The great point about this grape is its flavour. I hope the professional nurseryman will forgive me if I say that his claims for his wares sometimes read better on paper than they turn out in fact; his colours blow brighter, his fruit tastes sweeter, and the vigour of his plants is beyond belief. But the Strawberry grape really does taste of strawberries – the little Alpine or wood strawberry. One unkind guest said it tasted of peardrops, but I stick to my conviction.

A single plant will cost you 10s. 6d., but will, I am sure, prove an investment paying a good dividend. It can be obtained from The Six Hills Nursery, Stevenage, Hertfordshire.

Another vine which is giving me great pleasure at the moment is *Vitis het-erophylla*, an East Asian. You can't eat it, but you can pick it and put it in a little glass on your table, where its curiously coloured berries and deeply cut leaves look oddly artificial, more like a spray designed by a jeweller out of dying turquoises than like a living thing. Yet it will grow as a living thing, very rapidly, on the walls of your house, or over a porch, hanging in lovely swags of its little blue berries, rather subtle, and probably not the thing that your next-door-neighbour will bother to grow or perhaps doesn't know about. There are some obvious plants which we all grow: useful things, and crude. We all know about them. But the real gardener arrives at the point when he wants something rather out of the common run; and that is why I make these suggestions which might turn your garden into something a little different and a little more interesting than the garden of the man next door.

A note on some special small trees for autumn colour may therefore not come amiss. *Crataegus crus-galli*, the Cockspur Thorn, turns as scarlet as you could wish in October, and is a tough little tree which will flourish anywhere; against the dark background of a hedge he will look splendid. *Disanthus cer-cidifolius* hangs itself with round leaves like golden coins. *Cornus kousa* and *Cornus florida rubra*; *Berberis thunbergii atropurpurea splendens*; *Parrotia persica*; *Prunus sargentii*; all these will flame throughout October until the leaves come off. It is a good plan to plant them where at some moment of the day they will catch the sunlight; and it is more effective to plant two or three in a clump than some isolated specimen. This advice applies to most plants, but especially to those designed to make a bonfire of colour in the rich, mellow days of autumn.

October 2, 1949

The blue trumpets of *Gentiana sino-ornata* have given great pleasure during September. Some people seem to think they are difficult to grow, but, given the proper treatment, this is not true. They like semi-shade (I grow mine round the foot of an apple tree, which apparently suffices them in this respect); they like plenty of moisture, which does mean that you have to water them every other evening in an exceptionally dry summer; and they utterly abhor lime. This means that if you have a chalky soil you had better give up the idea of growing these gentians unless you are prepared to dig out a large, deep hole and fill it entirely with peat and leaf-mould.

It is a safe rule that those plants which flourish in a spongy mixture of peat and leaf-mould will not tolerate lime; and the gentians certainly revel in that sort of mixture. As a matter of fact, I planted mine in pure leaf-mould and sand without any peat, and they seem very happy. Perhaps they would have been even happier with some handfuls of Sorbex peat thrown in. But I am quite satisfied, and so are they. The boxful of plants I set out last autumn, the gift of a kind friend in Scotland who says she has to pull them up like weeds in her garden (lucky woman), have now grown into so dense a patch that I shall be able to treble it next year.* For the gentian has the obliging habit of layering itself without any assistance from its owner, and I have now discovered that every strand a couple of inches long has developed a system of sturdy white roots, so that I can detach dozens of little new plants in March without disturbing the parent crown, and, in course of time, can carpet yards of ground with gentian if I wish, and if my supply of leisure, energy, and leaf-mould will run to it.

Gentiana sino-ornata is very low-growing, four inches high at most, but although humble in stature it makes up for its dwarfishness by its brilliance of colour, like the very best bit of blue sky landing by parachute on earth. By one of those happy accidents which sometimes occur in gardening, I planted my gentians near a group of the tiny pink autumn cyclamen, *Cyclamen europaeum*, which flowers at exactly the same time. They look so pretty together, the blue trumpets of the gentian and the frail, frightened, rosy, ears-laid-back petals of the cyclamen: they share something of the same small, delicate quality. It is one of the happiest associations of flowers.

So please plant *Gentiana sino-ornata* in a leaf-mould shady bed in your garden, with an inter-planting of *Cyclamen europaeum*. The same conditions will suit them both. The gentian may cost you anything up to 16s. 6d. a dozen; but even half a dozen will give you as many plants as you need in a year's time; and as for the cyclamen, its brown bun of a corm seems immortal, with a rich progeny of seedlings coming up all over the place.

October 16, 1949

Some friends of mine planted a small peach tree six years ago. They stuck it in and left it to make what it could of itself. This year they have picked over nine hundred peaches from it, fine large fruits, excellent for dessert, for jam or for bottling. We usually associate peaches with a sunny wall – and how warm the rosy fruit looks, hanging against old brick of much the same colour – but this tree stands out in the open, unsheltered, unprotected, and unpruned. The branches had to be propped, they were so heavy; but apart from a generous mulch of manure, that was all the attention it got. A good reward, I thought, for so little trouble.

* I have.

Of course, if you could find a sheltered corner, say in the angle formed by two hedges, giving protection from cold winds, it might do even better; and there is no doubt that if you threw a veil of tiffany or butter-muslin or even some old lace curtains over the blossom when frost threatens in April or May, you would be doing much to safeguard the crop. This would apply especially in a hard winter and a draughty spring. My friends treated their tree rough: they let it take its chance, and it took it. So I thought I would advise other people to try the same experiment.

After all, what do you risk? A guinea to buy the tree. Then you wait for a year or two, and then you start to pick the fruit. You get a couple of dozen after three years. After six years you get nine hundred – not a bad investment. It would certainly succeed in the Home Counties and in the South, and I have heard of a regular orchard of peaches in Essex, though I should not like to venture an opinion about the North. But, given a reasonably mild district, there seems no reason why this experiment should not be turned into profit as well as pleasure. The importation of foreign fruit has not improved the English market, but the home grower can still sell peaches or nectarines for anything up to eightpence each, and nine hundred eight-pences would make a useful contribution to the current expenses involved in keeping up a garden.

The peach my friends grow is called *Grosse Mignonne*, and that has proved its quality; but varieties specially recommended for this rather unorthodox method, i.e. not fan-trained against a wall, are *Peregrine*, *Sea Eagle*, and *Duke of York*.

I have mentioned nectarines. This most delicious fruit could, of course, be grown in the same way, as a bush in the open. *Early Rivers* and *Humboldt* are both good varieties.

October 30, 1949

It always surprises me that we in this country should neglect to plant some of the fruits which are now seldom to be seen save as survivals in some old garden. For example, the common quince. In some parts of France you see it growing as a hedgerow plant, its great yellow pear-shaped fruits heavily hanging for any thrifty villager to pick and turn into jelly or quince-cheese. It grows in the hedgerows there as thick as blackberries in an English lane. Why don't we plant it in our gardens here, as our grandfathers did?

It is of the easiest possible cultivation, and will do in almost any type of soil, though naturally it will be happiest in a nice light loam with plenty of humus. It appreciates moisture, so long as it is not completely waterlogged. It requires no pruning or spraying. So far as I know, it suffers from no form of disease.* It is self-fertile. Birds do not attack it, and the fruit ripens too late for the wasps. The blossom comes late, and thus seldom has to endure danger from frost. It lives to a great age and is a regular and reliable cropper. It makes all the difference to stewed apples or to an apple-pie. It can, and should, be turned as I have said into delicious jelly, marmalade, or cheese. If it is on its own roots, as it usually is, it can be readily increased from its own suckers. To this catalogue of excellences, add that it is very beautiful, both in May when it flowers and in October when it ripens, and you will not wonder that I should demand a revival of planting the common quince.

So far as its beauty goes, I think there are two ideal situations to choose for it. One would be near water, so that the branches would hang over and be reflected in a pool, a stream, or even a pond. The other would be immediately beneath a bedroom window, so that in the spring you could look down into the wide upturned faces of the shell-pink blossom amongst the young leaves and the wiry tangle of very black twigs, and in the autumn on to the fat golden fruits. Only the occupant of that upper room could tell the delight of observing the quince throughout the cycle of the seasons.

Then, as a postscript, I might put in a good word for the bullace. This, like the quince, is a tree seldom seen except in old gardens. It is, I believe, the child of a marriage between a damson and a plum. It has no ornamental value, but crops inordinately every year, small purple fruits which bring a good marketing price if you have the patience and leisure to pick them, and can also be used to make bullace wine.

As for the cherry-plum, or *myrobalan*, the medlar, and the various gages, including the old greengage, I must leave those for another article.†

October 1, 1950

I know I am continuously grousing about the dearth of plants, apart from annuals and herbaceous stuff, to enliven the garden in August and September, so it was with a startled pleasure that I observed three bushes growing in a cottage garden as I drove along a secret lane. They looked like pink lilac. Tall, pyramidal in shape, smothered in pointed panicles of flower, they suggested a bush of pink lilac in May. Yet this was September . . . Puzzled, I stopped by the roadside to investigate.

It was *Hydrangea paniculata grandiflora*, sometimes called the plumed hydrangea. In its native country, Japan, it is said to attain a height of twenty-five feet, but in this country it apparently limits itself to something between six and eight feet; and quite enough, too, for the average garden. Do not

* Note: see pp. 89–90.   † Addresses of fruit-growers will be found on p. 272.

confuse it with *H. hortensis*, the one which sometimes comes sky-blue but more often a dirty pink, and which is the one usually seen banked up in Edwardian opulence against the grandstand of our more fashionable race-courses. *H. paniculata grandiflora*, in spite of its resounding name, is less offensively sumptuous and has a far subtler personality.

It reveals, for instance, a sense of humour, and even of fantasy in the colouring it adopts throughout its various stages. It starts off by flowering white; then turns into the pink I have already described as looking like pink lilac. Then it turns greenish, a sort of sea-green, so you never know where you are with it, as you never know where you are with some human personalities, but that makes them all the more interesting. Candidly white one moment; prettily pink the next; and virulently green in the last resort . . . As I was leaning over the gate, looking at this last pink-green inflorescence, the tenant of the cottage observed me and came up. Yes, he said, it has been in flower for the last three months. It changes its colour as the months go by, he said. He knew it was a hydrangea, though he couldn't remember its second name. He was very proud of it. He was a dark man, a foreigner: and although he spoke fluent English he had a thick, peculiar accent which I could not identify. As I was talking to him across his gate, a circus passed with all its caravans and roundabouts; and I thought that the foreign man, and the circus, and the English cottage garden were all very much of the same thing; and that I would certainly order *H. paniculata grandiflora* to grow in a damp, shady spot next year, and hoped it would do as well as his.

October 8, 1950

My apologies for the delay in sending the Irish nurseryman's address. I have only just returned from abroad to find many letters of inquiry. I am now only hoping that he may be able to cope with the orders he receives, and that no one may be disappointed.

It was too late in the year to find many wild flowers in the mountains or in Italy, though in France the meadows were mauve with the autumn crocus and in the Apennines the woods and banks were stippled a shy pink with the little cyclamens. It was tantalizing to pass hill-slopes green with what appeared to be turf, but which on investigation proved to be a solid mat of *Gentiana acaulis*. I arrived in Tuscany with a bag full of seed and bulbs, corms and tubers; goodness knows whether they will consent to flower next year in England or what some of them will turn out to be; but at least one shining flower reminded me of itself, with a kind of reproach for not being more common in our gardens. This was *Sternbergia lutea*, the lily-of-the-field. They toiled not,

Vita Sackville-West, 1916

Above, Vita Sackville-West with her sons at Long Barn, Weald, Sevenoaks, 1924, and (*below*) broadcasting for BBC Radio, 1934

Right, Vita Sackville-West at her writing table in the Elizabethan Tower, 1948. *Below,* Vita Sackville-West, 1958

Vita Sackville-West at Sissinghurst Castle, 1948

neither did they spin, but they were certainly arrayed in beauty as they spread themselves in a gilded carpet under the black cypresses framing a distant view of Florence.

Sternbergia lutea might easily be mistaken for a crocus. It is, in fact, neither a crocus nor a lily, despite its scriptural association; it belongs to the family of the amaryllis. It is a most brilliant yellow, varnished as a buttercup, rising crocus-like amongst its narrow leaves. It likes a rather rich, gravelly soil, well drained, with as much sun-baking as possible. It does not like being disturbed; it likes being left for years in a clump to develop, with a little protection of bracken or leaf-litter through the winter in this country. It costs about 1s. 3d. a bulb, or 12s. a dozen, from English nurserymen. It is a very old plant in English gardens, having been mentioned by John Parkinson in the reign of Charles the first; Parkinson called it the Great Autumn Daffodil, though of course it is no more a daffodil than it is a crocus or a lily. I shall think of it always as I saw it growing in its golden sprinkle on that Florentine terrace, beneath the cypresses framing the cupola of the Duomo and the tower of the Palazzo Vecchio, romantic, floodlit; the lily tower of Florence.

May I remind readers that the WVS makes a special autumn appeal for plants, herbaceous or otherwise, which gardeners may now be discarding? It is better, surely, that they should go to beautify some stark pre-fab. or bare housing estate than perish on the bonfire? Your local WVS will collect them, with no expense to yourself, if you will kindly advise them.

October 15, 1950
The autumn garden . . . It has its beauty; especially, perhaps, a garden with an old orchard attached to it. When I was very small, about four years old, I suppose, a line of poetry entered into my consciousness, never to leave it again:

> Rye pappels drop about my head.

I had no idea what rye pappels might be, but they held a magic, an enchantment for me, and when in later life I identified them as the ripe apples of Andrew Marvell's poem they had lost nothing of their enchantment in the process of growing up.

Coming home from abroad, after an interval when the season had time to change from late summer into autumn, it struck me how *pink* and green the autumn garden was. Not bronze and blue, the colours we associate with the turning woods and the hazy distance and the blue smoke of bonfires along the hedgerows. The woods had not turned yet, but in the orchard the apples were rosy and in the garden the leaves of the peonies were pink, and so were the leaves of the common azaleas, and so were the leaves of *Parrotia persica* and the leaves of that other little tree with the lovely name *Liquidambar*, and the leaves of *Prunus sargentii*, so soon to drop, alas, from the row in which I had planted them along the top of a rosy-red brick retaining-wall.

The naked, reddish stems of the Belladonna lily (*Amaryllis*) had shot up in that surprising way they have, and were opening their clusters of pink flowers. This is a bulbous plant well worth growing, for it is reasonably hardy in the open ground in a sunny, well-drained position, preferably at the foot of a wall, and it supplies flowers for picking at a time when choice-looking flowers are rare. What it likes is lots of water in the early summer, while it is making its leaves, and then it likes to be left alone while the leaves disappear and nothing is seen until the flowering stems shoot up all of a sudden on an October morning. It may seem a bit expensive to buy (1s. 9d. to 2s. 6d. a bulb); but once you have got it you have got it for keeps, which is more than can be said for a two-and-sixpenny seat at a cinema.

The Michaelmas daisies were also rioting pink in the garden. All the sorts called *Beechwood, Beechwood Charm, Beechwood Challenger*, and that specially good one called *Harrington's Pink*. Some people tell me that *Harrington's Pink* is not a good doer. I can say only that it does very well here in ordinary conditions, and that I have no complaint to make against it. It thrives, adding its bit of brighter pink to the rich scale of colouring leaves in the incarnadine symphony of October.

October 22, 1950

In my garden I have an awkward little border. It is awkward only in the sense that I have never made up my mind how best to use it. I have tried many things, and nothing has ever looked right, except the wine-coloured and ruby-coloured wallflowers in the spring. These have to be torn out towards the middle of May, when they are over, and the little border is then left blank and empty, piteously clamouring for something to restore life to it during the summer. My little border, about a yard wide, happens to run along the foot of an old wall, this garden being largely a walled garden; but there are many narrow borders running under the house-wall, warm and sheltered, where one would wish to make the gayest possible display from April up to the autumn. The wallflowers are *right*; but what comes later? I have tried Korean chrysanthemums; no, they were too tall. I have tried annual carnations; no, they were too floppy. So now I have had another idea.

It was suggested to me by coming again across that pretty word: mixty-maxty. The dictionary defines it as 'incongruously or promiscuously mingled; jumbled together; mixed; confused'. Very well, I thought, a mixty-maxty border it shall be. I will buy many packets of annuals, and sow them on the ground as soon as the wallflowers have been thrown away; but I shall not sow them according to the usual method, a patch of larkspur at the back, a patch of candytuft at the front, all regulated by their different heights and colours; I shall tear open all my packets and pour all the seeds out into an old tobacco tin, and shake them up together, and then sow them and let them take their chance. Very odd effects may result. I may get a tall spire coming up in front, and a dwarf hidden at the back, but I shall not care. The fun of gardening is nothing unless you take reckless risks.

All the same, despite recklessness, one must also be sensible. Let us now come down to brass tacks. One must draw up a list of annuals for sowing. One might include some half-hardy annuals, since they will not be sown until the latter half of May. Here is a rough draft of my list, my half-sensible, half-temerarious list, of the seeds I propose to order and shake up in a tin and scatter broadcast along that narrow border. They are all seeds which can be obtained at a very low price from any of the big seedsmen.

Phacelia campanularia. Cornflower. Salpiglossis. Zinnias. Cosmea. Coreopsis. Clarkia. Eschscholtzia. Love-in-a-mist. Petunias. Godetia. Salvia patens. Scabious. Larkspur. Verbenas.*

October 29, 1950

October is the time for the garden to be taken to pieces and replanted if necessary for next year. It is also the month that ushers in the long dark evenings when one makes seed lists under the lamp, pure pleasure and no worry; no slugs, no rabbits, no moles, no frosts, no damping-off. An interesting and unusual plant which should find a place is *Cobaea scandens*, which sounds more attractive under its English name of cups-and-saucers. This is a climber, and an exceedingly rapid one, for it will scramble eight to ten feet high in the course of a single summer. Unfortunately it must be regarded as an annual in most parts of this country, and a half-hardy annual at that, for although it might be possible with some protection to coax it through a mild winter, it is far better to renew it every year from seed sown under glass in February or March. Pricked off into small pots in the same way as you would do for tomatoes, it can then be gradually hardened off and planted out towards the end of May. In the very mild counties it would probably survive as a perennial.

* July 1951. Do not follow this advice. It was a complete failure.

85

It likes a rich, light soil, plenty of water while it is growing, and a sunny aspect. The ideal place for it is a trellis nailed against a wall, or a position at the foot of a hedge, when people will be much puzzled as to what kind of a hedge this can be, bearing such curious short-stemmed flowers, like a Canterbury Bell with tendrils. Unlike the Canterbury Bell, however, the flowers amuse themselves by changing their colour. They start coming out as a creamy white; then they turn apple-green, then they develop a slight mauve blush, and end up a deep purple. A bowl of the mixture, in its three stages, is a pretty sight, and may be picked right up to the end of October.*

If you are now thinking that a half-hardy annual such as *Cobaea scandens* is too much trouble, and perhaps want something more permanent than you can get out of a seed packet, do consider the rose called *Nevada*. It got an Award of Merit from the RHS in 1949, and well it deserved it. I do not think I have mentioned it before, and as it is a fairly new rose, you may not have come across it. This is not a climber, but a shrubby type, forming an arching bush up to seven or eight feet in height, smothered with great single white flowers with a centre of golden stamens. One of its parents was the Chinese species rose *Moyesii*, which created a sensation when it first appeared and has now become well known. For those who are interested in such pedigrees, the other parent was *La Giralda*, a cross between that grand old Hybrid Perpetual, *Frau Karl Druschki*, and *Mme Edouard Herriot*. The grievance against *Moyesii* is that it flowers only once, in June; but *Nevada*, unlike *Moyesii*, has the advantage of flowering at least twice during the summer, in June and again in August, with an extra trickle of odd flowers right into the autumn.† One becomes confused among the multitude of roses, I know, but *Nevada* is really so magnificent that you cannot afford to overlook her. A snowstorm in summer, as her name implies. And so little bother. No pruning; no staking; no tying. And nearly as thornless as dear old *Zéphyrine Drouhin*. No scent, I am afraid; she is for the eye, not for the nose.

---

* The seed is obtainable from Messrs Thompson & Morgan, Ipswich, Suffolk, or from Mr Thomas Butcher, Shirley, Croydon, Surrey.
† For *Rosa moyesii* and *Nevada* see also pp. 127–8.

November

Judging by the number of letters I received, my recommendation to plant the
Alpine strawberries seems to have aroused some interest among readers of
The Observer. I now venture, therefore, to recommend the hardy vine, or outdoor grape. I did just refer to this in an earlier article, but as a wall-covering
rather than as a fruit, laying very little emphasis upon its edible qualities. It
does not appear to be generally known that vineyards were once common in
the southern counties, that the grapes ripened, and that wine was made from
them; so that what man has done once, man can do again.*

The wine-making part is of dubious value today, when wine-making
means sugar; but there is no doubt that vines producing small, sweet bunches
may profitably be grown against a south wall, say the wall of the house. There
are several varieties which may be relied upon to ripen in any normal English summer – the non-summer of 1946 was, in fact, the only summer in
which my grapes went mouldy, or shrivelled, or in some other way made
themselves entirely useless. Of the several varieties I would recommend, in
order of merit, *Royal Muscadine, Muscatel, Golden Drop, Dutch Sweetwater*. *Royal
Muscadine* I have found by far the best, though *Muscatel* runs it close.

Royal Muscadine, moreover, has a romantic history: it was discovered at
Cahors by Henry of Navarre on his way to Paris to become Henry IV of
France, and was taken by him from Cahors to Fontainebleau, where it
became known as the *Chasselas de Fontainebleau*. It is a Chasselas grape, meaning an ordinary little greenish grape of the type you see so plentifully displayed in greengrocers' shops in France and Italy, but none the worse for that,
if you have the patience to pick it off berry by berry, or are so impatient as to
cram a whole handful of berries into your mouth at one go. It is well worth
growing in our southern counties against a warm wall for it means that you
can pile a dish of grapes in August and September on your breakfast table.

The hardy vines are also very useful for making vinegar. You can use any
of the hardy fruiting vines for this purpose, but if you want to obtain the real
red wine vinegar I would recommend planting *Vitis vinifera Brandt*. This produces a dark, almost black grape, which turns into vinegar by the simple

* Since this article was written a most interesting book has appeared, *The Grape-vine in England*, by Edward Hyams, published by the Bodley Head, 16s., illustrated.

method of squashing the fruit into a wooden tub, leaving it to ferment for ten days or a fortnight, and then straining off the juice into bottles. Do not cork the bottles; put in a twist of paper to keep out the dust and flies.

Figs and peaches will likewise ripen in the south more readily than is sometimes supposed. There is no need to regard them as luxury fruits. The figs *Brown Turkey* and *Brunswick* are especially reliable against a wall.

A small shrub which I should like particularly to recommend is *Caryopteris Clandonensis*. It flowers from August onwards, bright blue and fringed, at a time when flowering shrubs are rare. Prune it, not very hard, at the end of February, and it will make a rounded bush from three to four feet high. If you cannot obtain the variety *Clandonensis*, the sorts named *Mastacanthus* or *Tangutica* will do as well. They like a sunny place but are not fussy as to soil; and in order to obtain the best effect I should plant at least three in a clump. At present-day prices, they cost from 4s. 6d. to 5s. 6d.

By the way, are you aware that many of the nurserymen now supply plant-tokens in the same way as booksellers supply book-tokens? The only difference is that whereas book-tokens can be exchanged in almost any bookshop, plant-tokens can be exchanged only at the nursery that issues them; but as the big nurseries have a wide choice of plants and seeds, this restriction does not much matter.

November 24, 1946

From the gardening point of view, those who live in the south of our island have certain undeniable advantages over those that live in the north. The climate is softer; a fact which undoubtedly influences those plants marked by an ominous little asterisk in nurserymen's catalogues, meaning 'suitable only for mild localities'. Nevertheless, those who live in the north need not despair; indeed, there are times when they may exult, for there are some things they can grow to greater perfection. What about *Tropaeolum speciosum*, the flame nasturtium, with brilliant red trumpets among the small dark leaves? This is the glory of Scottish gardens, defeating most efforts to grow it in the south, even on the cool north side of a hedge. And what about the autumn gentian, *sino-ornata*, which will do also in the south, in a lime-free bed of almost pure leaf-mould, but which is even better in the cooler conditions of the north? There are few lovelier plants for the shortening days of autumn; low, brilliant trumpets of the purest blue, increasing rapidly into large clumps that can be pulled to pieces and replanted or given away.* The coloured primroses and polyan-

* See also pp. 78–9 and 90–1.

tha also seem to favour a cool climate; indeed, many of the old-fashioned double primroses have now become so rare as to be obtainable only from a few Scottish nurseries.

The tropaeolum, the gentian, and the primrose are plants for every purse; but where a few extra shillings can be afforded they might well be expended on the magnificent Himalayan lily, *Lilium giganteum*, which the well-informed gardener always tried to obtain from Lord Stair's garden at Lochinch, Stranraer. Here, grown in light woodland, they were seen at their best. Eight to ten feet tall, they lifted their spires heavily hung with white trumpets, and as heavily spiced with scent. One of these spires, cut and put in a room, scents the air almost too strongly for the average person to endure.

They are expensive to buy, about 5s. for one three-year-old bulb, that is a bulb of flowering size; but they are more economical than they sound. For one thing, you may buy younger bulbs at a much cheaper rate, and grow them on for yourself; and for another thing, a full-grown bulb (which dies after its first flowering) will give you a whole cluster of little bulbs round it, which you can plant out in a nursery bed and thus, in three years' time, obtain ten or twelve for a fine group. Dig it up in October or November, to divide and replant. After this, you need never be without them. They like semi-shade; a rich mixture of leaf-mould and loam; manure if you can supply it, buried deep enough for their roots to reach; and a little bracken or other litter thrown over them to protect their tips against spring frost.*

The study of illustrated books, such as Sir Herbert Maxwell's *Scottish Gardens*, will readily convince the pessimistic that a wealth of perennial plants and flowering shrubs will flourish in northern latitudes. This book, out of print, I fear, but obtainable from libraries, is particularly valuable in that it not only includes many coloured illustrations, but starts off with a chapter on Scottish gardens in general and concludes with a list of shrubs recommended for northern planting. There is also a book by Reginald Farrer, that great collector and gardener, on his own garden in the Lake District. *My Rock Garden* is the title.

November 13, 1949

I have been getting myself into trouble, and must put it right. Writing about quinces,† I said that they were not liable to disease, *so far as I knew*. By that cautious little phrase I hoped to safeguard myself, and indeed my own experience of quince trees and all the books I consulted endorsed my opinion. It now appears that I was wrong. It appears that they are occasionally liable in

* See also pp. 137–8.   † See pp. 80–1

wet summers to 'a fungus rejoicing in the name of *Entomosporium maculatum*', which attacks both the foliage and the fruit; also to brown rot, which attacks the fruit; also to a fungus called cluster cups, which attacks the leaves and fruit of both the quince and the medlar. This fungus has an alternative host in the Savin juniper, and spores from the juniper can infect the quince and medlar, or vice versa. The moral obviously, and for once an easy one to observe, is to refrain from planting a Savin juniper in the near neighbourhood. I am much indebted to the East Malling Research Station for all this information.

The medlar is not a fruit I care much about; by the time it is ready to eat, it bears far too close a resemblance to a rotting or 'bletted' pear. It can, however, be made into a preserve, and the little tree certainly has a definite garden value, for in a favourable autumn the leaves turn into a motley of very beautiful variegated colours – pink, yellow, green, and brown, freckled with the russet fruits which always remind me of those knobbly objects you see attached to leather thongs on the flail-like hand-weapons of medieval warfare.

But although I may have no great affection for the medlar as a fruit, my affection for the cherry-plum or *Myrobalan* knows no bounds. I wish it could be planted more widely. It has every virtue. It grows quickly; it is pretty in the spring, with its white blossom; it reaches its supreme beauty when its fruit ripens in midsummer and its branches droop with the weight of fruit almost to the ground. The branches then seem loaded with fat jewels of amber and topaz, like a tree in an oriental fairy-tale.

It crops generously, most years. Its fruit makes delicious jam, especially if you put in the kernels of the stones, when you get a sharp almond flavour, reminding you of kernels left in apricot jam. It also makes a good hedge. It is, I feel sure, a tree to plant both for your immediate pleasure and for the pleasure of your children after you.

Plant the gages, too. The old greengage and all the other gages, the *Cambridge*, the *Early Rivers*, the *Transparent*. This (November) is the time to order and plant them.

November 27, 1949

Some weeks ago (to be precise, on p. 78) I wrote that the blue trumpets of *Gentiana sino-ornata* had given great pleasure during September. I little knew, then, how I was underestimating their value; so, in fairness to this lovely thing, I would like to state here and now, on this eighteenth day of November when I write this article, that I have today picked at the least two dozen blooms from my small patch. They had avoided the gales by cowering close to the ground, but they had suffered some degrees of frost; they looked miserable and shut up; I hesitated to pick them, thinking that they were finished for the year; but now that I have brought them into a warm room and put them into a bowl under a lamp they have opened into the sapphire-blue one expects of the Mediterranean.

This mid-November bowl has so astonished me, and made me so happy, gazing at it, that I felt I must impart my delight to other people in the hope that they would begin to plant this gentian.

It is not easy to find flowers for this time of year. November and December are the worst months. One has to fall back upon the berried plants, and amongst these I think *Cotoneaster rugosa Henryii* is one of the best. It is a graceful grower, throwing out long, red-berried sprays, with dark green, pointed, leathery leaves of especial beauty. It is not fussy as to soil and will flourish either in sun or shade, in fact, it can even be trained against a north wall, which is always one of the most difficult sites to find plants for in any garden. *Berberis thunbergii*, either the dwarf form or the variety called *purpurea*, both so well known that perhaps they need no recommendation, will also thrive in sun or shade, and at this time of year flame into the sanguine colours of autumn. They should be planted in clumps in some neglected corner, and be left to take care of themselves until the time comes to cut them for what professional florists call 'indoor decoration', but what you and I call, more simply, something to fill the flower vases with. They have the additional merit of lasting a very long time in water.

The leaves of the rugosa rose, *Blanc de Coubert*, in either the single or the double form, also turn a very beautiful yellow at this time of year and are good for picking. This rose has every virtue; the flowers are intensely sweet-scented, they persist all through the summer, they are succeeded by bright red hips in autumn, as round as little apples, and the whole bush is a blaze of gold in November. The only disadvantage, for a small garden, might be the amount of room the bush takes up; it is a strong grower, like most of the rugosas, and will eventually spread to a width of four or five feet and to a height of a tall man. It is, however, very shapely, with its rounded head, and it never straggles.

November 5, 1950

A correspondent makes the helpful suggestion that I might write an article on how to fill up the cracks and spaces in stone paving. I take it that she means either crazy paving or square-stone paving, or paving made from slabs of cement, poured in on the spot between a framework of wooden slats and left to 'set' with some wrinkled sacking laid over them to roughen the surface. This is a very economical home-made method; it also enables you to vary the size and shape of the slabs; and, especially if you incorporate into the wet cement some small pebbles known as 'beach' by builders, is almost indistinguishable from real stone once it has weathered.

I must assume, however, that my correspondent's paving is already laid, and is just waiting, stark and bare, to be planted with something that will take away the bareness. The first essential is that it shall be something which does not mind being walked upon. There was once a play called *Boots and Doormats*, which divided people into two categories: those who liked to trample and those who enjoyed being trampled. Today, in modern jargon, I suppose they would be called tramplers and tramplees; I prefer boots and doormats as an expression of this fundamental truth. Many big boots will walk down a paved path, and there are some meek doormats prepared to put up with such gruff treatment. The creeping thymes really enjoy being walked on, and will crawl and crawl, spreading gradually into rivulets and pools of green, like water slowly trickling, increasing in volume as it goes, until they have filled up all the cracks and crevices. The thymes are the true stand-by for anybody who wants to carpet a paved path.

There are other tramplees also. *Pennyroyal* does not mind what you do with it, and will give out its minty scent all the better for being bruised underfoot. *Cotula squalida* is much nicer than its name; it has tiny fern-like leaves, cowering very close down; no flower, but very resistant to hard wear and very easy to grow. All the *Acaenas* are useful; *Acaena buchananii*, a silver-green, or *Acaena microphylla*, bronze in colour. A pity that such tiny things should have such formidable names, but they are neither difficult to obtain nor to establish. John Scott, whose address is given on p. 271, supplies a useful list in his catalogue.

November 12, 1950

Writing last week in this column about crawly plants to grow in the cracks of paving-stones made me think how prettily this notion could be extended in a rather original way. I imagine a level plot of ground, the size and shape of which would naturally depend upon the space available; I would hope only that it need not be *too* small. It could be square, round, oval, or rectangular. It should not be under the drip of trees, but part of it could be in the shade, for the shade-loving plants, and part in the sun for the sun-lovers. I imagine the whole of this plot well dug in preparation, with a couple of inches deep of sharp sand spread on top of the soil to keep away the weeds, or at any rate to facilitate their removal. Then you lay your stones, or your home-made cement slabs as I suggested. Of course, real stone is the gardener's ideal, but it is expensive, working out at about ten shillings a square yard, which is more than most of us can afford.

It will not matter much what you make your paving of, for it will soon get covered up with plants and will not show through. I imagine that you will keep the middle of this paved plot for walking on, and that you will there plant the plants that do not object to being trodden underfoot and crushed – the thymes, and the small mints, and the other things I recommended. But in this new imaginary garden-plot you will have scope to plant all sorts of things round the edges where they are in no danger of being walked on.

I imagine lumps of Thrift, green cushions of the particularly pleasing sort called *Armeria corsica*, or the variety called *Vindictive*; I imagine also clumps of the low-growing daisy, *Bellis Dresden China*, as pink and pretty as its name suggests; and sun-roses (*helianthemum*) foaming in all the delicate colours of terracotta, buff, yellow, and rose; and the little trailing *Gypsophila fratensis*, a cloud of minute shell-pink blossoms; and some mounds of saxifrage, interplanted with the tiny iris-like *Sisyrinchium angustifolium*, sometimes called Blue-eyed Grass, which sows itself everywhere; and I should have also some tufts of the small iris *pumila*, in blue or violet, and a plant or two of the shrubby little *Aethionema Warleyensis*.

The small bulbs would also find a place – the bright blue scillas, the darker grape-hyacinths, chionodoxa or Glory of the Snow, the miniature narcissi, crocuses both spring and autumn flowering. All of them love the cool root-run they find between stones. There is no end to the choice, and no reason why you should not achieve colour and interest throughout the seasons. The main thing to remember is that what you are really trying to do is to make a rock garden on the flat.

November 19, 1950

What, I wonder, do you feel about rock gardens? Personally, I am against them, even when they are on a very grand scale. They seldom look right. Of course, if your garden happens to include a disused quarry there is nothing you can do but make a rock garden out of it; but few of us are thus favoured. Most of us are reduced to some lumpy bank, over which we dispose all the oddments of old stone we can collect and plant them up with such common tufts as aubrietia and yellow alyssum. It will be an artificial thing, pretending to be something it isn't.

Nevertheless, there is something to be said for rock-gardening provided you do it tactfully and do not pretend to be reproducing a bit of the Alps or the Himalayas or one of the more remote valleys of China where they were never intended to occur. The best claim to be made for rock-gardening is that it enables you to grow things according to the conditions which please them best. You can, in short, make up pockets of soil between the stones to suit individual plants. You can make a pocket of pure leaf-mould for *Gentiana sino-ornata*. You can make a sharp, gritty, sunny pocket for South African bulbs, the *ixias*, for example, or for the Mexican *tigridias*. You can fill one pocket entirely with limy rubble to please your dianthus; and another pocket with peat and leaf-mould to please your shrubby daphnes. In this way you can cut plants off, one from the others. You can prevent them from getting lost, as small things are apt to get lost in the open ground, and can also control any invasive neighbour – a vegetable neighbour, I mean, not a human one or a feline one.

You will observe that not all the plants I have mentioned are Alpines. This is because I never can see why one should be mesmerized into believing that Alpines should be the only occupants of a rock garden. The only rule to follow, I think, is that whatever looks right *is* right. Obviously, herbaceous plants will look wrong, and so will many of the annuals; but the pockets are ideal places for the small bulbs, nor is there any reason why they should not come up through a carpeting of saxifrage or androsace or arenaria or *Dryas octopetala* or the prostrate rosemary. I like to see the miniature narcissi grown in such a way, and the striped Lady Tulip (*T. clusiana*), and our native yellow tulip, *Sylvestris*, and the little green-and-white *Tulipa tarda*, sometimes called *dasystemon*, and that lovely Greek, *Tulipa orphanidea*, and the scarlet Persian *Tulipa linifolia*; and some fritillaries, too, not only our native Snakeshead, *Fritillaria meleagris*, but also *F. pyrenaica*, with its odd colouring of bronze and green; and, of course, the little early *Iris reticulata*. But I must desist. The bright picture growing up so rapidly in my mind already threatens to exceed the canvas allowed me.

November 26, 1950

A week ago I was writing in this column about rock gardens. Wildfire ideas swept across me, like a prairie alight. My own small blaze was not comparable to that. I just got excited about the things one could do in a rock garden, which is a mild little thing to get excited about; but, after all, the point is not what you get excited about, but the fact that in middle age you can still get excited at all. There is nothing like gardening to keep one young. It is the most rejuvenating of all occupations. One is always looking forward to next year, or five years hence.

I thought I would write this time about dry-wall gardening. Fortunate indeed are those whose lot is cast in one of our counties where low stone walls solidly crammed with soil already form part of the local landscape – in the Cotswolds, for instance. But even if you do not live where you may hope to find a ready-made dry wall, there is no reason why you should not build one in a place which seems to demand it.

A dry wall, it seems scarcely necessary to say, is a wall in which no hard mortar is used to fix the stones, but only soil to set them.

A retaining wall is the ideal, holding up a bank or a terrace, because then you will be able to build it with a *batter*, which in gardening terms does not mean a sort of Yorkshire pudding but a receding slope, lying backwards from bottom to top; this gives strength to the wall, which, if it were upright, would almost certainly fall down in course of time. Tilt each individual stone slightly backwards also, choosing the biggest stones to set along the foot. Fill the space at the back of the wall with good soil, a mixture of fibrous loam (well-rotted turves are excellent), some sharp sand, some peat, and compost if you have it, and also pack every crevice with the same mixture as you go. The more crevices you are able to leave, consistent with safety, the better.

It is a good plan to put in your plants while you build, and far easier and more satisfactory than poking them in afterwards. It enables you to spread out the roots instead of cramming them, and also to water them in, should the weather be dry. Some sort of planting plan in advance is advisable, to get the colours right, and also the shape and habit of the various plants; for example, if you decide to grow some of the *Lewisias*, or the long-sprayed saxifrage known as *Tumbling Waters*, you will not want them to get smothered eventually under a great beard of aubrietia.

December

I find, and do not doubt that most people will agree with me, that November and December are quite the bleakest months of the year for finding 'something to pick for indoors'. A flowerless room is a soul-less room, to my thinking; but even one solitary little vase of a living flower may redeem it. So in this note I propose to suggest some things that everybody can grow with a prophetic eye on next winter so that the usual blank period may not occur again. These will be things that flourish out of doors. I am not here concerned with greenhouses.

Viburnum fragrans will start producing its apple-blossom flowers in November, and unless interrupted by a particularly severe frost will carry on until March. It is a shrub growing eventually to a height of ten or twelve feet; it is extremely hardy; easy-going as to soil; and has the merit of producing a whole nursery of children in the shape of young self-rooted shoots. Picked and brought into a warm room, it is very sweet-scented.

The Christmas roses, *Helleborus niger*, are in flower now. They don't like being moved – in gardening language, they 'resent disturbance' – so even if you will take my advice and plant some clumps in early spring, which is the best time to move them, directly after they have finished flowering, you may have to wait a year or two before they begin to reward you with their greenish-white flowers and their golden centres. They are worth waiting for, believe me.

They like a rather shady place; moist, but well drained. A western aspect suits them. Once planted, leave them alone. They will grow in strength from year to year. I have a plant in my garden which to my certain knowledge has been there for fifty years. It was bequeathed to me by an old countrywoman of the old type, who wanted me to have the enjoyment of it after she had gone.

Hamamelis mollis. This is the Witch-hazel, a small tree which begins to flower on its bare branches in January. It is a real tough, which will grow anywhere – any soil, any aspect – though the better you treat it the better it will do. This applies to most plants, as to most people. The Witch-hazel will give you scented twigs for picking at a very early age.*

Then there is *Prunus subhirtella Autumnalis.* This is a little tree which, as its name suggests, ought to flower in autumn. As a matter of fact, in this country

* See also pp. 115–16.

96

it flowers in November or December, and is very useful on that account. Pick it in the bud; bring it indoors; and it will open into a fountain of bridal-looking blossom. It is said to strike very easily from cuttings taken in early summer from the current year's growth. I prefer it grown as a bush, not as a standard.

I should like to put in one last word for that very common plant, the pink-flowering currant, *Ribes sanguineum*. Nothing could be easier to grow, and it is sometimes despised on that account; but those who have the wit to cut some long stems of it in January, and to keep them in water in a dark cupboard, and to bring them out into the light in March, will find not a pink but a snow-white sheaf, a bride's sheaf, to reward them.

December 7, 1947
We are now in process of restoring a small herb garden after years of war neglect. During the war years we managed to keep a table-cloth-sized herb garden going, just outside the kitchen door: a few chives, a solitary plant of lovage, some thyme, some apple-mint, and a clump of garlic. This meant that the wise cook could dash out of the kitchen and quickly grab a handful of something that would turn the salad or the sandwiches into something that made guests ask what on earth has been put into them.

My answer to this was always, simply and monosyllabically, 'Herbs.' Why don't English women use more herbs in their concoctions? They are easy to grow, take up little room, and make all the difference. *Lovage*, with its leaves finely shredded, will convert a dull lettuce into a salad worthy of a good French restaurant. *Chervil* will serve the same good purpose, and has the additional attraction of meaning 'the leaf that rejoices the heart'. It can be made to rejoice the heart also in soups and stews. *Chives*, those little brothers of the onion, are so accommodating that they can be grown even in a window-box in a city. *Tarragon* can be used in omelettes and scrambled eggs with great advantage to the omelette and the eggs; and if you put a leaf of it into a bottle of vinegar the vinegar will greatly benefit.

Hamburg parsley is not really a herb, nor is it really parsley. It has a prolonged root like a turnip that has gone in for slimming; can be stored in sand for the winter; and can either be cooked or shredded raw into salads when it has a nutty flavour. The *Cucumber-apple* is not an apple though it looks like a very pale one, but is definitely a cucumber much better than the normal green kind. It, also, can be put into salads. (So can slices of raw apple. Try.)

All these are ideas which lead me naturally on to salads. We all grow lettuces, but why stick always to the same sorts? Why not grow *Green Jade* or *Tom*

Thumb, quite as easy as the others and far better. Stout little lettuces, with solid hearts.

December 11, 1949

At this great planting season of the year we should do well to consider the vast tribe of Pinks, or *Dianthus*, for there are few plants more charming, traditional, or accommodating. In old kitchen gardens one used to see long strips of *Mrs Sinkins* bordering the paths, and what could be more desirable than that ragged old lady heavily scenting the air? She is a very old lady indeed. Some people think she may be as much as 140 years old, though others would make her a mere eighty or so, and say that she had her origin in a workhouse garden at Slough. Whatever the truth about Mrs Sinkins may be, she appears proudly on the armorial bearings of the borough of Slough, firmly held in the beak of a swan.

She has a daughter, *Miss Sinkins*, less well known, but tidier and more prim in her habits, a retiring Victorian maiden whom you are unlikely to find in a search through most nurserymen's catalogues. In all the pile of catalogues on my table I can find only one nurseryman who lists her;* and he tells me that his stock is small, although he hopes to raise a larger supply next year. Do not worry about this, for there are plenty of the family to choose from. Our native Cheddar Pink, *Dianthus caesius*, is almost as heavily scented as *Mrs Sinkins* herself, and is as easy to grow.

This applies to nearly all the pinks. They make few demands. Sun-lovers, they like a well-drained and rather gritty soil; and if you can plant them with a generous supply of mortar rubble they will be as happy as the years are long. This means, of course, that they prefer growing in lime or chalk, an alkaline soil; but they don't insist on it; they exact so little that they will put up with almost anything except a waterlogged place. They hate that; and will revenge themselves on you by damping off.

The only other fault they have, a most endearing fault, revealing an all too generous nature, is that they may flower themselves to death in your service. You must be on the look-out for this, and cut the wealth of flowers hard back to the grey-green clumps, to protect and save them from their own extravagant generosity.

I wish I had more space to write about the pinks. I would like to devote fifteen articles to them. But at least I can recommend a book to you: *The Dianthus*, by Will Ingwersen (Collins, 10s. 6d.). This is the book for everyone who wishes to grow the *Dianthus* in his or her own garden, so Mr Ingwersen must

* W. H. Ingwersen, Birch Farm Nurseries, Gravetye, East Grinstead, Sussex.

take my place as an adviser. The illustrations alone are tempting enough, apart from the text, which is informative, practical, and delightfully written.

December 25, 1949

Why was it called golden, and why a bough, that grey-green tuffet, pearled and dotted with tiny moons? Apparently because it will turn golden if you keep it long enough, but as in this country mistletoe usually comes down with the rest of the Christmas decorations it never gets the chance of assuming this different aspect of beauty.

Shakespeare called it baleful; but, as everybody knows, it is possessed of most serviceable properties if only you treat it right. It can avert lightning and thunderbolts, witchcraft and sorcery; it can extinguish fire; it can discover gold buried in the earth; it can cure ulcers and epilepsy; it can stimulate fertility in women and cattle. On the other hand, if you do not treat it right it can do dreadful things to you. It may even kill you as it killed Balder the Beautiful, whose mother neglected to exact an oath from it not to hurt her son 'because it seemed too young to swear'.

The important thing, therefore, seems to be to learn as quickly and thoroughly as possible how to treat it right.

You must never cut it with iron, but always with gold. You must never let it touch the ground, but must catch it in a white cloth as it falls. This seems easy compared with the first stipulation, since even in these days most people do still possess a white cloth of some sort, a sheet, or a large handkerchief, whereas few of us can command a golden bagging-hook or even a knife with a blade of pure gold. You must never put it into a vase but must always suspend it, and after every traditional kiss the man must pick off one fruit – which is not a berry, although it looks like one – and when all the fruits have gone the magic of the kiss has gone also.

Folk-tales? He would be a bold man who attempted to explain or to explain away such ancient and widespread superstitions, ranging from furthest Asia into Europe and Africa. Mysterious and magical throughout all countries and all centuries, these tales may be read in Sir James Frazer's monumental work in which he honoured that queer parasite, the mistletoe, with the title *The Golden Bough*.

So here let me concentrate rather on some botanical facts which Sir James Frazer disregards, and try to correct some popular misconceptions about the nature of the mistletoe.

We think of it as a parasite, but it is not a true parasite, only a semi-parasite, meaning that it does not entirely depend upon its host for nourishment, but gains some of its life from its own leaves. It belongs to an exceptional family, the *Loranthaceae*, comprising more than five hundred members, only one of which is a British-born subject – *Viscum album*, the Latin name for our English mistletoe.

The mistletoe, as we know it, grows on some trees and not on others. The worst mistake that we make is to believe that it grows most freely on the oak. It seldom does; and that is the reason why the Druids particularly esteemed the oak-borne mistletoe, for this was a rarity and thus had a special value. The mistletoe prefers the soft-barked trees: the apple, the ash, the hawthorn, the birch, the poplar, the willow, the maple, the Scots pine, the sycamore, the lime, and the cedar. It is seldom found on the pear, the alder, or the beech; and is most rare on the oak.

Another popular mistake concerning the propagation of this queer plant. It is commonly believed that birds carry the seeds. This is only half true. What really happens, by one of those extraordinarily complicated arrangements which Nature appears to favour, is that the bird (usually the missel-thrush) pecks off the white fruit for the sake of the seed inside it, and then gets worried by the sticky mess round the seed and wipes his beak, much as we might wipe our muddy shoes on a doormat, and thereby deposits the seed in a crack of the bark, where it may, or may not, germinate.

Such are a few, a very few, legends and facts about the strange and wanton bunch we shall hang somewhere in our house this Christmas.

December 3, 1950

Many people have a limited garden space. They want to make the best of it and to get as much colour and variety as possible, yet the area they command restricts them. They have perhaps a front garden with a path running up it to the front door, and on either side of this path they have either a lawn of grass or some flower-beds, or both; and under the house they may have other beds, with a path running horizontally from left to right. This does not leave much scope for extra plants. I suggest, therefore, that gardening in tubs might be helpful, interesting, and amusing.

You acquire your tubs – barrels sawn in half. I would not paint them in the conventional colour, which in this country seems to be a most virulent arsenic green, swearing violently with all the greens of Nature; I would paint them the colour of coffee with far, far too much milk in it; and I would paint the bands round them the colour of coffee with no milk at all. This neutral coloration makes a much better foil to the colour of flowers than that wicked green.

You must now fill your tubs. Good drainage is essential, meaning a number of holes bored in the bottom, and then a two-inch layer of broken crocks (old flower-pots smashed up), and then a thick layer of fibrous leaf-mould half the tub deep; and then on top of all that the main soil in which your plants will have to grow for years and years. Give them a rich diet. Turfy fibrous loam and some compost and some bone-meal or some hop-manure, and some sharp sand to keep it open, all mixed up together. Fill the tubs to within two or three inches of the top, remembering that the soil will sink as it settles. Then the only thing left to do is to plant; and, of course, to water when watering becomes necessary. This is perhaps the only disadvantage of tub-gardening: you must keep a careful watch to see that your plants do not dry out.

Everyone will have his own ideas about what to grow. Some people will like tulips or other bulbs for the spring, followed in summer by annuals such as the purple petunia, which, sown in May, gives a sumptuous display from July to October. Others will prefer more permanent things such as fuchsias. Whatever you choose, tub-gardening does seem to be a solution for those who have not as much ground space as they would like and who, by setting their tubs where they want them, can prolong the flowering season in many odd corners.

December 10, 1950

A lady writes to ask what she can grow as an edging to her rose-beds. She wants something out of the ordinary, something that will flower all the summer, something that will require no attention, and, of course, it must be a perennial. Is that, she says, asking too much?

This inquiry rather put me on my mettle. I did not dare to suggest anything so obvious as catmint (*Nepeta mussinii*), which would have fulfilled all her demands with the single proviso that by way of 'attention' she would have to cut it right back to the base in early spring. Clearly, it is difficult to find something that will at least look neat when not in flower. The rock-roses perhaps provide as long a flowering period as anything, but there again you would have to clip them back after their first rush of bloom (which does last for at least two months) in order to make them break out again later on, and this operation might also come under the heading of 'attention'. The Cheddar Pink, *Dianthus caesius*, I thought, would look neat and gay as an edging, with the additional charm of the exceedingly sweet smell from its masses of pale rosy flowers. Two little speedwells, *Veronica repens* and *Veronica rupestris*, would be pretty in their mats of china blue; and the rather taller *Veronica incana*, with darker blue spikes, would offer the advantage of tidy silvery leaves. *Gypsophila fratensis* and *Tunica saxifraga* would both trail in a foam of pink, like small clouds touched by sunset. Or, if my correspondent desired a stronger colour, the low-growing *Viola Huntercombe Purple*, most intense and imperial, would glow in a manner to attract notice even from a distance. Or, if she desired no colour at all, the beautifully shaped *Viola septentrionalis*, pure white, with leaves like a violet.

But, I added in my reply to my correspondent, why restrict your rose-beds to a mere edging? Why not allow the plants to encroach all over the beds? It will do the roses no harm, in fact it will supply a living mulch to keep the ground moist and the roses cool at the roots. It was, I think, that great gardener William Robinson who first advocated and practised this revolutionary idea. His roses certainly throve in spite of, or because of, it. When one murmured something about manure, he snorted and said that it was quite unnecessary. I fancy, however, that in these days of compost-heaps he would have agreed to some generous handfuls being inserted as a top-dressing annually between the plants; or even some organic fertilizer such as bone-meal.

December 17, 1950
Shady places often worry the amateur gardener, but, as a matter of fact, there are plenty of plants which thrive all the better for some shade. There are degrees of shadiness, and I suppose the ideal is a broken light, where the shadow is not too dense but is still sufficient to give protection from the hottest rays of the sun. In such a place, especially if the soil tends to be moist, all the coloured primroses and polyantha will be happy as a groundwork; and, if really moist, should be the perfect home for the taller primulas such as the Japonica hybrids, or the mealy mauve *P. capitata*, or the yellow Tibetan *P. florindae*, or the coppery *P. bulleyana*. These are all very easily raised from seed or division. Phlox enjoy shade and a deep, cool soil; so do the peonies. The columbines will put up with quite a lot of shade, and there are some very beautiful hybrids: *Longissima*, a fantastically long-spurred golden yellow; *Crimson and Gold*; *Crimson Star*; and a huge-flowered blue and white called *Azure Fairy*. Foxgloves are perhaps too obvious to be worth mentioning, but these also can be obtained now in different varieties: the Excelsior strain which flowers all round the stem, and the really lovely one called *Apricot*, well named, because it is exactly the pinky-amber of a ripe apricot turning its cheek to the sun. I think also that the pure white foxglove looks very handsome in a clump, towering above the colour of lower flowers. All obtainable from Messrs Sutton.

If you prefer shrubs for your shady corner or border, the choice is wide. Azaleas, provided you have a lime-free soil; rhododendrons, which enjoy the same conditions, are mostly too space-taking for the average garden. Some of the daphnes are woodland, leaf-mould-loving plants, especially the murrey-coloured *D. mezereum* and its white form, *alba*; and *D. tangutica*; and the fine hybrid, *D. Somerset*. And then there are the hydrangeas, many of which look far better, I think, shrouded in a little dusky mystery than exposed to a glaring light.

I have no room here to go into details about the hydrangeas; I wish I had. The best I can do is to recommend a book just published called *The Hydrangeas*, by Michael Haworth-Booth (Constable, 26s.). He has spent many years in expert study, and this is the first specialized work to be written in the English language on the subject. Serious gardeners will feel compelled to add it to their gardening library; and those more frivolous gardeners, who like joky gardening, will delight in his paragraph on page 164, telling them how to produce miniature hydrangeas two inches high in pots.

December 24, 1950

This article will appear, I suppose, on Christmas Eve when nobody's mind is attuned to hard work out of doors. It therefore seems a suitable moment to take up the challenge of a gentleman in Staffordshire who wants me to write something in defence of Lazy Gardeners.

It is an amusing letter, quite indefensible, yet with some grains of truth in it. He toils not, he says, but all the same gets a lot of pleasure from his neglected garden. His trousers become golden with buttercup pollen as he walks across his unmown lawn. He stares out of his windows in astonishment that a fourpenny packet of seed could produce so many marigolds. He has had neither the time nor the energy to prune his rambler roses, but is enchanted to find that they are still flowering riotously. He enjoys the few perennials left by the previous tenant. In fact, he doesn't expect anything to grow and is thrilled when it does.

This not being at all my own idea of gardening, I gasped at first, but on reflection perceived that there was something to be said for his contentions. It was nearly true, as he remarked, that the lazy gardener has time, peace, and leisure to look at his garden, whereas the active gardener has only work and is far too busy to enjoy anything. It was true also, though he did not say this but only implied it, that tidiness could be overdone. Nobody likes to see nettles, docks, or ground-elder; but a certain disorder among the flowers is surely preferable to too rigid a regimentation. Staking, for example, is a thing which requires to be done with a rare tact; one does not want to see the tall asters beaten down in a sodden mass on the ground, but neither does one wish to see them bound to their stake like the head of a birch broom to its handle. As for grass, nothing can excel the beauty of perfect turf; but unless this can be achieved over a wide expanse, I like to see it enamelled with some daisies – not plantains, thank you, or dandelions.

My correspondent has formed the commendable habit of reading gardening books in the winter evenings, even if he has no intention of putting their instructions into practice, which reminds me that I am often asked to recommend a practical, straightforward, comprehensive book and have no hesitation in advising *The Amateur Gardener*, by A. G. L. Hellyer, published by Collingridge Ltd, price 25s. Even if this seems rather expensive I am sure it is worth the money. Eight hundred pages of text and many photographic illustrations.

December 31, 1950

This may seem an odd time of year to write about irises, those velvet-warm flowers we associate with June – the very word *June* warms me as I write it. Outside all is bleak; the grass looks starved and dingy; this wintry weather is as unbecoming to the garden as to the human face. We all looked pinched and shrammed. But the longest night and the shortest day have gone with December 21st; we have left our darkest days behind us.

These reflections have been induced in me by receiving a copy of the *Iris Year-Book*, published by the Iris Society. I suppose we all grow irises, of one sort or another, even if we are neither experts nor specialists. Most of the irises are the most obliging of plants, putting up with poor treatment, asking for little more than a place in the sun, a modest demand, which we should all enjoy if we could get it. All iris growers would be well advised to join the Iris Society, 10s. 6d. for the yearly subscription, which entitles the member to a free copy of the *Iris Year-Book*. Address: N. Leslie Cave, Summerlea, Sugden Road, Thames Ditton, Surrey.

I have written about irises in this column before now, but never, I think, have I mentioned the *Oncocyclus* and *Regelia* species. I hesitate to do so, because they are not so easy to grow, so I write this note only for gardeners who are prepared to take some extra trouble, quite a lot of extra trouble. You should grow them on a raised bed if possible, under a south wall, in very gritty soil with lots of mortar rubble in it because they like lime and good drainage; and mortar rubble supplies both. If you have a warm, sheltered corner under a house wall, where you can build up a little raised bed and fill it with the sort of soil I have suggested, plant a few rhizomes of *Iris susiana*, the so-called Mourning or Widow Iris, a black-and-white enormous flower, a fantastic flower that doesn't look true, price about 2s. One calls it black-and-white, but it is in fact grey veined with very dark purple, as you can see if it is held up to the light. Seen like this, the veining suggests an anatomical drawing; or, more poetically, the leaden tracing in a stained-glass window.

Plant also a few rhizomes of Charon, or Hoogiana, or Korolkowi. I do not pretend that you will get a lot of bloom, and I do not deny that you may get some disappointments, but the pride of your successes will compensate. The main things to remember are: (*a*) good drainage; (*b*) a sun-baking; (*c*) avoidance of damp in summer, by placing a pane of glass over the dormant rhizome. These irises come from desert countries, so one must try to reproduce their natural conditions as nearly as possible.

A Little Flower Book

A Little Flower Book

There came recently into my possession a little shabby manuscript book. On the fly-leaf was inscribed:

THE
FLOWER GARDEN
or a discovery shewing
What the Power of Man, with the
Co-operation of Nature, can
now (since Man's fall, and
God cursing the earth
therefrom) pro-
duce in propa-
gating and
improving
of Flow-
ers.

Bound in brown leather, it measured only six inches by four, and its 164 pages were filled with a seventeenth-century script, tiny, but of exquisite legibility. Each page had been given its own heading, and moreover had been carefully ruled with red lines to allow for marginal glosses. It was thus a brown and red little book, for the ink also had faded to brown and some of the pages were slightly foxed. I looked at it and wondered.

Quietly, it preserved its anonymity. There was no name, no date, if you except the words Fra³ Wright, Nottingham, 16th March, 1831, written on the inside of the cover. I was not much interested in Mr Francis Wright, of Nottingham, for it seemed unlikely that without enormous research, possibly into the Nottingham Parish registers, I could ever discover anything about him, let alone find out how the little book had found its way into his library. No, it was the identity of the author I was after. Who was he, this patient, meticulous man, with his beautiful handwriting, his ruler and his red pencil, his extreme neatness, his manifest leisure and his piety? That he was both censorious and pious I quickly discovered from the first page of the introduction, for after a reference to 'this rude lumpe and confused heape' the Earth, which has been brought into form and beauty by Almighty God, he proceeds to a condemnation of his own times, 'wherein Wickedness superabounds and as it were forceth God to withhold the rain, to send the Mildew, the Caterpillar, and other his inferiour officers to correct us'. I turned then to the index, which was characteristically most full and conscientious, and read under the letter H:

> Heaven. must needs be hard to obteyn when our
> Gardens are so difficult to be made and Kept.

The pathos of that entry endeared him to me. Here is a man, I thought, who may be a bit of a moralist, even a bit of a prig, but who does at any rate appreciate the balks of gardening. How well I knew the mildew, the caterpillar and other inferior officers of God! How well I knew how difficult our gardens were to be made and Kept! even without the complication of obtaining Heaven.

Still, I asked myself, fingering his little book, who was this man, and what exactly were his own times when Wickedness superabounded? What sort of a man was he? And when did he live? I imagined some disgruntled old Cromwellian growling round his garden in disapproval of the Restoration and its ways. My quest for his identity followed a detective story on approved lines; I looked for clues. There were references to Sir Kenelm Digby's *History of the Vegetation of Plants*: this, I discovered, had first been delivered as an address at Gresham College in 1661, republished in 1669. Then there was a reference to 'the new-invented cucurbit glasses', which might be set mingled with honey and beer to entice wasps and flies which waste the store. This, I discovered, was a direct, almost a verbatim, quotation from John Evelyn's *Kalendula Hortensis*, 1664; yet there was no mention of John Evelyn in the text, and no acknowledgment under the letter E to Evelyn in the index. The index was detailed and conscientious. Why, then, did my unknown anonymous gardener suppress this acknowledgment to Evelyn? Had he a mean character, that would not acknowledge a debt to other people? I sought him down his tiny pages. I read his marginal glosses; and in one of these I found one which amused me particularly, because it concerned an ancestor of my own in the way he made his hot-bed: *The Earl of Dorset useth this way*, it said; and that in itself helped me to date my little book by internal evidence.

There were many other references I followed up, until I narrowed the date down to the later decades of the seventeenth century. One linguistic discovery interested me – the word 'avid' written in the same hand on a loose sheet; yet the first mention of this adjective, I found, was given in the *OED* as 1769. Perhaps my author was an experimentalist in words as well as in horticulture?

A man of education evidently; he knew and quoted Greek. He could also command the graphic image: 'You should prune and train wall-trees like the ribs of a skreen fan or ye fingers of a hand displayed.' The Snowflake, which he has flowering in February, he calls 'ye little early summer foole'. He had, I thought, some sense of humour, for he puts ants or pismires, earwigs or battler-wigs, under the heading of 'annoyances'. Anticipating the needs of 1950, he gives directions for growing and curing your own home-grown tobacco. He knew all about cloches, which he calls cap-glasses or casements. He knew about using weed-killer on paths, which, denied our advantage of buying pro-prietary preparations in a tin, he had to compose for himself: brine, potashes and water, or a decoction of tobacco refuse. He was sceptical about the influ-ence of the moon on seed-sowing, but conceded that gilliflowers should be sown at the full moon to produce double flowers.

He enjoyed experiments. To make gilliflowers large, he says, you use camomile, valerian, flag-roots and celandine leaves, and beat them all into a salve together and apply it to the roots and water them with the same juice, when the gilliflowers will grow to 'a wonderful bignes and sometimes alter the colour thereof'; and similarly if you wish to alter the colour of tulips you must anoint their roots with a mixture of herbs, sheep's dung and pigeon's dung, all beaten up together. A practical man, he has much to say about the sowing of seeds and propagation by offsets, 'only take care that the Dame be not destroyed in her delivery'. A kind-hearted man, evidently, to take so sym-pathetic a view of women in childbirth. A man of parts, with his Greek and his practical unsentimental love of his plants and his lists of flowers and fruit trees all growing somewhere in his garden, sometime between 1661 and 1700.

What was he, I still asked myself – this man who kept bees and had his gar-den, demanding so few tools? A water-pot, a tub, a spade, a pair of shears, some mats to put over tender plants – that was all he required. Who was he, who listed 'the great fox-grape', the iron-coloured foxglove, the cowslips tawny, murrey, yellow and blush, the great double white daffodil of Constan-tinople, the apples with their now forgotten names – the Golden Doucet, the Belle Bonne, the Ladies' Longing?

Who was he? I had composed a picture of him in my mind: he wore a big straw hat, and went about his garden grumbling against the Government. In his little book he had used the old word, *grutch*, meaning a complaint; and I thought of him as a grutching person, perhaps an old retired soldier or civil servant. Then, to my surprise, I had suddenly to revise all my ideas. My old Cromwellian vanished in one revealing phrase, explicit rather than refined. The author of my little manuscript was not a man, but a woman.

Note to A Little Flower Book

My ignorance and lack of scholarship are much to blame. One cannot, how-ever, know everything; and I render grateful thanks to Mr E. G. R. Taylor for informing me that I can probably date my little book a bit more closely, since he says it was Dr Thomas Burnet who described the post-diluvian world as a rude lump and a confused heap, in his *Sacred Theory of Earth*, first pub-lished in an English edition in 1684. This puts my little book to a later date than 1684; it becomes more and more of a chronological detective story.

What odd things happen when a tiny thing out of the past comes acci-dentally into one's hands! What unexpected connections strike up! Even the mysterious Fra^s Wright of Nottingham, that previous owner, has been iden-tified for me without any research through the Nottingham registers. I received from his great-grandson a letter accompanied by a most interesting book on their family history. His great-grandfather would, he says, have approved of the religious views held by the author of *The Flower Garden*.

Some Flowers

Some Flowers

Hamamelis Mollis – Witch-Hazel

Hamamelis mollis is perhaps more familiar to many people when they meet it in a bottle under the name Witch-hazel or Hazeline, but to the gardener it means a small shrubby tree, covered in the early part of the year with curly spider-like flowers on its naked branches. There is a particular charm about all trees which carry their flowers before their leaves, such as the almond or the judas: they have a cleanness of design, undisturbed by tufts of green; they allow us to observe the fine tracery of the twigs, while at the same time offering us some colour to look at. The Witch-hazel is certainly a tree which everyone should grow, for its merits are many, and if it has a fault I have yet to discover it, except that it is a slow starter.

Mollis, a Chinaman, is the best of the family, which includes also two Americans (*Virginiana* and *vernalis*) and a Jap (*Japonica*), and *arborea*, which is the tallest of all but whose flowers are inferior to those of *mollis*. *Mollis* is perfectly hardy and even the flowers do not wilt in a heavy frost. It likes a sunny place, where it has room to develop, and although it will not revenge itself upon you by perishing outright in a poor soil but will struggle manfully even against the stickiest clay, it will also show its gratitude for a good loam with some leaf-mould mixed in. Another of its virtues is that it starts flowering at a very tender age, so that there is none of that long weary wait of years until the plant has reached a certain size before embarking on the business which made us desire it. From the very first it is possible to pick it for indoors, and there are few things more welcome at the churlish time of the year when it occurs. New Year's Day may see it open; perhaps even Christmas Day. The queer, wriggly, yellow petals with the wine-stained calyx at their base will last for quite ten days in water, especially if you bring it indoors while still just in the bud, and will smell far more delicious than you would believe possible if you had only caught it out in the cold winter air. So delicious is it, that the owner of one small new tree begins to long for the day when he can cut big generous branches instead of the few twigs which is all that he can get at first. Every one of these twigs, however, will be doing its best, and flowering on all its little length.

The leaves come later, at the ordinary time for leaves, and you can forget comfortably about your Witch-hazel during all the months when so many other things give you flowers for your garden and your vase. You need remember it again only when your supply has failed and in despair you go out to look for something to keep you company indoors. And there they will be, those curly yellow petals, ready once more to scent the room and put brightness on the table.

Iris Reticulata

When flowers come so thick in summer that one hesitates which to pick among so many, one is apt to forget the bare cold days when the earth is a miser offering only one or two, take it or leave it. Wrapped in mufflers and overcoats we go and peer about for a stray sprig of winter-sweet, a splashed and muddy hellebore, a premature violet – anything, anything to fill one solitary glass with some pretence of spring long before spring has really arrived. There are the bulbs, of course, which one has carefully plunged in ashes or placed in a dark cupboard, according to the instructions in the garden books and catalogues: but somehow there is always something a little artificial about any flower which has been compelled to bloom before its time. Even though we may not number ourselves among the rich who languidly fill their rooms on an order to the florist with lilac at Christmas and tulips on New Year's Day, there is still, I think, a great difference between the flowers which we force and those which we have the patience to wait for at their proper season. For one thing, the forced flower always slightly spoils our delight in its outdoor successor when it normally arrives; and for another, the forced flower itself, however welcome, is always something of a fake. To the true lover of flowers, these arguments are disturbingly potent.

The moral of all this is, that we especially welcome any flower which lightens the gloom of winter of its own accord. The more fragile and improbable-looking, the better. Such a flower is *Iris reticulata*. It seems extraordinary that anything so gay, delicate, and brilliant should really prefer the rigours of winter to the amenities of spring. It is true that we can grow *Iris reticulata* in pots under glass if we wish to do so, and that the result will be extremely satisfying and pretty, but the far more pleasing virtue of *Iris reticulata* is that it will come into bloom out of doors as early as February, with no coddling or forcing at all. Purple flecked with gold, it will open its buds even above the snow. The ideal place to grow it is in a pocket of rather rich though well-drained soil amongst stones; a private place which it can have all to itself for the short but grateful days of its consummation.

Reticulata – the netted iris. Not the flower is netted, but the bulb. The bulb wears a little fibrous coat, like a miniature fishing-net. It is a native of the Caucasus, and there is a curious fact about it: the Caucasian native is reddish, whereas our European garden form is a true Imperial purple. Botanists, including Mr W. R. Dykes, the greatest authority on irises, have been puzzled by the Mendelian characteristics exhibited by this group. Mr Dykes received bulbs from the Caucasus, which were always reddish, the garden form was purple, and yet the seedlings he raised from the garden form were always reddish again. It was only in the fourth generation, raised from seed, that he re-obtained the purple form, and even that differed slightly in colour from the fixed garden type.

It is unlikely that many of us will wish to experiment with our own saved seeds in this way, but still I throw it out as a suggestion to those who have the inclination and the leisure. (Let me warn those enthusiasts that they will have to wait for at least four years between the sowing of the seed and the flowering of the bulb.) In the meantime I do suggest that every flower-lover should grow a patch of the little *reticulata* somewhere in his garden. The variety *Cantab*, a pale turquoise blue, flowers about a fortnight earlier as a rule; *Hercules*, a subfusc ruby-red, comes at the same time as the type.

Fritillaria Imperialis – The Crown Imperial

Like the other members of its family, the stateliest of them all has the habit of hanging its head, so that you have to turn it up towards you before you can see into it at all. Then and then only will you be able to observe the delicate veining on the pointed petals. It is worth looking into these yellow depths for the sake of the veining alone, especially if you hold it up against the light, when it is revealed in a complete system of veins and capillaries. You will, however, have to pull the petals right back, turning the secretive bell into something like a starry dahlia, before you can see the six little cups, so neatly filled to the brim, not overflowing, with rather watery honey at the base of each petal, against their background of dull purple and bright green. Luckily it does not seem to resent this treatment at all and allows itself to be closed up again into the bell-like shape which is natural to it, with the creamy pollened clapper of its stamens hanging down the middle.

It always reminds me of the stiff, Gothic-looking flowers one sometimes sees growing along the bottom of a medieval tapestry, together with irises and lilies in a fine disregard for season. Grown in a long narrow border, especially at the foot of an old wall of brick or stone, they curiously reproduce this effect. It is worth noting also how well the orange of the flower marries with rosy brick, far better than any of the pink shades which one might more naturally incline to put against it. It is worth noting also that you had better handle the bulbs in gloves for they smell stronger than garlic.

It was once my good fortune to come unexpectedly across the Crown Imperial in its native home. In a dark, damp ravine in one of the wildest parts of Persia, a river rushed among boulders at the bottom, the overhanging trees turned the greenery almost black, ferns sprouted from every crevice of the mossy rocks, water dripped everywhere, and in the midst of this moist luxuriance I suddenly discerned a group of the noble flower. Its coronet of orange bells glowed like lanterns in the shadows in the mysterious place. The track led me downwards towards the river, so that presently the banks were towering above me, and now the Crown Imperials stood up like torches between the wet rocks, as they had stood April after April in wasteful solitude beside that unfrequented path. The merest chance that I had lost my way had brought me into their retreat; otherwise I should never have surprised them thus. How noble they looked! How well-deserving of their name! Crown Imperial – they did indeed suggest an orange diadem fit to set on the brows of the ruler of an empire.

That was a strange experience, and one which I shall never forget. Since then, I have grown Crown Imperials at home. They are very handsome, very sturdy, very Gothic. But somehow that Persian ravine has spoiled me for the more sophisticated interpretation which I used to associate with them. Somehow I can no longer think of them solely as the flowers one sees growing along the bottom of a medieval tapestry. I think of them as the imperial wildings I found by chance in a dark ravine in their native hills.

Note: The disadvantage of this fritillary is that it is apt to come up 'blind', i.e. with leaves and no flower. I noted with interest that this occurred also in its native habitat.

Fritillaria Meleagris – The Meadow Fritillary

Our native fritillary is one of those strange flowers which does not seem indigenous to our innocent pastures at all. There are some such flowers – the wild arum, for instance, and many of the orchises, whom nobody would take for anything but exotics. The fritillary looks like something exceedingly choice and delicate and expensive, which ought to spring from a pan under glass rather than share the fresh grass with buttercups and cowslips. Its very nicknames have something sinister about them: Snakeshead, the Sullen Lady, and sometimes the Leper's Bell. Yet it is as much of a native as the blue-bell or the ragged robin.

Some people mistake it for a kind of wild tulip, others for a daffodil; Gilbert White of Selborne is one of those who fell into the latter error. Miss Mitford does even worse, in calling it 'the tinted wood anemone'. It belongs, in fact, to the *liliaceae* and so might accurately be called our own private English lily of the fields. Its curious square markings explain several of its various names: *fritillus*, for instance, is the Latin for dice-box, which in its turn had been named from a chess- or chequer-board; and *meleagris* derives from the Latin for the guinea-fowl, whose speckled feathers so vividly reminded our ancestors of the fritillary that Gerard in his *Herball* (1597) frankly calls it the Ginny-hen flower.

It is unfortunately becoming rarer every year, and is extremely local in its distribution. That is to say, where you find it at all, you find it by the acre, and where you do not find it you simply have to go without. Unlike the orchises, there is no chance of coming across a few here and there: the fritillary knows no half measures. When you have once seen it by the acre, however, it is a sight not likely to be forgotten. Less showy than the buttercup, less spectacular than the foxglove in the wood, it seems to put a damask shadow over the grass, as though dusk were falling under a thunder-cloud that veiled the setting sun. For when it grows at all, it can grow as thick as the blue-bell, sombre and fuscous, singularly unsuitable to the water-meadows and the willows of an Oxfordshire or a Hampshire stream. In wine-making countries one has seen the musty heaps of crushed discarded grape-skins after the juice has been pressed from them. Their colour is then almost exactly that of the meadow fritillary.

In its native state the bulb grows very deep down, so taking a hint from Nature we ought to plant it in our own gardens at a depth of at least six to eight inches. There is another good reason for doing this: pheasants are fond of it, and are liable to scratch it up if planted too shallow. Apart from its troubles with pheasants, it is an extremely obliging bulb and will flourish almost anywhere in good ordinary soil, either in grass or in beds. It looks best in grass, of course, where it is naturally meant to be, but I do not think it much matters where you put it, since you are unlikely to plant the million bulbs which would be necessary in order to reproduce anything like the natural effect, and are much more likely to plant just the few dozen which will give you enough flowers for picking. For the fritillary, unless you are prepared to grow it on the enormous scale to which it naturally inclines, is a flower to put in a glass on your table. It is a flower to peer into. In order to appreciate its true beauty, you will have to learn to know it intimately. You must look closely at all its little squares, and also turn its bell up towards you so that you can look right down into its depths, and see the queer semi-transparency of the strangely foreign, wine-coloured chalice. It is a sinister little flower, sinister in its mournful colours of decay.

Tulipa Clusiana – The Lady Tulip

She is familiarly called the Lady Tulip, but always reminds me more of a regiment of little red and white soldiers. Seen growing wild on Mediterranean or Italian slopes, you can imagine a Lilliputian army deployed at its spring manoeuvres. I suppose her alleged femineity is due to her elegance and neatness, with her little white shirt so jimply tucked inside her striped jacket, but she is really more like a slender boy, a slim little officer dressed in a particoloured uniform of the Renaissance.

Clusiana is said to have travelled from the Mediterranean to England in 1636, which, as the first tulips had reached our shores about 1580,* is an early date in tulip history. Unlike Lars Porsena, she has nothing to do with Clusium, but takes her name from Carolus Clusius (or Charles de Lecluse) who became Professor of Botany at Leiden in 1593. Her native home will suggest the conditions under which she likes to be grown: a sunny exposure and a light rich soil. If it is a bit gritty, so much the better. Personally I like to see her springing up amongst grey stones, with a few rather stunted shrubs of Mediterranean character to keep her company: some dwarf lavender, and the grey-green cistus making a kind of amphitheatre behind her while some creeping rosemary spreads a green mat at her feet. The rosemary should normally be in flower at the same time as the tulip, i.e. towards the second half of April, and a few neighbouring clumps of the blue *Anemone apennina* would associate perfectly both as to colour and to quality with the small pale bluish-lilac flowers of the rosemary. A grouping of this kind has the practical advantage that all its members enjoy the same treatment as to soil and aspect, and, being regional compatriots, have the air of understanding one another and speaking the same language. Nothing has forced them into an ill-assorted companionship.

If the extent and disposition of one's garden allows one to indulge in such luxuries as these little pockets of 'regional gardening', how lucky one is! Half the secret of planting lies in happy association. Some plants 'go' together; others, most definitely, do not. There can be no rule, for it is essentially a question of taste and flair, but if a rule can be made at all it is that Nature's own arrangements are usually the best. Think only of the innumerable tiny

* There is the possible exception of the golden *T. sylvestris*, which some believe to be a native of England.

Alpine gardens all over the high pastures of the mountains, to see how perfectly and effortlessly the job is done. A solitary huge boulder, a cushion of *silene* pressed against it, a few mauve violas blowing lightly a foot away, a dab of pink thrift, some blue lances of *Gentiana verna*, and there it is, complete. No overcrowding, no anomalies. Just three or four square yards of minute perfection round which you could put a picture-frame, detaching them from the sunny immensity and leaving them self-contained, self-sufficient . . .

In this way one may steal sections out of one's own garden and make self-contained satisfactory small enclosures, such as the scrap of Mediterranean hillside, in which to grow the scrubby lavender, the bushy cistus, the creeping rosemary, the blue anemone, and the slim little Lady Tulip who is more like a boy.

Primula Auricula

Auriculas are of two kinds, one for the rich man and one for the poor. There is no denying that the kind known as the Show auricula, which demands to be grown under glass, is the more varied and exquisite in its colourings and markings and general strangeness. Above the mealy stems and leaves, looking as though they had been dusted with powdered chalk, rise the flat heads, curiously scalloped with a margin of contrary colour, it may be of white or gold or green, or of purple or a reddish bronze, all as velvet as a pansy:

> Their gold, their purples, scarlets, crimson dyes,
> Their dark and lighter-haired diversities,
> With all their pretty shades and ornaments,
> Their parti-coloured coats and pleasing scents . . .
> In double ruffs, with gold and silver laced,
> On purple crimson, and so neatly placed.*

So greatly did the old florists esteem the Show auricula, that they used to stage it in miniature theatres, something like Punch and Judy, painting pictures in the interior of the theatre in order to give interest to their gardens when the plants were not in flower.

But although we may have modestly to content ourselves with the outdoor or Alpine Auricula, we have nothing to complain of, for it is not only the painter's but also the cottager's flower. It is indeed one of those flowers which looks more like the invention of a miniaturist or of a designer of embroidery, than like a thing which will grow easily and contentedly in one's own garden.

* Rev. Samuel Gilbert, *The Florist's Vade-mecum*, 1683.

In practical truth it will flourish gratefully given the few conditions it requires: a deep, cool root-run, a light soil with plenty of leaf-mould (some of the old growers recommended the soil thrown up from mole-hills), a certain amount of shade during the hotter hours of the day, and enough moisture to keep it going. In other words, a west or even a north aspect will suit it well, so long as you do not forget the deep root-run, which has the particular reason that the auricula roots itself deeper and deeper into the earth as it grows older. If you plant it in shallow soil, you will find that the plant hoists itself upwards, away from the ground, eventually raising itself on to a bare, unhappy-looking stem, whereas it really ought to be flattening its leaves against the brown earth, and making rosette after rosette of healthy green. If your auriculas are doing this, you may be sure they are doing well, and you may without hesitation dig them up and divide them as soon as they have ceased flowering, that is to say in May or June, and re-plant the bits you have broken off, to increase your group next year.

It is well worth trying to raise seedlings from your own seed, for you never know what variation you may get. The seed germinates easily in about ten days or a fortnight; sow it in a sandy compost, barely covering the seed; keep the seedlings in a shady place, in pots if you like, or pricked out on a suitable border till they are big enough to move to their permanent home. At one time, auricula seed was worth ten guineas an ounce, so perhaps this reflection ought to inspire us with some reverence for the quantity which Nature supplies gratis.

Auriculas have a long history behind them. It is suggested that they may have been known to the Romans, as a plant whose native home was the Alps. With more certainty we know that they derive their name from the supposed resemblance of their leaves to the ears of bears: *Oreille d'ours* in French, *Orecchio d'orso* in Italian; a somewhat far-fetched resemblance, I think, but one which obtained general credence. Huguenot refugees popularized them in England, and by the latter half of the seventeenth century many new varieties had been raised, to which some charming and fanciful names were given, such as the Fair Virgin, the Alderman, the Matron, Prince Silverwings, and a white novelty called the Virgin's Milk. The most pleasing and descriptive of all names, however, is the old Dusty Miller, more pleasing even than the name Vanner's Aprons, as they were called in Gloucestershire, no doubt in allusion to the tough leathery texture of the leaves. They appear also to have been called Baziers, but Baziers is a word I cannot trace, even in the big *Oxford English Dictionary*. I wonder if it can possibly have any reference to aprons made of baize. I don't know and offer the suggestion for what it is worth. One author suggests, perhaps more plausibly, that it may be merely a corruption of Bear's Ears.

Punica Granatum – The Pomegranate

Of all fruits the pomegranate is surely one of the most romantic. I never know whether I prefer it entire, with its polished leathery rind and oddly flattened sides, or split open, revealing the gleaming pips, each in its watery envelope with the seed visible through the transparency. We can never hope to grow such fully developed fruits in this country, but the tree itself is hardier than usually supposed. It will even flower, producing coral-coloured blossoms among the dark pointed leaves; it will produce miniature versions of its fruit in the autumn, too, but it is not for the sake of its fruit that I grow it. I grow it for the sake of its leaves and its blossoms; and for the sake, also, of its reddish twigs in spring, and of the young leaves which are as transparent as cornelian against the light before they have properly unfolded. I can think of no other shrub having quite such luminous tips, especially if it is growing above eye-level (as one often sees it on the tops of terrace walls in Italy) so that, looking up as we pass along, we catch it between us and the sun. I give it a warm corner, in the angle formed by a south and an east wall; in the winter I heap ashes over its roots, and provide a warm coat in the shape of a Russian mat tacked across the angle of the two walls. I planted a bush of myrtle beside it, thinking that they went well together both as to appearance and general character, wherein I was indeed right, though it was only some years later that I discovered that some botanists consider the myrtle and the pomegranate to be actually allied. Being no botanist, I had merely remembered the groves of myrtle and pomegranate in which I had slept in Persia.

The pomegranate is a native of Persia and Afghanistan, but has made its way so freely into other countries that it is difficult to say now whether it really grows wild there also or not. Some hold a theory that it has been found in a fossilized state in Pliocene beds in Burgundy, but even without going back to prehistoric times for evidence of its antiquity we can trace a long enough pedigree through history, mythology, literature, and art. It has its name in Sanskrit; it appears in sculpture in Assyria and Egypt; it is mentioned in the Old Testament and in the *Odyssey*. Nausicaa knew it, and her maidens. In Phrygia it shared with the almond the distinction of having enabled the virgin mother of Attis to conceive her mighty son by putting a ripe pomegranate (or almond) into her bosom; in Greece it was held to have sprung from the blood of Dionysos. The Romans got it from Carthage, and called it *malum punicum* in consequence. The sculptors of the Renaissance, like those of Assyria and Egypt, recognized it as one of the most decorative of fruits – the symbol of poetry and fertility. One really does not know whether to call it romantic or classic: it would provide quite a good starting-point for an argument on those two eternally disputed terms.

Verbascum – Cotswold Varieties

I suppose every gardener is familiar with the Great Mullein (*Verbascum thapsus*), that ubiquitous weed which appears in likely and unlikely places, sometimes in the middle of a rich flower-bed, where it will profit by the good soil to grow three or four feet in height, sometimes in a starved dry wall, where it will not attain more than a few inches. It seeds itself everywhere, and becomes a nuisance and a problem, because in good conditions it is almost too handsome a weed to root out. So handsome is it, in fact, with its woolly grey leaves and yellow spike of bloom, that were it not set down as a weed we should regard it as a decorative border plant. Besides, considered purely as a herb, it possesses many varied qualifications. There seems to be practically no ill which its decoctions will not cure. Mullein tea has a long tradition as a remedy for coughs and lung troubles; it is also reputed to cure such diverse ailments as ringworm, warts, toothache, headache, earache, and gout. There are also other uses to which it may be put. It will drive away the evil eye. It will dye the hair to a rich gold, as Roman women discovered long ago. Witches made wicks from its leaves for their Sabbaths. Poachers threw its seeds into the water to intoxicate the fish. The poor wore its leaves inside their shoes for warmth. It seems ungrateful to consider so serviceable a plant as a mere weed.

And then again, it goes by so many and such picturesque names in this our country. Some of these names are simply descriptive of the plant and its woolly characteristics: Our Lady's Flannel, or Blanket Herb, or Beggar's Blanket, or Adam's Flannel. There are other names which derive from its practical uses: the Candlewick Plant, or Hag's Taper, with their reference to its utility as tinder when dry. All these considerations ought to add to our tolerance of the Great Mullein when it arises unwanted as a grey and yellow torch in the middle of our carefully planned garden.

Luckily there are some relations of the common mullein which we may legitimately grow as border plants, to be obtained under such names as *Verbascum* Cotswold Gem or Cotswold Queen. It does not much matter which variety you specify, for they are all equally desirable. They are all dusty, fusty, musty in colouring – queer colours, to which it is impossible to give a definite name: they are neither pink, nor yellow, nor coral, nor apricot, but a cloudy mixture between all those. They look as though a colony of tiny buff butterflies had settled all over them. They are not to be planted in a brilliant garden of orange and scarlet, but in some private enclosure where they may associate with other faded colours which will not swear at them or put them to shame. Their flowering season, which is a long one, extends from June into July, therefore they might well be associated with some of the old roses, such as Tuscany or the old Red Damask or the purple Moss.

If only one were as good a gardener in practice as one is in theory, what a garden one would create!

Do not expect your mulleins to do anything much for you during their first year after planting. They will be too busy making roots and leaves to think of throwing up a flower spike, and if they do throw up a flower spike it will be a meagre one, not worth having, so you had better cut it off and let the plant concentrate all its strength for the next season. Be content, for the first year, with a strong rosette of leaves only, and next year you can look forward to a group of flowers four feet high. You will have to stake them and, moreover, to stake them early, for they are apt to get blown about by any stray wind which may arise. Four or five sticks and some string will do it, and of course if you have time to cut off the seeding stalks the more likely you are to get a second crop. I have very little hope that you will be able to follow my advice. I proffer it only knowing that it is right, which does not mean that I follow it myself. There is always so much to be done, that these small jobs are bound to get neglected. The lupins stand heavy with seed-pods and so do the delphiniums, but where are the necessary two, three, four hours to come from? What chance for the mulleins, who are less showy but more subtle and quite as deserving?

Dianthus Caesius – The Cheddar Pink

> Mid the squander'd colour
>   idling as I lay
> Reading the *Odyssey*
>   in my rock-garden
> I espied the cluster'd
>   tufts of cheddar pinks . . .

Robert Bridges was not being quite accurate in his statements on that occasion, however tenderly he may have expressed his sentiments. His Cheddar Pinks did not grow in a rock garden at all, but in two long bands down either side of a path at his home at Boar's Hill. At least, that is how I saw them. He may

125

have had them in a rock garden also, but if so I never saw it. Fortunately for me, the Laureate was not absorbed in the *Odyssey* that evening, but in an affably hospitable mood was more disposed to exhibit his pinks to an appreciative guest. Dressed in the true Tennysonian tradition in a sort of shepherd's cloak and large black hat, he had already emerged startlingly from among the rhododendrons – or were they laurels? – to open the gate for me on my arrival, and now proposed to extend his courtesy by taking me round his garden. I was charmed, alarmed, and rather overwhelmed. He was so old, so tall, so handsome, so untidy, so noble. And so childishly pleased with his pinks.

They were, indeed, a revelation to me in my ignorance. I had seen them growing wild on the cliffs of the Cheddar Gorge, but had never visualized them massed like this, giving off their scent so warmly to the summer evening. The Laureate marched in all his stateliness between them, pretending to be less pleased than I could see he was. Every now and then he bent his enormous length to pick some, snapping the stalks very delicately with his sensitive fingers, and having collected a generous bunch he offered it to me, solemnly and even ceremoniously, looking at me very hard meanwhile as though he were sizing me up, which again was an alarming experience. 'They make a pleasant tussie-mussie,' he said as he gave them, and I saw a twinkle in his eye which seemed to indicate that he was testing me on my reception of the unusual word. I was far too much intimidated to suggest that a tussie-mussie really meant a mixed bunch, so I let it go and just said thank you. Looking back, I think he would have liked me better had I bravely corrected him. He would have been amused. One makes these mistakes when one is young, as I then was, and over-anxious to be polite.

Next morning after breakfast he took me into his private room, and read me some passages from the manuscript of a poem he was then writing. He expounded his ideas about its peculiar rhythm in terms so technical as to be completely beyond my comprehension. The poem, when completed, he thought would be called *A* (or possibly *The*) *Testament of Beauty*. Again I was alarmed and overwhelmed. It was altogether too much like being growled at by Lord Tennyson in his later years.

Anyhow, he did introduce me to the virtues of the Cheddar Pink, and I immediately ordered a packet of seed and grew it down my own garden path in the same way, not so much from any desire to imitate the Laureate as from a desire to reproduce that same delicious smell on a warm summer evening. And in doing so I learnt from experience a lesson which he had omitted to give me. For two summer seasons my Cheddar Pinks were a great success, and I thought they were going on for ever, but, after that, they died out. I investigated indignantly and discovered that our native pink does die out when planted in ordinary garden soil, i.e. grown down the edge of an herbaceous border as Dr Bridges was growing it. Its only chance of perennial survival is to live in starvation in a crack of a wall, where it may flourish happily year after year. This does not mean that it cannot be grown down the border path also; it means only that you have to renew your supply by fresh seedlings every alternate year – not an excessive trouble to take, when you remember the grey-green clumps which so agreeably throw up the colours of other flowers, and then the pinks themselves while they are blooming and giving off that special, incomparable smell which for me will always be associated with a June day and the cloaked figure of a beautiful, agèd poet.

Rosa Moyesii

This is a Chinese rose, and looks it. If ever a plant reflected all that we had ever felt about the delicacy, lyricism, and design of a Chinese drawing, *Rosa moyesii* is that plant. We might well expect to meet her on a Chinese printed paper-lining to a tea-chest of the time of Charles II, when wall-papers first came to England, with a green parrot out of all proportion, perching on her slender branches. There would be no need for the artist to stylize her, for Nature has already stylized her enough. Instead, we meet her more often springing out of our English lawns, or overhanging our English streams, yet *Rosa moyesii* remains forever China. With that strange adaptability of true genius she never looks out of place. She adapts herself as happily to cosy England as to the rocks and highlands of Asia.

'Go, lovely rose.' She goes indeed, and quickly. Three weeks at most sees her through her yearly explosion of beauty. But her beauty is such that she must be grown for the sake of those three weeks in June. During that time her branches will tumble with the large, single, rose-red flower of her being. It is of an indescribable colour. I hold a flower of it here in my hand now, and find myself defeated in description. It is like the colour I imagine Petra to be, if one caught it at just the right moment of sunset. It is like some colours in a rug from Isfahan. It is like the dyed leather sheath of an Arab knife – and this I do know for certain, for I am matching one against the other, the dagger-sheath against the flower. It is like all those dusky rose-red things which abide in the mind as a part of the world of escape and romance.

Then even when the flowers are gone the great graceful branches are sufficiently lovely in themselves. Consider that within three or four years a single bush will grow some twelve feet high and will cover an area six to eight feet wide; long waving wands of leaves delicately set and of an exquisite pattern, detaching themselves against the sky or the hedge or the wall, wherever you happen to have set it. Never make the mistake of trying to train it tight against a wall: it likes to grow free, and to throw itself loosely into the fountains of perfect shape it knows so well how to achieve. Do not, by the way, make the mistake either of industriously cutting off the dead heads, in the hope of inducing a second flowering. You will not get your second flowering and you will only deprive yourself of the second crop which it is preparing to give you: the crop of long bottle-shaped, scarlet hips of the autumn. Preserve them at all costs, these sealing-wax fruits which will hang brighter than the berries of the holly. If you have a liking for rose-hips, you would be well advised to mix some bushes of *Highdownensis* with your *Moyesii*, for *Highdownensis* (which is, in fact, a chance seedling of *Moyesii*) produces even finer hips – amongst the finest of any roses in cultivation. And if you are going in for mixtures, plant *Rosa fargesii* too. This is probably another child of *Moyesii*, of a lighter and more brilliant shade. I am never quite sure whether the parent and the child go very well together, or not. Perhaps not. Perhaps on the whole it would be better to plant them in separate clumps, with something dark to divide them, say rosemary, or a couple of Irish yews: the black-green of the yews would be the ideal background for the precise and delicate luxuriance which the roses will throw up.

Both *Fargesii* and *Highdownensis* suggest that *Moyesii* may produce other children in future. *Moyesii* has not been for very long in cultivation in European gardens, having been first observed on the Tibetan frontier in 1890, rediscovered in 1903, exhibited in 1908 and put on the market in 1910, so we have as yet had but little time to exploit her possibilities. It seems to be fairly well established that she will not root readily (if at all) from cuttings, so it is evidently on seed that we shall have to depend, and everybody knows how exciting and unexpected seedlings can be. Every amateur among rose-growers might well make a few experiments.

We already have the variety called *Geranium*, of stockier growth, and the beautiful white *Nevada*, which is not a chance seedling but a deliberate cross.

Even the greatest botanists such as Reginald Farrer derived satisfaction from giving their name to a new plant. It is not given to all of us to find *Gentiana farreri* for the first time, but there does seem to be some hope for all of us of raising a new seedling of *Rosa moyesii* from our own garden, however humble that garden may be.

Rosa Centifolia Muscosa – The Moss Rose

There has lately been an enthusiastic revival of what we call 'the old roses', to distinguish them from the more fashionable varieties, such as hybrid Teas, hybrid Perpetuals, Polyantha, and Wichuriana. I have no wish to disparage these varieties, which include many very eligible things amongst them, but anyone who falls under the charm of the old roses will seldom find his heart among the newer ones again. This charm may be partly sentimental, and certainly there are several things to be said against the old roses: their flowering time is short; they are untidy growers, difficult to stake or to keep in order; they demand hours of snipping if we are to keep them free from dead and dying heads, as we must do if they are to display their full beauty unmarred by a mass of brown, sodden petals. But in spite of these drawbacks a collection of the old roses gives a great and increasing pleasure. As in one's friends, one learns to overlook their faults and love their virtues.

Having enumerated their faults – or, rather, their disadvantages – what are those virtues? A sentimental association: they recall everything that we have ever read in poetry, or seen in paintings, in connection with roses. A more personal association, possibly: we may have met them, neglected and ignored in the gardens we knew in childhood. Then, they usually smell better than their modern successors. People complain that the modern rose has lost in smell what it has gained in other ways, and although their accusation is not always justified there is still a good deal of truth in it. No such charge can be brought against the Musk, the Cabbage, the Damask, or the Moss. They load the air with the true rose scent.

The Musk may excel the Moss in this respect, but since the Moss is only a form of the Cabbage it shares the deep, velvety scent of its relation, with the added attraction of its own furry calices and shoots. Nobody knows when first a Cabbage rose turned itself into a Moss, but the first gardener to observe the freak must certainly have thought with alarm that his bushes were affected by some unknown disease. And so, in a sense, they were. Mr Edward Bunyard, who has done so much to restore the old roses to current favour, puts it neatly in his book, *Old Garden Roses*, 'The moss is a proliferation of the glands which are always present in the Cabbage roses.' Proliferation was an unfamiliar word to me, although the context showed me what Mr Bunyard meant, but on looking it up in the dictionary, I arrived at the more precise meaning: 'Proliferate: reproduce itself, grow by multiplication of elementary parts; so, proliferation.' Well, the Moss rose as we know it has proliferated itself from the Cabbage by a multiplication of the elementary parts or glands. It seems a dry and rather medical way of putting it, but how lucky for us that the freak became fixed into a permanent and enchanting form.

Some rosarians cling firmly to the maxim that the rose which fades from red to lilac is a bad rose, an undesirable rose, a rose instantly to be abolished from our gardens; but others, less conventionally minded, hold that the bishop's-purple of its dying hours invests it with a second beauty. In the case of the Moss, we must agree. I have two bushes of the Moss, *William Lobb* (incidentally they have attained a height of twelve feet), and as they reach the stage where some of the flowers are passing while others are still coming out, they look as though some rich ecclesiastical vestment had been flung over them. The dull carnation of the fresh flowers accords so perfectly with the slaty lilac of the old, and the bunches cluster in such profusion, that the whole bush becomes a cloth of colour, sumptuous, as though stained with blood and wine. If they are to be grown in a border, I think they should be given some grey-leaved plant in front of them, such as *Stachys lanata* (more familiarly, Rabbit's Ears), for the soft grey accentuates their own musty hues, but ideally speaking, I should like to see a small paved garden with grey stone walls given up to them entirely, with perhaps a dash of the old rose prettily called *Veilchenblau* (violet-blue) climbing the walls and a few clumps of the crimson clove carnation at their feet.

Rosa Mundi

The Wars of the Roses being fortunately over, making one war the less for us to reckon with, we are left to the simple enjoyment of the flower which traditionally symbolizes that historic contest. The only question is, which rose are we really to regard as the true York-and-Lancaster? For the one which most people hail cheerfully by that name in gardens, very often turns out to be not York-and-Lancaster at all, but *Rosa Mundi*.

There is no adequate reason why this confusion should have arisen, for apart from the fact that they both have variegated petals, the two roses are not really very much alike. The Rose of the World (*Rosa Mundi*) is a Gallica; the Rose of the Wars (York-and-Lancaster) is a Damask, but in case that classification is not of much practical use to you, here are two other ways by which you may tell them. York-and-Lancaster is a very pale pink, almost white; a few petals are variegated, but not all; a washy thing, not worth having. *Rosa Mundi* is far more striking. She is of a deeper pink, and *all* the petals are stained with a true carmine. She is also far more free-flowering. It does not very much matter if people, wrongly, like to go on calling her York-and-Lancaster, as they always do and no doubt always will. What matters is that we can now buy a rose which is variously called *Rosa Mundi* or York-and-Lancaster by the ignorant, and, so long as we are quite sure in our mind that it is *Rosa Mundi* we have acquired, can depend upon getting something which will increase in luxuriance from year to year. Striped and splotched and blotted, this fine old rose explodes into florescence in June, giving endless variations of her markings. You never know what form these markings are going to take. Sometimes they come in red orderly stripes, sometimes in splashes, sometimes in mere stains and splotches, but always various, decorative, and interesting. They remind one of red cherry juice generously stirred into a bowl of cream. A bush of *Rosa Mundi* in full flowering is worth looking at. It is not worth cutting for the house unless you have the leisure to renew your flower-vases every day, for in water it will not last. Even out of doors, blooming on its own bush, it does not last for very long. It is a short-lived delight, but during the short period of its blooming it makes up in quantity what it lacks in durability. It gives the best of itself for about a fortnight, and then it seems to have expended its total effort for the whole year.

Perhaps all the foregoing makes it sound rather unsatisfactory and not worth while. On the contrary, it is very much worth while indeed. For one thing, you can stick it in any odd corner, and indeed you will be wise to do so, unless you have a huge garden where you can afford blank gaps during a large part of the year. You can also grow it as a hedge, and let it ramp away. Mix some Moss roses with it, and you will soon have a rose-hedge so thick and romantic that all the nightingales of the neighbouring woods will come to press their breasts in song against the thorns. But the companion which really suits it best is Tuscany, who gets a section to herself in this book.

A word as to pruning. The true York-and-Lancaster scarcely needs any pruning at all, except at the interval of a few years, when the bush threatens to become straggly. *Rosa Mundi*, on the other hand, needs all weak shoots to be cut out after the flowering time is over, and in the spring the remaining shoots should be shortened to within half a dozen buds.

A further word as to suckers, those long, strong, thorny growths which most healthy roses throw up from the base of the bush, and which must be cut away unless the bush is to revert entirely to the original briar (or wild rose) stock on which it has been budded. It is sometimes difficult to decide whether the new shoot is a sucker or a valuable fresh addition supplied by the rose itself. Roughly speaking, a sucker springs from below ground-level (i.e. it springs from the *root* of the rose), and this, although not conclusive, is always an indication that the shoot should be regarded with suspicion. The sucker will

usually be found to carry larger and more vicious thorns than the rose proper,
and the leaves, if closely examined, will be found to differ. The most useful
hint of all was given to me verbally by Mr Bunyard – one of those simple
rules which for some reason are never to be found in books: 'Remember', he
said, 'that a sucker can never have more than seven leaves on a single stalk,
and that therefore any shoot bearing more than seven leaves cannot possibly
be a sucker.'

Rosa Gallica – Tuscany

I fear that my choice among the old roses may be regarded as somewhat
arbitrary and limited. Limited it admittedly is, and I regret it. There is scarcely
a variety I should not have liked to discuss, from the tight and tiny De Meaux
to the lyrically named Cuisse de Nymphe Emue, but a sense of apportion-
ment forbade it. I could not put in too many roses to the exclusion of other
flowers, and this is why I have restricted myself to *Rosa Mundi*, the Moss Rose,
and the Gallica rose called Tuscany.

There seems to have existed once a rose known as the Velvet Rose. Nobody
knows with any certainty what particular rose was meant by this name, but it
is supposed that it must have been a Gallica. Nobody knows the place of its
origin: was it truly a wildling in Europe, or had it been imported into cultivation from the East? These are mysteries which have not as yet been resolved.
All that we can say is that the name is very descriptive of its supposed descend-
ants, amongst which we must include Tuscany.

The Velvet Rose. What a combination of words! One almost suffocates in
their soft depths, as though one sank into a bed of rose-petals, all thorns ideally
stripped away. It is improbable that we shall ever lie on a bed of roses, unless
we are very decadent and also very rich, but we can imagine ourselves doing
so when we hold a single rose close to our eyes and absorb it in an intimate
way into our private heart. This sounds a fanciful way of writing, the sort of
way which makes me shut up most gardening books with a bang, but in this
case I am trying to get as close to my true meaning as possible. It really does
teach one something, to look long and closely into a rose, especially such a
rose as Tuscany, which opens flat (being only semi-double), thus revealing the
quivering and dusty gold of its central perfection.

Tuscany is more like the heraldic Tudor rose than any other. The petals,
of the darkest crimson, curl slightly inwards and the anthers, which are of a
rich yellow, shiver and jingle loosely together if one shakes the flower.

No photograph can give any idea of what this rose is really like. Photographs make it look merely funereal – too black, almost a study in widow's crêpe. They make the flower and the leaf appear both of the same dark colour, which is unfair to so exquisite a thing. If you saw a photograph you might well wonder why I mentioned Tuscany as a suggested companion to *Rosa Mundi*. I did so because these two complement each other so perfectly, both sharing the same medieval quality. Just as the faces of one century differ in some subtle and indefinable way from the faces of another century, so do these two roses differ from any rose which could possibly be called modern.

As, like *Rosa Mundi*, Tuscany is a Gallica, it needs the same kind of pruning; it will never make a very tall bush, and your effort should be to keep it shapely – not a very easy task, for it tends to grow spindly shoots, which must be rigorously cut out. Humus and potash benefit the flowers and the leaves respectively.

Abutilon Megapotamicum or Vexillarium

This curious Brazilian with the formidable name is usually offered as a half-hardy or greenhouse plant, but experience shows that it will withstand as many degrees of frost as it is likely to meet with in the southern counties. It is well worth trying against a south wall, for apart from the unusual character of its flowers it has several points to recommend it. For one thing it occupies but little space, seldom growing more than four feet high, so that even if you should happen to lose it you will not be left with a big blank gap. For another, it has the convenient habit of layering itself of its own accord, so that by merely separating the rooted layers and putting them into the safety of a cold frame, you need never be without a supply of substitutes. For another, it is apt to flower at times when you least expect it, which always provides an amusing surprise.

You should thus grow it where you are constantly likely to pass and can glance at it daily to see what it is doing. It is not one of those showy climbers which you can see from the other side of the garden, but requires to be looked at as closely as though you were short-sighted. You can only do so in the open, for if you cut it to bring into the house it will be dead within the hour, which is unsatisfactory both for it and for you. But sitting on the grass at the foot of the wall where it grows, you can stare up into the queer hanging bells and forget what the people round you are saying. It is not an easy flower to describe – no flower is, but the Abutilon is particularly difficult. In despair I turned up its botanically official description: 'Ls. lanc., 3, toothed. Fls. 1½, sepals red, petals yellow, stamens long and drooping (like a fuchsia).'

133

Now in the whole of that laconic though comprehensive specification there were only three words which could help me at all: *like a fuchsia.* Of course I had thought of that already; anybody would. The flower of the Abutilon *is* like a fuchsia, both in size and in shape, though not in colour. But it is really a ballet dancer, something out of *Prince Igor.* 'Sepals red, petals yellow' is translated for me into a tight-fitting red bodice with a yellow petticoat springing out below it in flares, a neat little figure, rotating on the point of the stamens as on the point of the toes. One should, in fact, be able to spin it like a top.

Abutilon megapotamicum has a companion, *Abutilon vitifolium,* a Chilean which is more frequently grown, but which is less interesting – at least, according to my taste – with its pale mauve flowers or their white variety.

Primula Pulverulenta – The Bartley Strain

The early years of this century, which introduced such an amazing crop of new treasures to English gardens, produced amongst other discoveries from Western China the Primula known as *pulverulenta* – the powdered or mealy primula. It rapidly and rightly became a favourite, but to my mind at least its crimson head is a crude thing compared with the delicate refinement of the Bartley strain which is its child. Mr G. H. Dalrymple, who bred the Bartley strain, has been kind enough to furnish me with an account of how it came into being:

'Among the first plants of *P. pulverulenta* raised in this country there appeared a pale pink sport . . . I was so greatly taken with this plant and was so anxious to own it that I tried hard to get seed as plants were then (1912) very expensive . . . I had to use the pollen of the type plant on the pink sport to get seed, and the resulting seedlings gave me ninety-nine per cent type colour and one plant that flowered pink. After some years of work on it I had increased the percentage of pink flowers appearing in each generation until 1921 when the drought killed off every plant except one which produced a few seeds. From these I had about one hundred seedlings to plant out . . . and the following spring I had about fifty per cent pink. Further selecting, and the next generation gave me a better percentage and from these I selected the best and started another generation which gave me I might say ninety-nine per cent pink shades. Another selection, and the type plant completely disappeared and has never appeared since.'

The uninitiated may be surprised at the years of patience required before any new flower is triumphantly put upon the market, but Mr Dalrymple's primula is so lovely, as to reward him now for any trouble he took to secure it. In its habit of growth, *P. pulverulenta* resembles *P. japonica*, rising in a straight stem from amongst a cluster of leaves, and then displaying itself in ring upon ring of flowers. No photograph can suggest what Mr Dalrymple's Bartley variety of *P. pulverulenta* is really like. Against the white floury stem as soft to the look as fur is to the touch, you must imagine the rings of pink, in perfectly toned association. It is difficult to give any exact idea of the colour in words; to compare it with the pink of peach-blossom would be to suggest something far too crude, with the pink of apple-blossom something far too washy, with the pink of a sunset-cloud something far too pink; nor is there any rose which will give me the precise shade I want. It really suggests a far deeper pink which has been dusted over with chalk, so that the original colour shows through, behind the slight veil which has been powdered over it by a puff or a breath of wind.

There is a way of growing this primula which will greatly enhance the beautiful straightness of the stems. You should set it on a steep low bank, so that it appears to rise in tiers of increasing heights. Thus, the plants towards the top will tower two to three feet above the ones at the bottom, creating a sheet of chalky pink, sloping down and far more effective than an equal mass of uniform height. At the top of the bank I suggest azaleas of suitable colour; and there are many.

Only one difficulty presents itself against this plan. It is the simple difficulty that steep banks usually mean natural drainage, and that these primulas prefer to grow in places which retain coolness and moisture throughout the summer. Therefore you must be quite sure that your steep bank is as cool and damp at the top as at the bottom, otherwise they will thrive in the lower reaches and die parched at the top. This sounds an impossibly ideal condition to impose, but you can fulfil it if your garden offers a bank facing north, well shaded by trees which protect from the blistering sun. Then both your azaleas and primulas can hide themselves from the midday glare; can flower happily, unparched, unscorched, and can ripen and develop towards another year.

A warning: should you wish to save the seed off your own plants, be careful that the mice do not take it before you do. *Pulverulenta* is the only primula which a mouse will attack in this way.

Primula Littoniana

The amateur gardener does not as a rule trouble his head very much with botanical groupings. Such names as 'scrophulariceæ' and 'crassulaceæ' merely inspire him with boredom and distaste. Yet I suppose that a few of the natural orders are instantly recognizable, and that to the roses and lilies we may safely add the great family of the primulaceae. Lacking it, we should be without the primrose, the cowslip, the auricula, the polyanthus, and the innumerable varieties of primula.

The absence of the primrose and the polyanthus alone, with their range of colours, would impoverish the spring garden perhaps more than we realize. Consider that we can now grow them in blue, mauve, magenta, yellow, white, ruby, bronze, orange; consider also that they spread their flowering over nearly two months in April and May; that even in autumn and throughout a mild winter you are liable to find a few stray blooms; that they may be increased indefinitely, either by self-sown seedlings or by pulling big clumps to pieces. There are few plants more obliging. The smallest rooted bit will grow, and it is even possible to transplant them while in full flower: they scarcely seem to notice the move. A cool soil and the same amount of shade as pleases our native primrose is all they ask.

Their grander relations, the tall primulas, vary of course in amiability. They are the aristocrats of the group and as such are entitled to their fancies. Some of them, indeed, appear to be so democratically minded as to accommodate themselves to our wishes as readily as the primrose and the polyanthus; thus, although *P. japonica* and the yellow *P. sikkimensis* have travelled across half the world before reaching England, they give themselves no airs on arrival but adapt themselves happily to the banks of our woodland streams, set a lavish store of seed for our use, and quickly grow themselves into dividable clumps as big as cabbages. With these, however, I am not for the moment concerned. I am concerned with the more unusual *Primula littoniana,** a native of Yunnan, which many people admire when they see it at flower-shows but seldom grow in their own gardens. It seems to be one of those plants which get so far as the compliment of an X pencilled against it in the nurseryman's leaflet, and stop at that. I do not quite know why. It is a very shapely thing, not difficult to grow with success. My illustration,† I think, gives quite a good idea of its quality, though of course not of its colour. The photograph does at least suggest the thimble-like effect of a cone set on the top of the flower, though it necessarily leaves out the red and violet diversity of the half-expanded flower. The photograph suggests also the conditions under which this primula likes to be grown; cool, shady, rather moist, with plenty of leaf-mould for its rather shallow root-run, and protection from a burning sun. Given these, a colony should flourish, but do not expect to be able to increase it by seed for it is not at all obliging in that respect. Your only hope is to increase by division of a sturdy plant.

* Now called *Vialii*.   † Which appeared in the first edition of *In Your Garden*.

Lilium Giganteum*

It is a contrast to turn from such small delicacies as the embroidery of the old roses, to the towering heroism of the Himalayan lily. Too splendid to be called vulgar, she is still very decidedly over life-size. Unconsciously, one sets oneself some kind of limit as to what size a flower ought to be, and here is one which exceeds them all. It looks almost as though she had adapted herself to the proportions of her tremendous home. For I suppose that there is no scenery in the world so appallingly majestic as that of the great mountains of Central Asia. Reginald Farrer found her in Tibet, and any reader of his books will have formed some distant idea of that remote and lonely region, scarcely travelled and practically unmapped, where men are few, but flowers are many, a ravishing population put there as it were to compensate for the rudeness of life, the violence of the climate, and the desolation of the ranges.

So the Giant Lily, not to be outdone, has matched her stature against the great fissures and precipices and nameless peaks. In an English garden she looks startling indeed, but out there a peculiar fitness must attend her, making of her the worthy and proportionate ornament, sculptural as she is with her long, quiet trumpets and dark, quiet leaves. I do not know to what height she will grow in her native home, but in England she will reach twelve feet without much trouble, and I have heard it said that in Scotland she will reach eighteen.

A group of these lilies, seen by twilight or moonlight gleaming under the shadow of a thin wood, is a truly imposing sight. The scent is overpowering, and seems to be the only expression of life vouchsafed by these sentinels which have so strange a quality of stillness. I should like to see them growing among silver birches, whose pale trunks would accord with the curious greenish-white trumpets of the flower-spike. Unluckily, few of us have a birch-wood exactly where we want it; and even though we were willing to make a plantation, the stem of the young birch lacks the quality of the old.

But failing either of these, any coppice say of hazel or chestnut will serve the purpose, which is to provide shade and coolness, for the Giant Lily will stand a good deal of both. Then you must dig out a hole two to three feet deep, and fill it with the richest material you can provide in the form of leaf-mould, peat, and rotted manure. This simple recommendation reminds me of the exclamation of a friend: 'It seems to me', she said, 'that this lily of yours has all the virtues and only four disadvantages: it is very expensive to buy; the bulb takes three years before it flowers; after flowering once it dies; and you have to bury a dead horse at the bottom of a pit before it will flower at all.'

* Now called *Cardiocrinum giganteum*.

Up to a point, these remarks are true. A bulb of flowering size does cost five shillings, it does then die, and it does demand a lot of feeding. On the other hand, it will produce a number of bulblets which you can grow on for yourself, thus arranging for an inexhaustible stock. The best plan is to buy as many three-year-old bulbs as you can afford, and also some second year bulbs which are cheaper. By the time your second year bulbs have flowered and died, you will have some third year bulbs ready for your own raising, and then you are safe indefinitely.

Having then dug your hole in October and filled it up again, you plant the bulbs so shallowly that the tip, or nose, just shows above the surface of the ground. It is wise to throw down some covering of leaves or bracken as a protection against late frosts. It is wise also to put in some tall stakes at the same time as you do the planting, for stakes will be needed, and by ramming them in later on you run the risk of damaging roots or even the bulb itself. When the leaves begin to appear in spring, put down slug-bait, for the slugs attack with vigour, and the glossy perfection of the huge leaves is a thing to be jealously guarded. You then wait for June, when you may expect your reward.

In the following October, you dig up the old bulb and throw it away, having first carefully saved the bulblets which you will find clustering round it like chicks round a hen.

Zinnias

Anthologists sometimes take especial delight in quoting the botanical howlers made by reputable authors, but (unless I have overlooked it, which is quite likely), no anthologist has yet put his finger on Walter Pater's howler when in *Marius the Epicurean* he makes his Romans go in search of zinnias wherewith to deck themselves. 'They visited the flower-market, lingering where the *coronarii* pressed on them the newest species, and purchased zinias [*sic*] now in blossom (like painted flowers, thought Marius), to decorate the folds of their togas.' Now either Pater had some botanical information drawn from Roman historians and subsequently mislaid by us, or else he was merely drawing on his imagination to find a flower which he thought suitable to decorate a toga. If he was just drawing on his imagination, he went absurdly wrong. For as the zinnia is a native of America and Mexico, and as Marius lived in Rome in the second century AD, Pater is out by about twelve centuries: he was, in fact, enriching Rome by a flower from a continent not due for discovery until some twelve hundred years later. I suppose this must be granted under the heading poetic licence.

In actual fact, the original zinnia, or *Zinnia elegans*, was introduced into European countries in 1796, and since then has been 'improved' into the garden varieties we now know and grow. Many flowers lose by this so-called improvement; the zinnia has gained. Some people call it artificial-looking, and so in a way it is. It looks as though it has been cut out of bits of cardboard ingeniously glued together into the semblance of a flower. It is prim and stiff and arranged and precise, almost geometrically precise, so that many people who prefer the more romantically disorderly flowers reject it just on account of its stiffness and regularity. 'Besides,' they say, 'it gives us a lot of trouble to grow. It is only half-hardy in this country, and thus has to be sown in a seed-box under glass in February or March; pricked out; and then planted out in May where we want it to flower. We have to be very careful not to water the seedlings too much, or they will damp off and die. On the other hand, we must never let the grown plant suffer from drought. Then, when we have planted it out, we have to be on the look-out for slugs which have for zinnias an affection greatly exceeding our own. Why should we take all this trouble about growing a flower which we know is going to be cut down by the first autumn frost?'

Such arguments crash like truncheons, and it takes an effort to renew our determination by recalling the vivid bed which gave us weeks of pleasure last year. For there are few flowers more brilliant without being crude, and since they are sun-lovers the maximum of light will pour on the formal heads and array of colours. The disadvantage of growing them in seed-boxes as a half-hardy annual may be overcome by sowing them where they are to remain, towards the end of May. Whether we grow them in a mixture (sold, I regret to say, under the description 'art-shades') or separate the pink from the orange, the red from the magenta, is a matter of taste. Personally I like them higgledy-piggledy, when they look like those pats of paints squeezed out upon the palette, and I like them all by themselves, not associated with anything else.

As cut flowers they are invaluable: they never flop, and they last I was going to say for weeks.

Tigridias – The Tiger-Flower

'May be grown with success on a hot, dry border.'

This is typical of the instructions given in gardening books and nurserymen's catalogues, which make the Englishman ask himself where he is going to find a hot, dry border in this country. Borders, as he well knows, are more apt to be chilly owing to the deficiency of sun, and wet owing to the excess of rain. He thinks with envy of those strips of soil at the foot of Provençal terraces, which might well be described as hot and dry, and, as such, fit homes for such sun-lovers as the Mexican Tiger-Flower. He thinks of that succession of blazing days, interrupted only by an occasional thunderstorm. (Thus do we idealize climates other than our own, and forget the disadvantages against which we do not have to contend.)

He may, however, take heart, for there are several ways in which he may improvise or at any rate substitute conditions such as those recommended. It is true that he cannot provide sunshine when the sun refuses to shine, but he can at least choose his border where any available sunshine will strike it, facing either south or east; and he can do a great deal towards the desirable dryness. He can arrange for dryness, i.e. good drainage, either by making his border on the sharp slope of a hill, or by raising it several inches above the natural level of flat ground on a bed banked up by a stone (or brick) surround, with a foundation of broken rubble or ashes under the soil. Both these systems entail trouble and labour. Far more simply, he can walk round his house and find a narrow strip of border facing south or east, which is almost entirely protected from rain by the overhanging eaves of the house. In such a position, only such summer rain as is driven in by an accompanying wind ever reaches the six or eight inches at the foot of the house wall; and this, provided the soil is sufficiently light and crumbly, is an ideal position in which to grow *tigridias*.

I imagine, therefore, a long narrow bed under the shelter of the eaves, entirely given up to this brilliant and ephemeral flower. Let me explain these two adjectives. Brilliant is frequently used of flowers too rashly and too unadvisedly, but of the *tigridia* with deserved justice, for a border of these Mexicans really resembles a colony of bright and enormous insects, settled upon green leaves but ready at any moment to be off. They look like gigantic butterflies, flat, open, wing-spread; white, yellow, orange, carmine, spotted, speckled, beautifully shaped. But ephemeral, short-lived. One would expect no less of such a butterfly flower. Within a few hours of opening, the individual flower has closed its petals in a saddened droop. Astonishing at breakfast, miserable at luncheon . . . Watching them, it seems tragic that so exquisite a form of creation should also be so wasteful, that the surprising bloom which one has discovered in the morning should be gone by the afternoon; but in splendid compensation another crop of poised insects is there next morning, like a renewal of reward after brief discouragement.

The moral of all this is, that the tiger-iris (for *tigridias* belong to the iris family) should be planted in dozens or in hundreds. Only by planting a quantity can you ensure a real display. Each plant will give generously, but it takes a quantity to keep up the daily, hourly supply. Like dahlias or gladioli, they had better be taken up for the winter and kept in a shed where the frost will not injure them and the mice will not get at them; but unlike dahlias or gladioli, they give no trouble as to staking, for they grow low to the ground, a great advantage over those more usual and obvious flowers, which are to be found in every garden, where *tigridias* are not.

Gerbera Jamesonii – The Transvaal Daisy

There are some flowers about which there is nothing interesting to say, except that they happen to have caught one's fancy. Such a flower, so far as I am concerned, is *Gerbera jamesonii*. It has no historical interest that I know of; no long record of danger and difficulty attending its discovery; no background of savage mountains and Asiatic climates. It carries, in fact, no romantic appeal at all. It has taken no man's life. It has to stand or fall on its own merits.

I first observed it in the window of a florist's shop, neatly rising out of a gilt basket tied with pink ribbons. No more repellent presentation could be imagined, or anything more likely to put one against the flower for ever, yet somehow this poor ill-treated object struck me instantly as a lovely thing, so lovely that I suffered on its behalf to see it so misunderstood. I went in to inquire its name, but the young lady assistant merely gaped at me, as they nearly always do if one makes any inquiry about their wares unconnected with their price. 'It's a dysy of sorts,' she said. It was only later, at a flower-show, that I discovered it to be *Gerbera jamesonii*, also called the Transvaal daisy. Neither name pleased me very much, but the flower itself pleased me very much indeed. It seemed to include every colour one could most desire, especially a coral pink and a rich yellow, and every petal as shiny and polished as a buttercup. Long, slender stalks and a clean, erect habit. It was altogether a very clean-looking flower; in fact it might have been freshly varnished.

The exhibitor was better informed than the florist's young lady. It was only hardy in this country, he said, if it could be grown in very dry conditions at the foot of a warm wall, in which case it might be regarded as a reasonably hardy perennial. I know, however, that nurserymen are frequently more optimistic in their recommendations than they should be, so privately resolved to grow it in an unheated greenhouse. This house is really a long lean-to, sloped against the brick wall of an old stable, and all along the foot of the wall runs a bed about six feet wide, which is an ideal place for growing things such as the *Gerbera* which cannot without a certain anxiety be left out of doors. I wonder indeed why those who are fortunate enough to possess such a lean-to, do not

141

more frequently put it to this use. It is true that it entails sacrificing all the staging down one side of the house, but the gain is great. Staging means pots, and pots mean watering, and 'potting on' if you are to avoid root-starvation, whereas plants set straight into the ground can root down to Australia if they like. You can, moreover, make up the soil to suit every separate kind; you can work under cover in bad weather; you can snap your fingers at hailstorms, late frosts, young rabbits, and even, to a certain extent, slugs. There is certainly a great deal to be said for this method of gardening.

I once saw a lean-to house which had been adapted in this way, with a special view to growing lilies. The wall had been distempered a light blue, of that peculiar shade produced by spraying vines with copper sulphate against the walls of farm-houses in Italy: in the centre was a sunk rectangular pool, with blue nymphaea growing in it and clumps of agapanthus at each of the four corners. The tall lilies rose straight and pure and pale against the curious blue of the wall. I liked best going into this house after dark, when the single electric reflector in the roof cast down a flood-lighting effect more unreal and unearthly than anything I had ever seen.

Salpiglossis

Sooner or later one has to make up one's mind as to whether half-hardy annuals are worth growing or not. They certainly take up a lot of time, and once the frost has cut them down they are gone for ever, and all our labour with them, for, unlike the hardy annual, they will seldom renew themselves in their self-sown children the following year. It is, of course, possible to diminish the labour by sowing the seeds in the open garden in May, instead of following the orthodox method of sowing in boxes under glass in early spring, but then one has to take the risk of a late frost which may blacken an entire bed of young plants in one night.

The salpiglossis arrived in this country from Chile as long ago as 1820 and is one of those flowers which has benefited incredibly from the attentions of horticulturists to the original form. There is now nothing which is not entirely lovely about it except its name. I wish it could acquire a decent English name, instead of this corrupt Greek (from *salpigx*, trumpet, and *glossa*, tongue), but if it possesses an English name I never heard it. Perhaps when it has been with us for another century the constant mis-pronunciations to which it is subjected will produce an unrecognizable variant, for there are few botanical names which give greater trouble in the arrangement of their vowels and consonants. It seems necessary for the English tongue to put in an additional *p* or *s* somewhere. I have heard it called 'salpiglopsis' and 'salsipiglossis' alternately, both, unfortunately, even more hideous than their original. I wonder what it is called in Chile?

Its name apart, it is, as I said, entirely lovely. To my mind it far exceeds its relation the petunia in every way. The range and richness of its colour is amazing. Like the Assyrian, it can come up in cohorts of purple and gold, or in ruby and gold, or in white and gold, when it has the milky purity, gold-embroidered, traditionally associated with the robes of saints and angels. Then you can also grow it in brown and gold, a very rare colour in flowers, for it is a true brown – the brown of corduroy, with all the depth of the velvet pile. The veining is drawn as though by the stroke of a fine brush; and, moreover, suggests what is in fact the truth: that the salpiglossis shows to great advantage as a cut flower. Out in the garden it is apt to look bedraggled rather too easily, for unless it has been carefully staked its brittle stems suffer badly from wind or heavy rain, but in a vase its intense livery glows unsullied. Place it for choice in a window or on a table where the sun will strike it, and then ask yourself whether it has not proved itself worthy of all the care it entailed.

For the same reason, try growing it as a pot-plant for the winter months. It adapts itself very graciously to this treatment. Of course you must keep it warm; forty to fifty degrees should be a safe temperature. In fact, you might try rescuing half a dozen plants from the garden in the autumn before the frosts come, potting them, and seeing whether they would not carry on, getting even sturdier as they grew older. Experiments are always interesting, but if you prefer the safer course sow a few seeds in pots in March and grow them on in what gardeners descriptively call a gentle heat.

Lilium Auratum

The various lilies present a problem to the amateur gardener. The advice offered to him by gardening books, nurserymen, and personal friends alternates between divergence and unanimity of opinion, both of which his own experience will prove to be wrong. He is told to plant shallow, and to plant deep; to supply manure and to avoid manure at all costs; to provide shade, and to choose the sunniest site possible. The Madonna lily (*Lilium candidum*) perhaps gives rise to the oddest combination of contradictions. On the divergent side we are told: (*a*) that the Madonna lily revels in a heavy mulch of manure, and (*b*) that manure is the one thing she cannot abide. We are told (*a*) to plant her among other growing things, that her roots may be shaded; (*b*) to plant her where the hot sun will ripen her bulbs. We are told (*c*) to lift the bulbs every two or three years; (*d*) never, at our peril, to move the bulbs at all. On the unanimous side we are told that the Madonna lily is the easiest of all lilies to grow with complete success, a contention which, as every gardener who has not the luck to be a cottager knows, is totally and miserably untrue.

Many explanations have been put forward as to why the Madonna lily reappears triumphantly every year in cottage gardens and peters out in the gardens of those whose home ranks as a house rather than as a cottage. It has been suggested (*a*) that cottagers habitually throw their pails of soap-suds over the lilies, (*b*) that the dust of passing traffic smothers the stems with purifying grit, (*c*) that the bulbs remain undisturbed year after year. Now I should be perfectly willing to throw soap-suds by the gallon over my lilies, and to collect trugs-full of grit for them from the lanes, and, above all, I should be willing and happy to leave them where they were for as many years as they saw fit. I ask no better. I can imagine nothing which would give me greater pleasure than to see a group of *Lilium candidum* increasing season after season, in the happy confidence that they would never be disturbed so long as I was in control of their fate. I would, in short, do anything to please them, but all my efforts have led me to the sad conclusion that the Madonna lily, like the wind, bloweth where it listeth.

There is a great deal more I could say on the subject of the Madonna lily, but I had started out with the intention of writing about *Lilium auratum*. Less wayward than *candidum*, in fact not wayward at all, there is no reason why the golden-rayed lily of Japan should not grow satisfactorily for all of us. It is said that the Japanese complacently ate the bulbs as a vegetable, much as we eat the potato or the artichoke, until, fortunately for us, they realized the commercial value to European gardens, when the slopes of Fujiyama started yielding a profitable harvest of bulbs timed to reach this country shortly after New Year's Day.

There are two ways in which we can grow this superb lily: in the open, preferably with the protection of shrubs, or in pots. I do not, myself, very much like the association of lilies with shrubs. It always looks to me too much like the-thing-one-has-been-told-is-the-right-thing-to-do. It savours too much of the shrubbery border effect, and suggests all too clearly that the lilies have been added in order to give 'an interest after the flowering shrubs are over'. This is not quite fair an accusation, since shrubs do certainly provide an ideal shelter for lilies, but still I retain a personal distaste for the arrangement. I cannot agree, for instance, that *Lilium auratum* looks more 'handsome' against a background of rhododendron or azalea; I think they look infinitely more handsome standing independently in pots set, let us say, on a flight of garden steps. Of course this method involves a little more trouble. It means carrying the pots to the desired position, and watering them throughout the growing season. Still it is worth while, and if they can be placed somewhere near a garden bench their scent alone is sufficient justification.

Luckily, they are very amenable to life in pots, provided the pots are large enough and are filled with a rich enough compost of peat and leaf-mould. It is as well to stake them when planting the bulbs, remembering that they may grow to a height of seven feet, especially the variety *platyphyllum* which is the finest of all. White and gold and curly, it unfolds to expose its leopard-like throat in truly superb and towering arrogance.

Hidcote Manor

Hidcote Manor*

Hidcote Manor, through the generosity of that fine gardener, Major Lawrence Johnston, was the first garden to be presented to the recently formed Committee for the preservation of gardens of outstanding merit under the joint auspices of the Royal Horticultural Society and the National Trust. It lies, secluded and remote, in the leafy country on the borders of Worcestershire and Gloucestershire, far from any considerable town, but within a few miles of Broadway and Chipping Campden, along winding and hilly lanes that could be nowhere but in the very depths of England. Its own farm surrounds it, including a tiny hamlet, extremely picturesque with thatched roofs, and cottage gardens in which I suspect Major Johnston of having taken a very practical interest; and from the top of the garden you command wide views over woods and meadows, with not a house in sight, right away to Bredon Hill on the opposite side of the valley. The manor house itself is charmingly unpretentious, in the Cotswold style, with a forecourt, and a chapel on one side.

When Major Johnston first acquired Hidcote forty-two years ago, he had nothing as a basis to his garden except one fine cedar and two groups of beeches. The rest was just fields, and I cannot believe that to any but a most imaginative eye it can have seemed a very promising site. There was no particular shape to it; standing high, it was somewhat windswept; there was nothing in the nature of old walls or hedges to afford protection; the soil was on the heavy side. It must have required immense energy, optimism, foresight, and courage to start transforming it into what it is today – a matured garden full of variety and beauty, the achievement of one man in his lifetime.

There are several points of view from which we may consider Hidcote. It appeals alike to the advanced gardener in search of rare or interesting plants, and on the aesthetic side to the mere lover of beauty, content to wander down broad grass walks flanked with colour, turning continually aside as the glimpse of little separate gardens lures him. The combination of botanical knowledge and aesthetic taste is by no means axiomatic, but Major Johnston possesses it in the highest degree. To my mind, Hidcote is a flawless example of what a garden of this type should be – but before going any further it would

* Reprinted from *The Journal of the Royal Horticultural Society*, vol. LXXIV, part II, November 1949.

be as well to define what we mean by 'a garden of this type', for Hidcote amongst its other merits displays a remarkable originality, and thus should perhaps not be associated with any 'type' at all.

Would it be misleading to call Hidcote a cottage garden on the most glorified scale? (It covers ten acres, but acreage has nothing to do with it.) It resembles a cottage garden, or, rather, a series of cottage gardens, in so far as the plants grow in a jumble, flowering shrubs mingled with roses, herbaceous plants with bulbous subjects, climbers scrambling over hedges, seedlings coming up wherever they have chosen to sow themselves. Now in a real cottage garden, where the limitations and very often the pattern – for example, the curve or the straightness of the path leading from the entrance gate to the front door – are automatically imposed upon the gardener, this delightful effect is both restrained and inevitable: it could not, we feel, be otherwise. It is very largely accidental. But in a big garden like Hidcote great skill is required to secure not only the success of the actual planting, but of the proportions which can best give the illusion of enclosure; the area must, in fact, be broken up in such a way that each part shall be separate from the other, yet all shall be disposed round the main lines of the garden in such a way as to give homogeneity to the whole. At Hidcote this has been achieved by the use of hedges, with openings cut for the convenience of communication, rather than by the use of walls and gates; tall living barriers which do much to deepen the impression of luxuriance and secrecy. In one such enclosure, I recollect, no larger than a fair-sized room, where moisture dripped and the paths were mossy and the walls were made of the darkest yew, scarlet ropes of *Tropaeolum speciosum* trailed all over the hedges, more amazingly brilliant in that place full of shadows, than ever it had appeared on a whitewashed cottage in Scotland.

The garden falls into six main portions. First the forecourt, which is lavishly planted all round the walls with hydrangeas, hypericum (the Hidcote variety), *Solanum crispum*, magnolias, buddleia, choisya, carpentaria, and *Schizophragma hydrangeoides* climbing beyond the first-floor windows. After passing through the house, you come out on to the old cedar spreading its branches over a couple of steps, and look down the wide grass walk which is the principal axis, terminating in a short flight of steps flanked by two little summer houses or pavilions with a slightly Chinese up-tilt at the corners of the roof, and leading finally to a wrought-iron gate between brick piers, commanding the view away to Bredon. On the right-hand side of this wide walk, and raised above it, lies a *very* large grass lawn, oval in shape, with a mound on which stand two or three big beech trees; another group of beech trees is at the opposite end; it is spacious, simple, and peaceful. Beyond this, concealed behind hedges, is the kitchen garden with the glass-houses and the collection of old-fashionable roses. On the left-hand side of the wide walk are most of the little separate gardens to which I have referred; and beyond them again, over a little stream gay with primulas, is the part of the garden known as the Wilderness – several acres of trees and shrubs, either for flowering in the spring or for colouring in the autumn.

I am aware that this dry tabulation can convey no idea whatsoever of the variety and beauty of the garden at Hidcote. Even now, I have omitted several features, such as the other wide grass walk between twenty-foot hedges of mixed beech and hornbeam; and the heath garden; for in truth, there is so much to say that it is impossible to compress it into a single article. This place is a jungle of beauty; a jungle controlled by a single mind; never allowed to deteriorate into a mere jungle, but always kept in bounds by a master hand. I cannot hope to describe it in words, for indeed it is an impossible thing to reproduce the shape, colour, depth, and design of such a garden through the poor medium of prose.

What I should like to impress upon the reader is the luxuriance everywhere; a kind of haphazard luxuriance, which of course comes neither by hap nor hazard at all.

I have already remarked on the originality of Major Johnston's garden. This originality displays itself in several ways. We must always remember that the fashion of one generation becomes the commonplace of the next; but that is no reason why we should not pay a grateful tribute to the person who had the first idea. We have all, in these difficult gardening years, turned towards the flowering shrubs and flowering trees and the roses-grown-as-shrubs; we have become used to seeing them no longer relegated to what used to be called the shrubbery – and a dingy thing that usually was – but mixed with other plants in that now almost obsolete thing, the herbaceous border. This method is now rapidly becoming customary, but I must recall the comment made on Hidcote by someone who saw it in its early days: 'This man is planting his garden as no one else has ever planted a garden.' The garden at Hidcote was bare then; it is no longer bare; it is packed and crowded; not an inch of soil is visible; and that is part of its originality.

Major Johnston maintains, moreover, and how rightly, that if you cram your beds and borders with what you do want, there is less room for what you don't want – weeds.

I have heard gardeners criticize the Hidcote garden because flowers of a kind are not grown in bold masses. It is almost a precept, usually a good one, that big clumps are preferable to small clumps, and that if you have twelve plants of a kind it is better to set all twelve together than to divide them into two lots of six or three lots of four. The advantages and disadvantages of this system are obvious: while the plants are in flower you obtain a more showy effect, but when they are out of flower you are left with a blank. Major Johnston has got the best of both methods, by distributing his plants so lavishly everywhere. Thus there is never a vast blank, and never a corner without colour. This must not be taken to mean that no bold massing occurs. It does, in some instances. The 'old' roses are massed, and many hydrangeas; primulas also, along the stream; *Paeonia peregrina* on either side of a path; fuchsias in a special garden of their own; and many other things too numerous to mention. But generally speaking you are likely to find a patch of humble annuals nestling under one of the choicest shrubs, or a tall metallic *Onopordon arabicum* (or was it *O. acanthium?*), towering above a carpet of primroses, all enhancing the cottage-garden effect to which I have already referred.

I remember in particular a narrow path running along a dry wall; I think the gardener called it the rock garden, but it resembled nothing that I had ever seen described by that name. At the foot of the wall grew a solid mauve ribbon of some dwarf campanula. It may have been *C. garganica* and this, of course, after the Hidcote principle, had been allowed to seed itself also in brilliant patches wherever it did not rightly belong. Out of the dry wall poured, not the expected rock-plants, but a profusion of lavender (the deep Hidcote variety, superior in every way to the common *Spica*) and wands of *Indigofera*; there was *Choisya ternata* also, and some Cistus; and an *Azara microphylla* on the bank at the top of the wall, which had been allowed to grow into a real tree quite fifteen feet in height; and there was a creamy, fluffy apparition of *Hydrangea integerrima* looking over the top of a hedge somewhere; but it is difficult to remember details in a garden so thick with detail. I remember also a particularly brilliant picture composed of Major Johnston's own climbing rose, originally known as 'Hidcote Yellow' but now called 'Lawrence Johnston', its rich butter-yellow holding its colour splendidly in conjunction with the flame-and-orange of *R.* 'Signora' its next neighbour on the wall. I ought to have taken more notes and trusted less to memory. Above all I regretted the absence of Major Johnston, who had always been my host on previous visits to Hidcote when no thought of writing an article was in my mind. He could have told me much.

No description of Hidcote would be worth anything without mention of the hedges, and here again the originality of the planter is apparent. There is a great deal of yew, but Major Johnston has not been content with plain yew, skilfully as he has employed it. On one place there is a mixed hedge of yew and box, an attractive combination with its two shades of green: he has realized how many different shades of green there are in Nature, not forgetting the value of dark pools of water with their *chatoyant* reflections, and has made use of all these greens in a way that would have delighted Andrew Marvell. Different textures of leaf have also been made to play their part, in the 'flatness' of yew contrasted with the interplanted shine of holly. Then there is one harlequin of a hedge, with five different things in it; yew, box, holly, beech, and hornbeam. Like a green-and-black tartan.

The hedges of copper beech entirely redeem the copper beech from its suburban associations; they may not inaptly be compared to a Persian carpet with their depths of rose-madder and violet, and the tips of young growth as sanguine as a garnet seen against the light.

There is just enough topiary to carry out the cottage-garden idea; just enough, and not so much as to recall the elaborate chessmen at Hever Castle or the tortured shapes at Levens Hall. The topiary at Hidcote is in the country tradition of smug broody hens, bumpy doves, and coy peacocks twisting a fat neck towards a fatter tail. It resembles all that our cottagers have done ever since the Romans first came to Britain and cut our native yew and box with their sharp shears. This is right for Hidcote, and just as it should be: Major Johnston has used the old tradition with taste and restraint, and has supplemented it with some arches of a serene architectural value.

Nor must I forget the quincunx of pleached hornbeam, set behind the two small garden-houses. It may not be an exact quincunx in the geometrical sense, but the word will serve. It gives a sudden little touch of France to this very English garden. Neat and box-like, standing on flawlessly straight little trunks, it has always been so perfectly clipped and trained that not a leaf is out of place.

I have but barely mentioned the large, thickly planted area known as the Wilderness. This is partly because in the month of June, when I was last at Hidcote, the Wilderness is not at its best; it is either a place for spring, with all its flowering trees, or for August with its massed hydrangeas (not the wig-like *H. hortensis* but the far more elegant *H. aspera maculata*), or for autumn when it becomes a bonfire of colour. I know of its spring beauty only by repute; in August I have seen the shrubby hydrangeas – and this, surely, is the way to grow them if you have the space, in a bosky place made secret by the overhanging trees, with a trickle of water somewhere invisibly near at hand, and the smell of damp peaty soil. A little later on, before the Wilderness had reached its autumn glory, I remember a huge colony of colchicums as you emerged on to the grass from a woodland path. I noted also a large tree of *Cercidiphyllum*; whether it was *japonicum* or *sinense* I do not know; but there could be no doubt that with its autumn colouring it must present a most astonishing sight. The Wilderness is indeed a worthy imaginative adjunct to the general design of the garden.

But on the whole I suppose it is as a botanist and plant-hunter that Major Johnston would wish to be thought of. He himself has travelled much in search of rare plants, and many others have been sent to him from all over the world by fellow collectors. The hardier subjects resulting from these expeditions are planted out, it may be at the foot of a wall where lights may be propped over them in winter; the tenderer subjects are roofed over in two plant-houses, with open sides throughout the summer. Here, again, I wished that he had been at hand to answer many questions. I remember the big yellow trumpets of a *Datura*, and the hanging bells of several varieties of *Abutilon*; a pale *Plumbago*; great pots of fine specimens of fuchsia, notably a rare variety of *F. corymbiflora alba*; a *Carpentaria* with the widest white flowers I had ever seen; a striped red-and-white gladiolus from Mount Kilimanjaro, it may have been *Watsonioides*; and a general impression of dripping luxuriance, but to speak of these exotic treasures in any detail is beyond my power.

Near the larger of the two plant-houses are the propagating frames and the greenhouse containing the collection of pelargoniums which were on show at Chelsea this year (1949). We are now in the kitchen garden, but in this kitchen garden are many things more worthy of contemplation than cabbages. Major Johnston is no orthodox gardener: he tips out the contents of his cornucopia everywhere. There is, I recollect, a raised circular bed round a Scotch pine, foaming with *Helianthemum* of every shade, a lovely surprise, as light as spindrift, shot with many colours the rainbow does not provide. There is a full-grown pink acacia near by, which I took to be *Robinia pseudoacacia Decaisneana*, judging by the rich pink tassels of its flowers; but I may have been wrong in my judgment, and it may have been *R. hispida macrophylla*. By that time I had become so wildly intoxicated by the spilling abundance of Hidcote that I was no longer in any mood to worry about exact nomenclature, but only in the mood to enjoy the next pleasure to be presented.

There were several next pleasures in that most original of kitchen gardens. There were nursery beds full of rose cuttings and young syringas. I remembered how, years ago, Major Johnston had sent me off with a huge bundle of syringas, saying, 'Take your chance of these. Some of them won't be worth keeping, but you may hit on some that will do.' He was right. I took my chance, and now have some fine kinds growing in my garden – children of Hidcote which I am proud to possess – a grand double-white, and a true pink one which particularly pleases me.

154

Down the centre path of the kitchen garden are the old roses, planted in wide rows three and four bushes deep. Major Johnston grew these enchanting varieties long years before they became the fashion, and his collection includes many which are still hard to obtain. There was the blackish-purple of the *centifolia* Nuits de Young (How did it come by that name? Was it called after Young's *Night Thoughts?*) and the slaty-purple of the *gallica* Cardinal de Richelieu; Roseraie de l'Hay; l'Evêque and William Lobb tangling their long sprays of amethyst; the pink Buttonhole Rose, with its sharp little pointed buds, also called Rose d'Orsay because that famous dandy affected it in his coat. I have never been able to find this in any nurseryman's catalogue. It would take pages to enumerate them all, so let me merely revive the memory of that June day and the loaded air, and the bushes weeping to the ground with the weight of their own bloom, a rumpus of colour, a drunkenness of scents.

It is a welcome thought that this lovely garden is now available to all. There are many lessons to be learnt from it, both for the expert gardener and the amateur. The expert will find his own interests, though I suggest that with Major Johnston's approval a more elaborate system of labelling might be devised, with special regard for the rarer plants. The amateur, after he has considered and absorbed the general beauty of Hidcote – which will take him through hours of a real treat-day – would be well advised to go back and study what he may learn for the benefit of his own garden. We cannot all aspire to gardens like Hidcote, either in extent or in particularity. But, as I have suggested, there is much in the Hidcote garden which is applicable to the more modest dwelling – the cottage, the week-end cottage, the manor house, and such diverse habitations as are to be found in our small country towns and even in the garden city. There are many hints to be taken. Why, I thought, had I not planted the pink acacia instead of the common white one, years ago? and out of this regret came the moral of Hidcote: choose always the *best* variety, or the *best* strain. Do not be content with the second or third best. Grow it under the conditions that suit it best, e.g. I recall a colony of *Primula* 'Garryard' under a north wall, planted in a rich moist bed of peat and sand: those plants were as big as the largest lettuces. I blushed as I looked at them, remembering my own poor starved samples which hitherto I thought were doing quite well thrust into ordinary soil. A made-up bed of peat and sand and compost should not have been beyond my scope; it was simply that I had not taken the trouble.

This article must not degenerate into a cautionary tale, so I desist, expressing only the hope that gardeners and garden-lovers will visit Hidcote in their thousands now that it is open to the public.

In Your Garden Again

Foreword

This is a second collection of articles contributed on Sundays to *The Observer*, covering the dates between February 18, 1951, and March 8, 1953. As in the previous volume, the months have been grouped together irrespective of the year in which the articles appeared. I am afraid this system may have the effect of bringing some rather repetitive remarks too close together, but on the whole it seemed the best system to adopt, and I would ask readers to remember that these articles in their original form were spaced seasonally at weekly intervals over two years.

As in the previous volume, I have added many names and addresses of nurserymen from whom the plants mentioned may be obtained. There is also an appendix of names and addresses at the end. There is also an index.

With great regret, I learn that Mr Ralph Cusack, for reasons of health, is obliged to give up his nursery. I have, however, left his name wherever it occurs, in the hope that his retirement may be delayed, or that some successor may carry on.

I would again like to thank *The Observer* for their courtesy in allowing me to reprint these articles in book form.

V.S.-W.
Sissinghurst Castle,
Cranbrook,
Kent.

January

It often happens that an old, rough hedge occurs somewhere in a garden; a hedge which presents a problem. Too heavy a job to grub out, too expensive to replace, and giving no pleasure to the eye, being composed of a thorny rubbishy mixture, usefully dense but unaesthetic. It is possible to add some interest and colour by planting climbers to ramble along and over this sort of inherited relic.

Obviously, these climbers will have to be tough. They will have a great deal of competition to put up with, a starved root-run, a spiteful host, and a slash of ungentle trimming in the autumn, probably administered by a countryman with a billhook and a pair of shears. Yet if you reflect on the survival of such things as the wild honeysuckle and the wild clematis, Old Man's Beard or Traveller's Joy, in precisely those conditions, you will see that it should not be impossible to devise a collection of slightly more sophisticated trailers to transform the old hedge from a dull thing into a thing garlanded, here and there, with some streaks of beauty.

A rough hedge, as a matter of fact, offers a real opportunity to the enterprising gardener. We should take a hint from Nature, and plant such things as normally thrive in such unkind circumstances. The wild honeysuckle suggests the garden varieties of climbing (as opposed to shrubby) honeysuckles; the wild clematis suggests the more tenacious of the garden sorts. I can imagine *Clematis montana*, either the white or the pink, throwing itself like a cloak over the top of the hedge; a single plant of this should cover an area of fifteen feet within a very few years. *Clematis flammula*, white and sweet-scented, should do as well, and should not too greatly resent being hacked about when the time comes for the autumnal brishing. Then, remembering how the wild dog-rose flourishes, we should try some rambling roses of the Wichuriana type, Albéric Barbier, creamy; Albertine, a coppery pink; François Juranville, pink-and-tea. One might also try a wistaria. It would be amusing to see some long tassels of wistaria dangling from amongst the common quick or thorn.

I can imagine also our disgraced and discarded old friend, the Virginia creeper, looking very fine in this novel position, or indeed any of the ornamental vines which colour well, if you can ensure that the hedge is not trimmed too early. *Celastrus articulatus* (or *orbiculatus*) with golden berries splitting open to reveal orange seed-pods, would perhaps be even more satisfactory growing horizontally than up a tree or over a shed, and it would certainly be easier to pick the berries.

January 13, 1952

As a rule I try to be practical in these articles, recommending only such plants as can be grown with some hope of success by the amateur gardener having no advantage of glass or any similar luxury. For once, however, I would like to introduce a climber which does demand shelter from frost, although it may stand out of doors in its pot happily throughout the summer, and, failing a greenhouse, could be safely preserved in a warm room in winter. To do this, you would have to keep it within reasonable bounds by training it round some hoops of sticks, when it makes the most charming pot-plant imaginable. It is so pretty, it flowers so continuously, and smells so deliciously sweet, that it justifies all this extra trouble.

Its name is *Jasminum polyanthum*, a fairly recent introduction from China where I believe it was discovered by Major Lawrence Johnston, that great gardener and creator of the garden at Hidcote. Not very well known here as yet, it may be obtained for the modest sum of 5s. 6d., and as it strikes very readily from cuttings a home-grown stock may be raised within a very short time if wanted. To look at, it resembles the familiar white summer-flowering jasmine, *officinale*, but the flowers are larger, the scent twenty times as powerful, and the rosy, pointed buds are so pretty among the dark green leaves as to be like little jewels in themselves. I have a sprig six inches long on my table, today in January, carrying twenty-two buds, so its name *polyanthum*, meaning many-flowered, is manifestly well deserved. On the parent plant, now standing in an unheated glass lean-to, a few flowers are already open, a real boon in January. I hope I have said enough to stir temptation.

In the milder counties it could, of course, be grown out of doors, and I have in fact seen a magnificent specimen reaching as high as the eaves of the house in Major Stern's famous garden, Highdown, near Goring-on-Sea, in Sussex. Here it has the wall to protect it from the north wind, and the sea-air which always means less frost. In Devon or Cornwall, or in some sheltered parts of Somerset, Dorset, and Wales, I imagine that it would grow exuberantly and to a great height. Like all such twining things, it tends to get into a tangle, which, as all gardeners know to their cost, leads to a lot of dead wood in the centre and is plaguy to control. The best way of thwarting this airless, lightless jungle is to train some strong shoots sideways, away from the main stem; otherwise we shall find ourselves with a task like unravelling several milesworth of mad hanks of string.

The Purple Border with lupins, roses, clematis and hardy geraniums, Sissinghurst Castle Garden, Kent, June 2007

Above, Scilla messeniaca and hellebores in Delos, March 2007, and (*below*) white cosmos, sweet peas and *Solanum* in the White Garden, Sissinghurst Castle Garden, Kent, July 2007

The Elizabethan Tower with frosted winter foliage in the foreground, Sissinghurst Castle Garden, Kent, December 2007

Above, *Clematis montana* var. *rubens* 'Tetrarose' and a view through an arch to the Yew Walk, May 2007, and (*below*) *Paeonia* 'Felix Crousse' in the Rose Garden, Sissinghurst Castle Garden, Kent, June 2007

For those whose interest I may have caught by this mention of the Chinese jasmine, I might end by a reference to the Cape jasmine, *J. angulare*, which is said to be even more fragrant. Both these jasmines may be obtained from Treseder's Nurseries, Truro, Cornwall.

January 20, 1952

Climbers are among the most useful plants in any garden. They take up little ground space, and they can be employed for many purposes: to clothe a boring fence, to scramble over a dead tree, to frame an archway, to drape a wall, to disguise a shed, or to climb lightly into a pergola. They demand comparatively little attention, once they have taken hold of their support, maybe a yearly pruning or a kindly rescue if they have come adrift in a gale.

The clematis is perhaps as popular as any, despite its distressing addiction to the disease known as *wilt*. Few garden-lovers can resist the splendid midsummer purple of the Jackmanii hybrids, but there are other forms to choose from, for instance *C. Spooneri*, an ivory-white with curly edges, or *Armandii Snowdrift*, pure white with pointed, evergreen leaves, or, if you prefer a cloud of smoky blue, *Perle d'Azur* and *Jouiniana Praecox*. If you would like a yellow, with hanging flowers like tiny Chinese lanterns, try *C. tangutica Gravetye Variety*; it may not be very showy, but it has its charm when you stand underneath it and look up into its little golden bells.

The enterprising gardener will, however, want to get away from the more obvious climbers, amongst which the clematis must, I suppose, be included. What about *Akebia quinata* and *Akebia trifoliata*, sometimes listed as *A. lobata*? They are not often seen, but they should be. They are both strong growers, semi-evergreen, with shamrock-like leaves and curiously coloured flowers. The flowers of *A. trifoliata* are brown, and the flowers of *A. quinata* are of a dusty violet, which might best be described by that neglected adjective, *gridelin*. Both kinds are hardy, and in a mild climate or after a hot sunny summer will produce fruits the size of a duck's egg, if you will imagine a duck's egg in plum-colour, with a plum's beautiful bloom before it has got rubbed off in the marketing. These fruits have the advantage that their seeds will germinate one hundred per cent if you sow them in a pot; at any rate, that has been my experience.

The Akebias will grow tall if you let them, but if you want something which will never exceed eight to ten feet let me recommend *Actinidia kolomikta* as a plant to set against a wall facing east or west. The small white flowers are insignificant and may be disregarded; the beauty lies in the leaves, which are triple-coloured, green and pink and white, so gay and decorative and unusual as to provoke friends and visitors into asking what it is.

January 27, 1952

I wrote about climbers last week, but there were many I had no space to mention. I wanted to put in a good word for the Passion flower, *Passiflora caerulea*, which is hardier than sometimes supposed, springing up from its roots again yearly, even if it has been cut down to the ground by frost and has apparently given up all attempt to live. Its strangely constructed flowers are not very effective at a distance, but marvellous to look into, with the nails and the crown of thorns from which it derives its name. It should be grown against a warm wall, though even in so favoured a situation I fear it is unlikely to produce its orange fruits in this country.* There is a white variety called Constance Elliott. I prefer the pale blue one myself; but each to his own taste.

Then the Bignonias. I know that I have often mentioned them in these articles, but they are so showy and so decorative that I must insist once again. Their big orange red trumpets make a noise like a brass band in the summer garden. They are things with a rather complicated botanical history, often changing their names. *Bignonia grandiflora* is now known as *Campsis grandiflora* (it went through a phase of calling itself Tecoma) and *Bignonia radicans* is now *Campsis radicans*. The best variety of it is *Mme Galen*; and as it has rather smaller flowers than *grandiflora*, a friend of mine calls it Little-nonia, a poor joke that will not appeal to serious gardeners, but may be helpful to the amateurs who wish to remember the difference.

They all want a sunny wall, and should be pruned back like a vine, that is, cut right hard back to a second 'eye' or bud, during the dormant season between November and January. Like a vine, again, they will strike from cuttings taken at an eye and pushed firmly into sandy soil.

Berberidopsis corallina, from Chile, whose second name describes the colour of its flowers, has the advantage of being evergreen and of not objecting to a shady wall, where its beautiful racemes will hang in a rich glow. I think this range of colours, orange or coral or red, gains in splendour from a shadowy place. *Berberidopsis* has, however, two disadvantages: it does not like any lime in the soil, and its hardiness is not above reproach. Given a sheltered corner, it should survive most winters, especially in the south or west.

---

* I must go back on this remark. Plants on two cottages near where I live, in Kent, produce a truly heavy crop of fruits. I could not think what they were till I stopped to investigate. The curious thing is that both plants are facing due east, and can scarcely receive any sun at all. See also February 10, 1952.

January 4, 1953

It has been asserted that, since we admire flowers chiefly because they are not green, it is natural that green flowers should fail to arouse much enthusiasm. If that allegation be true, then our two native hellebores must be ruled out. But I dispute it. The green rose, *R. viridiflora*, gives me much amusement; and I have always longed to come across a plant of the green primrose. I like green flowers, especially when they are of a bright apple-green as in *Helleborus viridis*, commonly called Bear's Foot, or in *Helleborus foetidus*, the Setterwort, even more commonly and certainly more rudely called the Stinking hellebore, found in beechwoods in company of *Daphne laureola* and the Dog's Mercury spurge. Besides, I like any plant that will surprise me out of doors with flowers in January or February.

Perhaps it may soften prejudiced hearts if I add that the hellebores belong to the same botanical family as the buttercups, the *Ranunculaceae*. Few of the English – a most sentimental race – can resist the appeal of the buttercup and those gold-besprent meadows of childhood, and the Kingcups growing along the banks of a stream.

Our two native hellebores are becoming rare now, so if you have the luck to find them growing wild in the chalky soil of the South Downland country, please do not dig them up, but make a note to order plants or seeds from a nurseryman* or seedsman. Seeds germinate quickly when they are freshly harvested. It is said that ants distribute them in Nature: but as we cannot rely on an obliging ant-heap it is better to buy a packet of fresh seed for ninepence and sow it at once in a seed-box and prick out the plantlings later in the usual way.

I will not contend that either of our two natives is as handsome a plant as the Corsican cousin, *Helleborus corsicus*, so strong and stout that its leaves alone have an architectural quality in the same sense as the Acanthus has an architectural or sculptural quality, quite apart from the beauty and value of the flowers. But I do contend that our two natives are worth adding to any collection of the hellebores. They are humble, and make few demands. They will put up with a considerable amount of shade, and they do not mind lime, in fact they like it, two considerations that ought to appeal to people with difficult patches in their gardens.

Do not be alarmed if *H. viridis* dies away in autumn; it is not dead, it is resting, and will revive. *H. foetidus*, on the contrary, is evergreen.

* Mr W. Th. Ingwersen has plants; address on p. 272. Messrs Thompson & Morgan have seeds; address on p. 272.

January 11, 1953

I went to a Christmas party given by a neighbour of mine, a member of a great hereditary firm of seedsmen, almost feudal in their family tradition. His baptismal name, most appropriate to the season, was Noel. All the things appertaining to a cocktail party were standing about, on tables; but the thing that instantly caught my eye was a pot-plant of cyclamen I had not seen for years.

Delicate in its quality, subtle in its scent, which resembles the scent of wood-violets, it stood there in a corner by itself, looking so modest and Jane-Austen-like among its far grander companions. It had a freshness and an innocence about it, a sort of adolescent look, rather frightened at finding itself in company of orchids and choice azaleas and glasses filled with champagne cocktails.

It was the little Persian cyclamen, in its original size before it had got 'improved' by nurserymen and swollen into its present inflated form. May I here make a protest against the fashion for exaggerating the size of flowers? Bigger, but not thereby better. Those vast begonias; those tree-trunk delphiniums; those mops of chrysanthemums, all those things called *giganteum* – does anyone really like them, except the growers who get the gold medals?

Ah, no, I thought, looking at the little Persian cyclamen, white, pink-tipped, shy, unobtrusive, demure; this is the way I like my flowers to be; not puffed up as though by a pair of bellows; not shouting for praise from gaping admirers.

I have never seen it growing wild in Persia. Apparently it grows wild also in Cyprus and in Rhodes.

I wish it were easier to obtain.* You can buy or be given the big cyclamen at any florist's shop, and I am not saying anything against them. They are a wonderful stand-by at this time of the year, and with due care their corms should last year after year, reviving again in July or August to start on their job of flowering once more before next Christmas. But handsome though they are, these big Christmas-present cyclamen, they do not possess the Tom-tit, Jenny-wren, leveret-eared character of the little Persian.

January 18, 1953

Not for the first time I find myself at a loss to know what to write about. January is a dead season, when one cannot get out to do anything active in the garden, so one is reduced to studying catalogues under the lamp and thereby being induced to order far more plants or seeds than one ought to.

* Small plants can be got from Messrs Blackmore & Langdon, Bath.

166

I have ordered a summer-flowering tamarisk, *Tamarix pentandra*. This will flower in August, I hope, during that month when flowering shrubs are few. We do not grow the tamarisks enough; they are so graceful, so light and buoyant, so feathery, so pretty when smothered in their rose-pink flower. The earlier-flowering one is *Tamarix tetrandra*; it comes out in April to May.

The seed catalogues are my undoing. I have grown wise, after many years of gardening, and no longer order recklessly from wildly alluring descriptions which make every annual sound easy to grow and as brilliant as a film star. I now know that gardening is not like that. Yet I can still be decoyed into ordering some packets of the Roggli pansies and the Chabaud carnations, having learnt from experience how good and repaying they are. The pansies, if sown in March under glass, will scarcely flower this summer, or at any rate not until September, but twelve months later they should have made fine clumps which will start flowering in May and should continue without remission until the first autumn frosts. The annual carnations, however, if sown in February under glass (a seed-box in a frame or under a hand-light) should fill bare patches during the ensuing summer and are as pretty and scented as anyone could desire. They can be had in self-colours, or flaked and striped like the pinks in old flower-paintings; with their old-fashionable look they associate perfectly with the Damask and Gallica and Cabbage roses.

'Carnation' is perhaps a misleading term, since to most people, myself included, carnation suggests a greenhouse plant of the Malmaison type; an expensive buttonhole for a dandy at Ascot or Lord's. The Chabaud carnations are more like what we think of as our grandmother's pinks.

Please make a point of getting the two strains I have recommended: the Roggli pansies, and the Chabaud carnations, whether annual or perennial. They are by far the best I know and the seeds may be obtained from Mr George Roberts, Davington, Faversham, Kent.

January 25, 1953

There are certain roses whose charm lies in their foliage as much as in their flowers. They are the roses whose foliage one can describe only by calling it fern-like; and by that I do not mean the ferns of woodland or damp places, but the so-called Maidenhair fern which used to be grown in company of smilax for the decoration of dinner tables at public banquets, and perhaps, for all I know, still is.

First among these tiny-leaved roses I would put *Rosa farreri persetosa*, otherwise known as the Threepenny-bit rose. It could not be better named, for its bright pink flower is no larger than the old silver thrup'ny bit we seldom have in our pockets or purses now, since it has been replaced by a solid twelve-sided coin of a baser metal. I am told that in Burma it is known as the four-anna-bit rose. The Thrup'ny-bit rose is a rare darling, a tiny treasure; not tiny as to growth, for it will go up to six or seven feet high; but tiny as to its leaves and its flock of miniature flowers in early summer. It comes from the South Kansu province of China, growing wild in the Ta-tung Alps, where it was found by Reginald Farrer in 1914. It is perfectly hardy, and renews its pretti-ness in autumn with small red fruits and colouring leaves.*

Other small-leaved roses, all of which will make a big loose shrubby bush, are *Hugonis* and *Cantabrigiensis*, smothered with butter-yellow flowers in May; *Rosa primula*, yellow; *Rosa rubrifolia*, whose beauty lies chiefly in the contrast between the grey-green leaves and stems the colour of a Victoria plum; *Rosa willmottiae*, pale pink, usually the first of all to flower and valuable on that score alone, but with the tiresome fault of making an exaggerated amount of dead twiggy wood armed with real little savages of thorns when one goes to clear it out for its own advantage. *Rosa omiensis*, white-flowered, has ferocious blood-red thorns, half an inch long, magnificent when the rising or setting sun strikes through them, so take the hint and plant this rose where it will catch the morning or the evening light.

There are other roses which may be chosen for their delicate foliage, their wildly generous growth, and their willingness to fill an otherwise wasted corner. I meant simply to give an indication of what can be found by the intelligent gardener looking through the descriptive catalogues issued by nurserymen who specialize in roses other than the well-known hybrid teas and ramblers. See addresses on p. 273.

May I add, to correct what seems to be a misapprehension on the part of many people, that roses can still safely be planted up to the beginning or mid-dle of March.

* Messrs T. Hilling stock it.

February

Once I wrote about flowering trees trained along wires in front gardens, and ended up with a hint about rose-hedges to grow along the pavement of a village street. Not necessarily a village, but a small country town, or even a suburb or a new housing estate; anywhere that demands a hedge to divide the front garden from the road.

In a gracious, small and ancient town near where I live, someone has had the imagination to plant just such a hedge of rambler roses. It occupies the whole of his road frontage, about 150 yards I believe, and in the summer months people come from all over the county to see it. I must admit that it is an impressive sight; a blaze of colour; a long, angry, startling streak, as though somebody had taken a red pencil and had scrawled dense red bunches all over a thicket-fence of green. A splendid idea; very effective; but, oh, how crude! I blink on seeing it; and having blinked, I weep. It is not only the virulence of the colour that brings tears to my eyes, but the regret that so fine an idea should not have been more fastidiously carried out.

The hedge is made of *American Pillar*, a rose which, together with *Dorothy Perkins*, should be for ever abolished from our gardens. I know this attack on two popular roses will infuriate many people; but if one writes gardening articles one must have the courage of one's opinion. I hate, hate, hate *American Pillar* and her sweetly pink companion *Perkins*. What would I have planted instead? Well, there is *Goldfinch*, an old rambler, very vigorous, very sweet-scented, and when I say sweet-scented I mean it, for I do try to tell the exact truth in these articles, not to mislead anybody. *Goldfinch* is a darling; she is my pet, my treasure; a mass of scrambled eggs. Then there is *Félicité et Perpétue*, white, flushed pink; and *Madame Plantier*, white, with larger flowers. Or *Albertine*, very strong and free-flowering, a beautiful soft pink that appears to have been dipped in tea; or *François Juranville* who has also fallen into a tea-cup.

February 25, 1951

Is the Winter Aconite too well known to deserve mention? Surely not. We cannot be reminded too often of so dear and early a thing. It started flowering here, in Kent, on January 20th; I made a note in my diary. Then frost came, turning it into tiny crystallized apricots, like the preserved fruits one used once to get given for Christmas. They shone; they sparkled in the frost. Then the frost went, and with the thaw they emerged from their rimy sugar coating into their full, smooth, buttercup yellow on a February day with its suggestion of spring, when the first faint warmth of the sun falls as a surprise upon our naked hands.

I am being strictly correct in comparing the varnished yellow of the Winter Aconite to our common buttercup, for they both belong to the same botanical order of the *Ranunculaceae*.

The proper name of the Winter Aconite is *Eranthis*. *Eranthis hyemalis* is the one usually grown, and should be good enough for anybody. It costs only 2s. 6d. a dozen, but if you want a superior variety you can order *E. Tubergenii*, more expensive, at 10s. 6d. or 12s. 6d. a dozen. I daresay this would be worth trying. Personally I am very well satisfied with the smudge of gold given me by *hyemalis* (meaning, of winter). It has the great advantage of flourishing almost anywhere, in shade or sun, under trees or in the open, and also of producing a generous mustard-and-cress-like crop of self-sown seedlings which you can lift and transplant. It is better to do this than to lift the older plants, for it is one of those home-lovers that likes to stay put, and, indeed, will give of its best only when it has had a couple of years to become established. So do not get impatient with it at first. Give it time.

There are many small early things one could happily associate with it; in fact, I can imagine, and intend to plant, a winter corner, stuffed with little companions all giving their nursery party at the same time: *Narcissus minimus* and *Narcissus nanus*; the bright blue thimbles of the earliest grape-hyacinth, *Muscari azureum*; the delicate spring crocus *Tommasinianus*, who sows himself everywhere, scores of little Thomases all over the place . . . but I must desist.

February 3, 1952

It suddenly occurred to me that I had never written about pergolas in this column nor am I quite sure that pergolas are altogether suitable for this country. They drip. Moreover, they are all too often used as a support for the less desirable kinds of rambler rose and their usefulness as a framework for more interesting climbers is often overlooked. Practically all the flowering climbers look fine thus seen overhead, and to them may be added the many sorts of ornamental vine, including the hardy fruiting vines, for what could be prettier than bunches of little grapes dangling, either green or black?

Even the people who prefer to stick exclusively to roses have a wide choice of very beautiful and vigorous varieties. There are old favourites amongst them: *Gloire de Dijon, Lady Hillingdon, Mme Alfred Carrière, William Allen Richard-*

son; but there are also some loose, huge single or semi-double flowerers: *Allen Chandler*, a blaze of red with golden centres; *Cupid*, a silvery shell-pink; *Emily Gray*, a butter-yellow with shiny dark leaves and reddish stems; and the well-known *Mermaid*, flowering late, a delicate yellow. Many of the favourite hybrid teas may also be had as climbers: *Crimson Glory, Etoile de Hollande, Ophelia, Mme Edouard Herriot*. Then there is *Paul's Lemon Pillar*, one of the most perfectly shaped roses I know, and of so subtle a colour that one does not know whether to call it ivory or sulphur or iceberg-green. A very rich yellow is *Lawrence Johnston*, once known as *Hidcote Yellow*; and for a mixture of yellow and red, giving an effect of the most brilliant orange, you have *Réveil Dijonnais*, greatly resembling the old Austrian Copper, which, in fact, is one of its parents, only with far larger flowers. Startling when it first opens, it has the fault of fading into a truly hideous pinkish mud.

These are only a very few of the substitutes I would suggest for my old enemies *American Pillar* and *Dorothy Perkins*.

I get grumbled at from time to time for recommending roses that don't figure in some rose-growers' catalogues, so may I refer the reader to some addresses given on p. 273 of this book?

February 10, 1952

A lady writes to say she has an ugly porch to her house, and what evergreen climber can she grow to cover it up? Her hope is to obscure the porch all the year round. No doubt many people find themselves in a similar predicament, so a note on the subject may be useful. The trouble is that few climbers, with the exception of ivy, are evergreen; and that those which are, tend to be only half-hardy. Amongst true evergreen climbers I can think of two honeysuckles, Giraldii and Henryii; one of each, planted either side of the porch, should soon grow up to intertwine overhead. But this does not take us very far, and it becomes necessary to look round for some substitutes.

We may find them amongst the tall-growing shrubs which can be treated as a kind of buttress or side-piers, and induced by means of wire to grow horizontally across the top. *Ceanothus rigidus* and *Ceanothus thyrsiflorus* both come to mind, with dark green leaves and powder-blue flowers; reasonably hardy, they will attain a height of twelve to thirty feet respectively. They could not, however, look so tidy as something which could be clipped into shape; and that makes me think of the Sweet Bay, *Laurus nobilis*. You know how sometimes on old country cottages one sees a kind of deep, dense porch, generally cut out of yew or box, giving an air of solidity and mystery to the entrance, which would be especially welcome in a brand-new, perhaps rather insubstantial, dwelling? There is no reason why the Sweet Bay, with its aromatic foliage, should not be used for a similar purpose, to frame and disguise the objectionable porch. It is of fairly rapid growth, and will put up with any amount of shaping. Within a few years it should provide the front door with a dark green cavern of shelter.

If my correspondent thinks this sounds gloomy, though personally I think that a bit of gloom is of immense value in a garden, as a foil to the bright flowers, she might try planting two of the poplar-like cherries as sentinels either side of her porch. True, they are not evergreen, but their mass of pale pink blossom is a delight of youthfulness in spring. *Prunus lannesiana erecta* is the name, or Amanogawa, meaning Celestial River, the Japanese equivalent of our Milky Way.

May I thank all those enviable people who have written to say that their Passion flower does produce its fruits in their gardens? Mostly west-country gardens, I may add, though there was one triumphant letter from Hampshire, which is not so very far west.

February 17, 1952

Amongst other seeds for spring sowing I ordered a sixpenny packet of *Mimosa pudica*, the Humble Plant. Most people, including some nurserymen, call it the Sensitive Plant, a name that should be reserved for *Mimosa sensitiva*, which contradictorily, is less sensitive than *M. pudica*. So humble is the Humble Plant, so bashful, that a mere touch of the finger or a puff of breath blown across it will cause it to collapse instantly into a woebegone heap, like the once popular Ally Sloper. One grows it purely for the purpose of amusing the children. The normal child, if not an insufferable prig, thoroughly enjoys being unkind to something; so here is a harmless outlet for this instinct in the human young. Shrieks of delight are evoked, enhanced by the sadistic pleasure of doing it over and over again. 'Let's go back and see if it has sat up yet.' It probably has, for it seems to be endowed with endless patience under such mischievous persecution.

I must admit that I would like to see it in its native home in tropical America, where, I have been told, acres of pigmy forest swoon under the touch of a ruffling breeze. Nominally a perennial there, it is best treated as a half-hardy annual here. This means that we must sow our sixpenny packet in a pot or a pan under glass or on the window-sill of a warm room. By late summer it will have grown up into quite a tall plant about a foot high; and then you may observe that, like most sensitive people, it is not only sensitive but prickly. It develops large spiky thorns, but still retains its shivering fright. It then becomes not only an amusement for children but a symbol for many of our friends.

If these joke plants interest you I have several more in mind. For instance, the Burning Bush, *Dictamnus fraxinella* or Dittany, which you can set alight into a blue flame, especially on a warm summer day, without any harm to the plant. The explanation of this apparent miracle is the presence of a volatile oil; but why seek for explanations when you can so easily entertain your young guests?

Seeds of *Mimosa pudica* and of the Burning Bush, *Dictamnus fraxinella*, can be bought from Messrs Thompson & Morgan, Ipswich; but it is better and quicker to get a plant of the Burning Bush at 1s. 9d. from W. Th. Ingwersen, address on p. 272.

February 24, 1952

Last Sunday in this column I was writing about joke plants, but had to stop short. I wanted to go on about the Marvel of Peru, *Mirabilis jalapa*, familiarly called Four o'clock, because it opens only at tea-time and shuts itself up again before breakfast. It is an old-fashioned herbaceous plant, seldom seen now, but quite decorative with its mixed colouring of yellow, white, red, or lilac, sometimes striped and flaked like some carnations. It can be grown as a half-hardy annual from seed sown in spring, and if you want to save the roots you will have to lift them in autumn like a dahlia. It seems simpler to grow it from seed afresh each year. Messrs Thompson & Morgan sell the seed.

Then there is the Obedient Plant, *Physostegia virginiana*. The form of amusement provided by this object is the readiness of its flowers to remain in any position you choose to push them round the stem. I never could get it to work, until a Scottish friend told me that I did not poosh it hard enough. If you look carefully, you will see that they have a sort of little hinge. A hardy perennial, of stiff habit, it grows about two feet high and flowers at a useful time in late summer. The variety usually offered by nurserymen is called *Vivid*, but to my mind this is not a very pleasing shade of pink. For those who share my distaste for pink tinged with magenta, there is a white form, *Alba*. Seed from Thompson & Morgan, or plants from Messrs Barr, 1s. 9d. each.

Perhaps the oddest plant of all is The Monarch of the East, *Sauromatum guttatum*. The name comes from *saurus*, a lizard, and *guttatum* means dotted or spotted. The flower, which resembles an arum lily in shape, is indeed dotted and spotted like some oriental lizards, only in different colours. The Monarch rejoices in the decadent livery of green and purple, with purple bruises on the pale green. Its colouring, however, is not the chief queer thing about it. The chief queer thing is the way it will agree to grow. You set the tuber down on a saucer, just like that, plonk! with no soil and no water, and quite soon it will begin to sprout, and within a few weeks will begin to show signs of flowering.

When it has flowered, you should plant the tuber out in a rather damp corner of the garden to let it develop its leaves during the summer. Then in August or September you lift the tuber, dry it off, and eventually put it back into its saucer, when it will perform again, year after year. The first tuber will cost you half a crown, but you should get many offsets if you want to increase your stock to give birthday presents to your nephews and nieces, or even to your own children, for the nursery window-sill. Mr Ralph Cusack, whose address will be found on p. 271, sells the bulb; I have not seen it listed elsewhere.

February 1, 1953

Is anybody, or perhaps everybody, suffering as we are suffering from the inexplicable mischief of birds? One always expected to find the bullfinches busy among the fruit-blossom, but never until this year and last have I found the ground beneath the forsythias green as a lawn with pecked-off buds. There will not be a single smudge of yellow on them this spring. The Winter-sweet was likewise stripped; and a neighbour tells me that every bud on her *Magnolia stellata* has been taken. It is not the bullfinches I complain of, but the sparrows. Can any ornithologist provide an explanation? The countrymen seem to think that the intensive spraying of orchards has destroyed so much of the birds' natural food in the shape of insects and grubs that they must turn elsewhere for nourishment. I love birds, but my affection is rapidly diminishing. I am told that spraying a plant with alum and water is a deterrent, but then one would have to repeat the dose after every shower of rain.

Meanwhile the snowdrops will soon be going over, and it is as well to remember that the time to divide them is immediately after they have finished flowering, and consequently to plant new bulbs also in March, if you can induce the bulb merchant to send them then. It is as well to remember, moreover, that there are different kinds besides the common snowdrop (only one hates to call it common). For instance, there is the finer variety called *Galanthus nivalis Viridi-apicis*, or green-tipped; and, of course, there is the double snowdrop, but I hope nobody would wish to grow that, for surely the whole beauty lies in the perfection of line of the single bell. Then there is the tall, large-flowered *Galanthus elwesii*, from the hills behind Smyrna, often seen in old cottage gardens but not so often planted by the modern gardener, a most graceful dangling thing, flowering rather later than the little *Galanthus nivalis*, the milk-flower of the snow. For people who want something really unusual, and are prepared to pay for it, there is *Galanthus ikariae*, which has the romantic peculiarity of growing in a wild state in only one place in the world: the small island of Ikaria or Nikaria in the Aegean Sea, where Hercules buried the ill-fated Icarus. It flowers in March, and much resembles the common snowdrop, except that the flower is a little larger and the leaves curl over backwards.

This by no means exhausts the list (there are fourteen different species), but if anyone should have so perverted a taste as to desire the sight of a snowdrop in autumn, there is *Galanthus olgae*, which comes from Mount Taygetus, near Sparta, and flowers in October. The leaves come after the flower; and this is a bulb which should positively be planted during the spring months. I fancy that it is the same as *Galanthus octobriensis*, under another name.

Galanthus corcyrensis, from Corfu, flowers in November, and *G. cilicicus*, from Syria and Asia Minor, in December.

February 8, 1953

A letter from America reminds me that people who wish to grow the ornamental gourds this summer should order the seeds now. Sutton & Sons, Reading, stock them, as also does Miss Hunter, see p. 274, and they can be had in a variety of shapes and colours from the great orange pumpkins (*potirons*), so familiar a sight as they lie hugely about in the fields of France, to the little striped white-and-green, no larger than a tennis ball. They should be grown under the same conditions as the vegetable marrow; picked when ripe; and lightly varnished with Copal varnish to preserve them for indoor amusement throughout the winter.

It appears that there is a Gourd Society in North Carolina. Our American friends never do things by halves; and although their fondness for a tricksy ingenuity may sometimes outrun ours, I thought I might pass on some of their ideas for the benefit of those who have the leisure and the inclination to carry them out. Thus the elongated Dutchman's Pipe gourd may be scooped out and transformed into a ladle. The circular, medium-sized kinds may be scooped out likewise and turned into bowls. A pleasant occupation for an invalid, possibly – what an extract from an American catalogue calls 'Fun for the shut-in'.

The supreme example of North Carolinan ingenuity comes from one competitor in the Society's exhibition. She had turned a vast pumpkin into a coach for Cinderella, drawn by eight mouse-sized gourds. What a hint for our Women's Institutes, at their autumn Produce Show, in this Coronation year!

More pleasing to our taste, perhaps, is the harvest festival the Gourd Society organizes for the thousands of people who flock to see it. Throughout the summer, members of the Society have grown ornamental grasses to mix with their gourds; and this reminds me that I had always wanted to grow a patch of *Phalaris canariensis*, in plain English, Canary seed, in my garden, partly for fun, partly because I could then give a dollop of seed to any friend who kept a canary, and partly and principally because this form of Shakers or Quaking Grass, whose 'floures do continually tremble and shake, in such sort that it is not possible with the most steadfast hand to hold it from shaking', was called in the first Elizabethan reign, when writers had some sense of vivid naming, the *Petty Panick*. We suffer from so many major panics nowadays that it is comforting to consider a petty one for a change.

February 15, 1953

Children have a gift for asking apparently simple questions to which there is no real answer. I was asked: 'What is your favourite flower?' The reply seemed almost to suggest itself: 'Any flower, turn by turn, which happens to be in season at the moment.'

Thus, I now find myself regretting that I did not plant more of the species crocuses which are busy coming out in quick succession. They are so very charming, and so very small. If you can go and see them in a nursery garden or at a flower-show, do take the opportunity to make a choice. Grown in bowls or Alpine pans they are enchanting for the house; they recall those miniature works of art created by the great Russian artificer Fabergé in the luxurious days when the very rich could afford such extravagances. Grown in stone troughs out of doors, they look exquisitely in scale with their surroundings, since in open beds or even in pockets of a rockery they are apt to get lost in the vast areas of landscape beyond. One wants to see them close to the eye, fully to appreciate the pencilling on the outside of the petals; it seems to have been drawn with a fine brush, perhaps wielded by some sure-handed Chinese calligrapher, feathering them in bronze or in lilac. Not the least charm of these little crocuses is their habit of throwing up several blooms to a stem (it is claimed for *Ancyrensis* that a score will grow from a single bulb). Just when you think they are going off, a fresh crop appears.

Ancyrensis, from Ankara and Asia Minor, yellow, is usually the first to flower in January or early February, closely followed by *Chrysanthus* and its seedlings *E. A. Bowles*, yellow and brown; *E. P. Bowles*, a deeper yellow feathered with purple; *Moonlight*, sulphur yellow and cream; *Snow Bunting*, cream and lilac; *Warley White*, feathered with purple. That fine species, *Imperati*, from Naples

176

and Calabria, is slightly larger, violet-blue and straw-coloured; it flowers in February. *Susianus*, February and March, is well known as the Cloth of Gold crocus; *Sieberi*, a Greek, lilac-blue, is also well known; but *Suterianus* and its seedling *Jamie* are less often seen. Jamie must be the tiniest of all: a pale violet with deeper markings on the outside, he is no more than the size of a shilling across when fully expanded, and two inches high. I measured.

I have mentioned only a few of this delightful family, which should, by the way, be planted in August.*

February 22, 1953

The courage of some small and apparently fragile flowers never ceases to amaze me. Here are we humans, red-nosed and blue-cheeked in the frost and the snow, looking dreadfully plain; but there are the little flowers coming up, as brave and gay as can be, unaffected by snow or frost. The winter aconite is a cheerful resister, coming through the white ground with puffs of snow all over his bright burnished face, none the worse in his January–February beauty, and increasing from self-sown seedlings year after year.

We all grow the Algerian iris – and I wish, by the way, that I could find a nurseryman who lists it in separate varieties, for there is no doubt that some clumps flower much earlier than others, even in November, whereas others do not arrive until March, and also there is a considerable difference in the colour, ranging from the usual pale lavender to a really fine deep purple. (According to William Robinson, this richly coloured variety would appear to be *speciosa*.) I imagine that the explanation lies in their place of origin, for Algeria is not their only native home, and they are to be found also in Greece, in Asia Minor, in Syria, and even so far east as the coast of the Black Sea. It is, however, not of this iris that I wished to write, but of the less familiar *Iris histrioides*, which to my mind has many advantages over *I. unguicularis*, or, as most people call it, *stylosa*. It is true that *histrioides* does not give us a prolonged flowering period, but flowers only once, in February, so that we cannot look forward to picking for many weeks in succession. Once we have granted *stylosa* the superiority in this respect, there is nothing but good to say of the brilliantly blue little actor from the north of Asia Minor. For one thing, it blooms before the leaves have come through, and even when the leaves do appear they are far neater than the frankly unsightly muddle which makes us relegate *stylosa* to a hidden corner. For another thing, the cobalt of its petals is intense and its capacity for resistance to the weather is unequalled. For three weeks now my small group has been exposed without any protection to gales and rain and cold and snow; I have

* Messrs Wallace specialize in them. See p. 271 for the address.

daily expected to find it sodden or tattered, but the valiant little thing – it is only four inches high, though the flower is comparatively large, much larger than its relation *I. reticulata* – has never faltered.

If it is happy, in a sunny place with some mortar rubble to provide it with lime, it should increase by means of the offsets which will form round the parent bulb; and as *Iris histrioides* is not at all easy to buy now, even at 5s. a bulb, it is advisable to preserve the offsets and grow them on in pots until they attain their flowering size, which may be in a year or two. This sort of gardening demands time and love, I know; but how great is the satisfaction and the reward.

March

March 4, 1951

A winter corner . . . Winter must here be taken as meaning January to the end of March. I wish we had a name for that intermediate season which includes St Valentine's Day, February 14th, and All Fools' Day, April 1st. It is neither one thing nor the other, neither winter nor spring. Could we call it wint-pring, which has a good Anglo-Saxon sound about it, and accept it, like marriage, for better or worse?

My wint-pring corner shall be stuffed with every sort of bulb or corm that will flower during those few scanty weeks. The main point is that it shall be really stuffed; crammed full; packed tight. The winter aconite (January–February) will flower first, with *Narcissus minimus*, sometimes called *Asturiensis*, coming up amongst it, and also the sky-blue *Muscari azureum*. There will be the spring-flowering crocuses; there will be *Iris reticulata*, the ordinary purple and gold sort, and the earlier flowering blue kind called *Cantab*; and the black-green *Iris tuberosa*; and I might also risk half a dozen *Iris histrioides*, not very reliable but so lovely that it is worth taking a chance.

There will be many miniature daffodils, and if anyone is particularly interested in these I would advise him to go to the RHS spring shows, where a Cornish bulb-grower, Mr Alec Gray, of Treswithian Daffodil Farm, Camborne, always devotes his stall to these tiny, exquisite things. There will be some early tulips, such as *Tulipa biflora* and *turkestanica* and *kaufmanniana*, the water-lily tulip, flowering in March. There will be *Scilla biflora* and *Scilla Tubergeniana*, both flowering in February; and as a ground work, to follow after the winter aconites, I shall cram the ground with the Greek *Anemone blanda*, opening her starry blue flower in the rare sun of February, and with the Italian *Anemone apennina*, who comes a fortnight later and carries on into March and is at her best in April. Terrible spreaders, these anemones; but so blue a carpet may gladly be allowed to spread.

If only *Cyclamen coum* were not so expensive, at 5s. a corm, I would like to include him, but at that price he is only for the millionaires. (The alternative is to grow him from seed; slower, but quite satisfactory in the end.) Otherwise, the winter corner should be cheap to plant; and needs, humbly, only a little patch of ground where you can find one. Let it be in a place which you pass frequently, and can observe from day to day.

March 11, 1951

A friend of mine, whose own fingers are of the greenest, reproaches me from time to time for making gardening sound too easy. My optimism, she says, is misleading. Yet I try to avoid recommending 'difficult' plants, or at any rate to accompany them always with a warning. The truth is probably that most plants are temperamental, except the weeds, which all appear to be possessed of magnificent constitutions. The mystery of the Madonna lily, for instance, has never been satisfactorily explained. *Daphne mezereum* provides another puzzle: you may observe all the rules, but nothing will make her flourish if she does not intend to do so. Then there is the case of the self-sown seedling, which, sprouting up in apparently impossible conditions, excels in health and vigour anything similar which you may have transplanted with the greatest care into a prepared bed of the most succulent consistency.

In my own garden I have a curious example of the perverse behaviour of plants. Two cuttings of a poplar, brought home in a sponge-bag from Morocco, were both struck and planted out at the same time. Same age, same parent, same aspect, same soil; yet, fifteen years later, one is only half the size of the other. Why? I can suppose only that like two children of identical begetting and upbringing, they differ in constitution and character.

It thus becomes evident that gardening, unlike mathematics, is not an exact science. It would be dull if it were. Naturally, there are certain laws whose transgression means disaster: you would not plant an azalea in a chalk pit. I do agree with my friend, however, that writers on gardening very often omit to make some elementary comments, pointing out possible causes of failure. This brings me to two things I wanted to say. The first is about snowdrops. The time to move them, if you wish to do so, is just after they have flowered; in other words, now. (Do not cut off their heads as they are very generous in seeding themselves.) The second thing is about mice. They eat bulbs, leaving large bare patches where one has planted snowdrops and crocuses. I asked an eminent nurseryman what one could do about this, and he replied that as one soaked peas in red lead before sowing them, he could see no reason why the same procedure should harm bulbs. It would be an experiment worth trying, because there is no doubt that distressing gaps do appear, for which I can find no explanation except mice. Besides, there are tell-tale little holes.

I am ashamed of having forgotten to mention the blue *Anemone hepatica* as occupants of a winter corner, last week. They should on no account be omitted.

March 18, 1951

The Dog's tooth violets (*Erythronium dens-canis*) should now be coming into flower, so this is the time to study these curly objects and to decide if you would like to order some for planting next autumn. There will probably be a fine display of them at the Royal Horticultural Society's fortnightly spring shows when anybody living within reach of Vincent Square, Westminster, can go and spend an hour of pure delight at this débutante festival. Of course one must expect everything to look better at a show than it will ever look in one's own garden. The exhibitors have chosen their best specimens, and have arranged them in a very becoming bed of moist dark-brown-velvet peat, showing them up to their best advantage.

The Dog's tooth violets should be there, beneath the great flowering cherries and almonds of the spring. They are small, they are low, they are humble in stature, not more than six inches high, but with their beautifully mottled leaves and reflexed petals like tiny martagon lilies they are more than worthy of their place. Some of them are natives of central Europe, some of North America; they belong to the lily family and have nothing to do with violets. 'Dog's tooth' is because of the tuber, which is white and pointed, like a fang. They prefer a little shade; light woodland is ideal for them; they like some sand and peat or leaf-mould in their soil, which should be moist but never waterlogged; they dislike being moved, so leave them alone for years once they have settled down. I have seen them flourishing and increasing even under beech trees, where few things will grow. You can get them in white, pink, purple, and yellow. They are inexpensive, at about 4s. a dozen.

The trilliums, or North American wood-lily, also called the Trinity Flower from its triangular shape, flower a little later but enjoy the same conditions of shade and soil. One does not very often see them, but I notice that they always attract attention. Claret-coloured or white, they grow to about a foot high and have the advantage of lasting a very long time, which seems to be true of most woodland things, I suppose because they do not get burnt up by a hot sun. Unfortunately the trilliums are rather expensive, at 3s. 6d. each according to my catalogues; but as they are very striking, a group of only three or four makes quite an effect, and after all one can always add a couple every year. They, as well as the Dog's tooth violets, are ideal not only for woodland planting but also for a cool shaded place in a rock garden.

The claret-coloured one is *Trillium erectum*. The white one is *Trillium grandiflorum*, which in its native home is known as Wake Robin, a name we commonly give to our wild arum or Lords-and-Ladies.

March 25, 1951

Easter-day, loveliest and youngest of feasts. I can hardly bring myself to think about summer, which to me always seems middle-aged compared with the adolescence of March, April, and even May. March is seventeen, though by no means always sweet; April is eighteen; May is nineteen; June is twenty to twenty-five; and then July leaps to thirty and thirty-five; and then August from forty to fifty; September to a mature, mellow sixty; October to an even mellower, yellower seventy; and then comes the leafless calm of the descending year.

Still, one must be practical, thinking of summer, if one is to fill up the gaps in one's garden, and I have been forcing myself to think about it in terms of the *hemerocallis*, or day-lily. This used to be regarded as a common old plant, almost a weed, when we grew the type which spread everywhere and was only a pale orange thing, not worth having. Now there are many fine hybrids, which may come as a revelation to those who have not yet seen them. They may be ordered now, for planting within the next two or three weeks, so this is the time to obtain them.

Some of them are to be had at very high prices, right up to £2 each for named varieties, but you need not pay that price for a collection of the hybrids. You can get them at 27s. 6d. a dozen for mixed hybrids. The firm of Amos Perry, of Enfield, Middlesex, has been responsible for much good hybridizing; and further fine varieties have been raised in America. They will grow either in sun or shade. They will grow in damp soil, even by the waterside if you are so fortunate as to have a stream or a pond in your garden, when their trumpets of amber, apricot, orange, ruddle, and Venetian red will double themselves in reflection in the water. They will grow equally well in an ordinary bed or border. They are, in fact, extremely obliging plants, thriving almost anywhere.

They are especially useful for the summer garden, flowering as they do from July into September. Mostly in July and August.

My search for an alphabetical glossary of botanical terms has been rewarded by the discovery of exactly what I wanted. *A Popular Dictionary of Botanical Names and Terms, with their English Equivalents*, by George F. Zimmer, is published by Routledge and Kegan Paul, Ltd, Broadway House, 68–74, Carter Lane, EC4, at the very reasonable cost of 5s.

March 2, 1952

It sometimes happens that people inherit, or acquire, an old dwelling house or cottage with a pool or even with the remains of a moat. Presumably, such surroundings are highly picturesque, and the fortunate owner wants to make the most of them. Let us assume also that no previous owner has bothered about suitable planting, and has left the waterside to ramp away into a terrible mess of unworthy weeds. So I thought I would devote my next two articles to this rather special problem.

Water is the making of a garden. It gives a rare chance to the gardener. He can grow things *in* the water, and *beside* the water, and even *on* the water – a triple pleasure, far more agreeable than the filling up of triplicate forms. I will take *in* and *on* the water first, and leave the higher marginal planting until next week.

Water lilies come first to the mind; and apart from the white and our native yellow one, there are hybrids in pink, red, and primrose. Twelve to eighteen inches of water depth is a safe rough guide, and full sun. The usual method is to sink the plants in an old basket, when they will root through the basket into the bottom mud; but they can also be tied between two turves and sunk (the right way up). Late May or early June is the time. If you think the leaves of water lilies too large for a small pond, there is the Water Hawthorn, *Aponogeton*, also the Bog-bean with small white flowers, floating; or *Villarsia*, with golden flowers four inches above the water level, or *Pontederia cordata*, like a pale blue arum. For the edges, where the water is not so deep, our native yellow flag iris is both lovely and reliable; the Flowering Rush, *Butomus umbellatus*, is an arrowy grower three to four feet high with rosy flowers; it looks exotic, but is in fact to be found wild in Britain. *Sagittaria*, the true Arrow-head, white flowers, associates well with this rather spiky group.

For something lower in stature on the boggy margin, the water Forget-me-not, *Myosotis palustris*, is a great spreader of a china-blue, paler than the garden varieties. The King Cup or Marsh Marigold will grow either in sun or shade, which is obliging of it.

Finally, the very brave could experiment with the ordinary white arum, the Lily of the Nile, which, if planted deep enough, should survive an average winter in the South of England. But if you want to grow arums out of doors in water, the Bog-arum, *Calla palustris*, is a less risky investment.

March 9, 1952

In choosing plants for the waterside, I think it is important to remember that their beauty will be doubled if you can arrange for them to be reflected in the water. If the water is covered by floating plants, such as water lilies, this will not be possible, though one can usually contrive to keep a bare zone round the outside to serve as a mirror. Much will depend, of course, on whether the

183

pond has banked-up sides, or fades away into a swampy level; these are differences which can only be considered on the spot.

For the marshy swamp I would suggest a drift of the moisture-loving primulas: *Sikkimensis, Florindae, Japonica, Chionantha, Bulleyana, Helodoxa*, known as the Glory of the Marsh. If economy is a consideration, as it usually is, these primulas are all easily raised from seed. The tall clematis-like Japanese irises, *I. kaempferi*, look most beautiful growing amongst them, but I always think their requirements are a little awkward to manage – wet in summer, dry in winter. Nature's water supply usually works the other way round. The blue *Iris laevigata*, on the other hand, does not mind boggy conditions all the year through. *Iris sibirica*, less large and handsome than the Japanese, is exceedingly graceful and pretty and most accommodating, though it does not like being too deeply drowned. *Iris delavayi* resembles it, and is useful because it flowers later, when *Sibirica* is over. The richer the soil, the better for all these irises, even to a mulch of rotted manure.

These are all tall-growing, but if you can spare a special corner, marking it off with a ring of rough stones, do try the little almost-black gold-veined *I. chrysographes*, a real gem; and *I. fulva*, a coppery-red.

So much for the waterside irises, but coming higher up on the bank, assuming that there is a bank, and that it is dry, I think one might plant the scarlet dogwood *Cornus alba*. Do not be misled by the name; *alba* in this case refers only to the flowers, which are silly, contemptible little things in summer. The glory of this plant is the red bark of its bare stems throughout the winter. Caught by the light of the sinking sun, reflected in water, it is as warming to the heart as a log-fire on the hearth after a cold day.

March 16, 1952

The other evening I had a strange and lovely experience. I found myself, never mind how or why, completely alone in the Royal Horticultural Society's hall in Vincent Square after the fortnightly show had been closed to the public for the night. There I was, by myself, with not so much as a stray kitten wandering about. The lights were on, turning that vast hall into a raftered church overhead, and shining down on the silent flowers beneath. It was like being in a cathedral paved with flowers, with the scent of thousands of hyacinths taking the place of incense. An old phrase from the fifteenth century came into my mind: 'The fair flourished fields of flowers and of herbs, whereof the breath as of balm blows in our nose, that ilk sensitive soul must surely delight.'

I write this, however, not so much to describe that experience as to urge you to take note now of the many small bulbous plants which grace this time of the year. The tiny crocus species, for instance, some so delicately feathered on their outer petals with a complementary colour – *C. susianus*, yellow feathered with brown, or *C. chrysanthus Snow Bunting*, white feathered with lavender. They are too numerous for separate mention here, but a good catalogue will give a descriptive list if you cannot manage to visit a nursery or a flower-show. Messrs R. Wallace, Tunbridge Wells, have a very long list. (See also under February 15, 1953.) Cheap to buy, they should, I think, be crowded all together into a special corner, or grown in a stone sink, or for the house in an Alpine pan. The miniature narcissi go well with them, and, of course, the small irises; there is a particularly fine wine-red form of *I. reticulata* called J. S. Dijt. The early grape-hyacinth, *Muscari azureum*, mixes its sky-blue spikes to perfection, it is nearly the same colour as *I. reticulata Cantab*.

The rest of this brilliant little company should not be too ruinous. A few shillings will go a long way for a start, and one can always add more during ensuing years. They take up so little room, and are so welcome in the months when spring seems to be so endlessly laggard.

March 23, 1952

Many years ago, in the high mountains of Persia, I collected some seed-pods off a mimosa which was most unaccountably growing there, some five thousand feet above sea-level, and some hundred miles from any spot whence it could possibly be considered as a garden escape. I do not pretend to explain how it came there, in that cold, stony, snowy, desolate region; all I know is that there it was, and that I brought seeds home, and now have a tree of it growing out of doors in my garden and a vase full of it on my table, smelling not of the snows but of the warm south.

I think it is probably *Acacia dealbata* and not a true mimosa at all, but it looks so like what we call mimosa in the florists' shops or on the French Riviera that the name may conveniently serve. Botanists may write to tell me that it is more likely to be *Albizzia Julibrissin*, a native of Persia, whereas the acacia is a native of Australia, which adds to the mystery of how it came to be growing on the Elburz mountains; but *Albizzia* it certainly is not.

All this preamble is intended to suggest that enterprising gardeners in the South of England might well risk a plant in a sheltered corner. Of course the ideal place is a large conservatory, but few people have large conservatories nowadays. It might not come unscathed through a terrible winter such as we had in 1947, but my tree at any rate has not so far turned a hair in frost, and the place where I found it growing was certainly more bleak and windswept than anything we can provide here. We take the precaution of wrapping its trunk and lower branches in trousers of sacking, and that is all the protection it gets. For greater safety, it could be trained fan-wise against a wall, if you started the training young enough. I should perhaps add that a high wall shelters it from the north, and that it is planted facing full south. I should add also that it is no good picking it before the flowers are fully out, in the hope that they will open in water; there are some things which refuse to oblige in that way, and this is one of them. You must wait till the clusters are as fluffy and yellow as ducklings.

It makes a charming pot-plant until it becomes too large and has to be transferred into a tub or else planted out into the open ground.

Anyone wanting to try the experiment can get this acacia from Treseder's Nurseries, Truro.

March 30, 1952

Nostalgia for the past has brought with it a revival of taste for the old-fashioned flowers: the flaked pinks and carnations, the double primroses, the old roses, the broken tulips, the double Sweet William. Perhaps it is not only nostalgia for an age which, rightly or wrongly, we esteem to have been happier than our own, as it was certainly more leisurely, but also a natural reaction against the exaggerated blooms we are offered today: size not subtlety. Who wants a begonia like a saucer?

Amongst the many plants thus returning to favour, the auricula finds its little place. I am not here concerned with the outdoor, or Alpine, auricula, so familiar in cottage gardens, but with what is known as the *Show auricula*, which must be grown indoors or under glass, not because it fails in hardiness but because the powder (*farina*) gets washed off in the rain and all its essentially cleanly character is lost. It cannot afford to get itself into a mess. Neatest and most exquisitely demarcated of flowers, it must keep itself as trim as the fireside cat. Given this opportunity, it will produce in April and May flower-heads which combine at one and the same time a demure simplicity and an appearance of extreme sophistication. Grey; green; white edged with green; scarlet edged with green; yellow edged with grey; the variations are manifold. The old growers used to put their pots on ranged shelves, sometimes fitted into a small home-made theatre with scenery painted behind it as a background.

Few of us have the leisure to indulge in such charming fancies, but it is still possible to treat ourselves to a hanging wall-bracket with four or five shelves, knocked up from some odd pieces of wood by any handy carpenter.

To be practical about raising the auriculas. They are expensive to buy as plants, but cheap to grow from a packet of seed from the best firm. Sow in

April in a pan of very finely sifted soil, and scarcely cover the seed. This is important: if too deeply buried the seed will refuse to germinate. Prick the seedlings out into tiny pots, and pot up singly into four-inch pots, never into a big pot. Keep them cool always, never exposed to a hot sun.

The House of Douglas, Edenside, Great Bookham, Surrey, supply seed.

March 8, 1953

I have just planted out a *Metasequoia glyptostroboides*. In case this name should by any chance sound unfamiliar, I should explain that it refers to a tree whose discovery was one of the romances of plant-collecting. It had been known for some time as a fossil going back to the Mesozoic era which I understand occurred some two hundred million years ago, but as no living specimen had ever been seen, botanists assumed that it had gone out of existence at about the same time as its contemporaries the giant reptiles. The surprise of a Mr T. Wang can therefore be imagined, when in the year 1946 three strange conifers were observed growing in a remote valley of north-eastern Szechuan. Their foliage corresponded to his fossil remains. Further exploration revealed the somewhat patchy presence of more, similar trees in the same area, growing for the most part beside streams in marshy places; seed was collected, and, since it germinates readily, this extraordinary survivor from a fantastically distant age may now be regarded as safe for future generations in Europe and America.

It seems unlikely that many owners of small gardens will feel inspired to plant one, for its eventual height of 130 feet may prove as intimidating as its name. Nevertheless, as young specimens can already be seen growing in some public and some private gardens, I might as well describe their appearance so that you can recognize a *Metasequoia* when you meet one. Pale green and feathery in spring and summer, it turns bright pink in autumn, a really startling sight when the sunshine catches it. Judging by my own experience from a tiny seedling given to me, it grows very fast, about six feet in as many years, especially if planted in the damp situation it loves.

I did not plant mine in a damp situation; I kept it in a pot, not knowing what to do with it; and it grew and grew, becoming more and more pot-bound, poor thing, but still thriving. It throve so well under these unkind conditions that I felt bound to reward it by letting it out into a damp gully in the middle of a field, where, if no cow eats it, I shall watch its progress with considerable interest.

If any brave person, or any enterprising municipal council, wants one of these living fossils, it can be obtained at a price varying from 15s. 6d. to £3 3s. od., according to size. Messrs Hillier supply them.

April

This, I fear, is not going to be a very practical article. It will be of no use at all to anybody who is making or planting a garden. But as it will appear on All Fools' Day I may perhaps be allowed a frivolity for once.

The frivolity concerns a nurseryman's catalogue dated 1838. Queen Victoria had recently come to the throne. One of her humbler subjects, Mr John Miller, of the Durdham Down Nursery, near Bristol, had just died as a bankrupt. His executors were carrying on his Business, for the benefit of the Creditors including the Bankrupt's immediate Relatives.

Poor Mr John Miller. He had a magnificent list of plants for disposal, not only roses, but pelargoniums, auriculas, pinks, orchids, herbaceous plants – pages and pages of them. It seems a shame that he should go smash so soon after his young Queen had embarked on a reign of over sixty years of prosperity. He should have prospered with her; evidently he did not.

The reason why I here revive his list is not so much because I feel sorry for Mr Miller, dead and lost 113 years ago, as because I think his catalogue may interest rose specialists and may also appeal to those who share my appreciation for such names as these, picked at random:–

Monstrous four seasons; *Belle sans flatterie*; *Black African*; *La belle Junon*; *Ninon de l'Enclos*; *Temple d'Apollon*; *Conque de Vénus.*

Where have they gone, these bearers of fantastically romantic names? If Edmond Rostand had known of them he would surely have put a great speech about them into the mouth of Cyrano de Bergerac. Where are they now? Lost, I suppose, for ever, unless they could be discovered in some ancient garden in England or France.

One of those queer quirks of memory that sometimes assail us made me take down from my shelves a copy of *The Rose Fancier's Manual*, translated from the French by Mrs Gore, once a best-seller amongst novelists. I found, as I expected, that Mrs Gore's book exactly corresponded in date, 1838, with the list of Mr Miller, deceased. She mentions a number of the same roses, but she also mentions others which Mr Miller had not got, or perhaps had sold out of. Her *Coupe d'amour* does not figure in Mr Miller's list; nor does *Tout aimable*; nor does the rose whose name, if truthful, makes me want to possess it more than any: *Rien ne me surpasse.*

Surely the most exacting should be satisfied with that.

April 8, 1951

Vegetables . . . Not cabbages or turnips or parsnips, sodden in water, insipid, tasteless, 'one mutt, two veg.', but rare, succulent vegetables which are quite as easy to grow. Most of them can be sown this month or next, and can be obtained from Miss Kathleen Hunter, who is the successor of the well-known Miss Eleanour Sinclair Rohde. Address on p. 274.

Calabrese is perhaps becoming better known, but is still not well known enough. It is a brassica much appreciated in America and with good reason. It serves a double purpose, because you first eat the small, cauliflower-like head, which is green instead of white, and then you keep continuously picking the side-shoots, which taste of asparagus. It is really and truly delicious, and most prolific. Sow seed in the open in April, or buy plants at 10s. a hundred, twenty-five for 3s., to be delivered June–July. It likes a rich soil, with manure.

Peas. Have you tried the *True French petit pois*, or the *Mange-tout*, which is so tender that you eat the whole thing, pod and all? 1s. a packet each.

Beans. The Golden butter-bean, a dwarf which needs no stringing. Sow it towards the end of May, and pick it when it is lemon yellow. 6d. a packet.

Onions. Have you tried the Tree-onion? It is a perennial, and grows its little edible onions at the top of the plant instead of in the ground. Plants cost 1s. each, or 11s. a dozen, and can be increased by planting out the little onions or by division of the roots.

Lettuce. Two of the best lettuces, I think, are *Brittle Ice* and *Green Jade*, nice names and crisp hearts. *Green Jade* may seem rather expensive at 2s. 6d. a packet, but it is exceptionally good. It should be sown at frequent intervals, because it is inclined to bolt, and it should never be transplanted, only thinned out. *Brittle Ice* costs less, at 6d. a packet. Both are of the cabbage type, not the Cos. Why anybody bothers to grow the Cos instead of the solid, curly cabbage sorts passes my understanding.

These are all more or less necessary vegetables, meaning that one must have brassicas, peas, beans, onions, and lettuce, in one variety or another, but there are many other things which the enterprising kitchen-gardener might grow as extras. *Hamburg Parsley*, for instance, of which you eat the root, grated or sliced, in salads, when it tastes like nuts; it will keep all through the winter. Sow in April, seed at 1s. a packet. The *Black Radish* can also be stored throughout the winter, 'big as a tennis ball, with a skin as black as soot and flesh as white as snow'. Sow in July, 1s. 6d. a packet.

Squashes and marrows ought to come into this article, but space runs out. I shall return to them next week, with a note on the ornamental gourds.

Meanwhile I must ask forgiveness from many correspondents who urged me to write an article about window-boxes or hanging baskets in town. I tried, but it was such a poor article that I tore it up. I don't know anything about town gardening; I have never had any experience of it; I am a country gardener not a town gardener; and if one values one's integrity in such matters one cannot pretend to a knowledge one does not possess. Sorry; but there it is.

April 15, 1951

Ornamental or edible, the great family of the *Cucurbitaceae* must have representatives in every garden. We all grow *Cucurbita pepo ovifera*. Do we? Yes, but we don't call it by that name: we call it the vegetable marrow. And how wrongly we treat it! Instead of picking and cooking it when it is only about four inches long, we encourage it to grow into something resembling a porpoise, a prize-winner at the local flower-show but a soapy, watery thing in the kitchen.

In this article I want to suggest some other types of the family. Have you, for example, ever tried growing the *Avocadella*? – not to be confused with the Avocado pear. You grow it as you would grow a marrow, but its fruit never grows bigger than a grapefruit in size. It will cost you 2s. 6d. a packet of seed. Sow it now, under glass, if you have glass; if not, sow it out of doors at the end of May. It likes a sunny place, and some manure in the soil. An old compost heap suits it nicely.

Then there is the *Apple cucumber*. This is a novelty I really recommend. Most prolific, it produces egg-sized fruits more constantly and reliably than any hen. Sow it in a frame now, or in the open in May. Seed costs 1s. 6d. a packet.

Then there are the *Cocozelle*. These are the *Zucchini* of Italy, well known to all travellers in that delectable country. You can get the seed at 1s. a packet, and grow it as you would grow a marrow. Then if you like squashes, you can now get the *Hubbard Squash* at 1s. a packet, or the *Custard Marrow* at 6d. a packet.

This is all very practical, culinary, and utilitarian. I would now like to put in a word for the ornamental gourds, which are no good to eat but which are just sheer fun. And what fun they are! What jokes! What fantasies! You get a mixture in a seed packet and you may get all shapes, colours, and sizes. Little turbans, little striped green-and-yellows, or round oranges; you may get, if you are lucky, named sorts, such as the *Warted Gourd*, the *Bishop's Mitre*, the *Hedgehog*, the *Powder Flask*, the *Hercules Club*, or the *Turk's Cap*, white or red. Whatever comes out of your shilling packet you may be sure of variety; and you can preserve them throughout the winter for house-decoration in bowls if you varnish them with a thin coating of Copal varnish.

But, before doing that, grow them over any rough fence or shed this summer. They provide a very quick covering, which your neighbour is unlikely to have thought of. Miss Hunter, whose address will be found on p. 274, supplies seed of everything mentioned here.

April 22, 1951

However popular, however ubiquitous, the clematis must remain among the best hardy climbers in our gardens. Consider first their beauty, which may be either flamboyant or delicate. Consider their long flowering period, from April till November. Consider also that they are easy to grow; do not object to lime in the soil; are readily propagated, especially by layering; are very attractive even when not in flower, with their silky-silvery seed-heads, which always remind me of Yorkshire terriers curled into a ball; offer an immense variety both of species and hybrids; and may be used in many different ways, for growing over sheds, fences, pergolas, hedges, old trees, or up the walls of houses. The perfect climber? Almost, but there are two snags which worry most people.

There is the problem of pruning. This, I admit, is complicated if you want to go into details, but as a rough working rule it is safe to say that those kinds which flower in the spring and early summer need pruning just after they have flowered, whereas the later flowering kinds (i.e. those that flower on the shoots they have made during the current season) should be pruned in the early spring. For further information I would refer you to Ernest Markham's book *Clematis*, which has just been republished by Country Life, Ltd, at 18s. and which includes a chapter on pruning by Mr George Jackman, whose father raised the well-known *C. Jackmanii* and its many hybrids, or indeed to Mr Jackman's own catalogue, obtainable from his nursery at Woking.

The second worry is *wilt*. You may prefer to call it *Ascochyta Clematidina*, but the result is the same, that your most promising plant will suddenly, without the slightest warning, be discovered hanging like miserable wet string. The cause is known to be a fungus, but the cure, which would be more useful to know, is unknown. The only comfort is that the plant will probably shoot up again from the root; you should, of course, cut the collapsed strands down to the ground to prevent any spread of the disease. It is important, also, to obtain plants on their own roots, for they are far less liable to attack. I see that Mr Markham agrees with this.

Slugs, caterpillars, mice, and rabbits are all fond of young clematis, but that is just one of the normal troubles of gardening. Wilt is the real speciality of the clematis.

There is much more to be said about this beautiful plant but space only to say that it likes shade at its roots, and don't let it get too dry.

April 29, 1951

In these ruinous days many people would like to make a little profit back from their gardens. In fact so many people are now selling surplus flowers and vegetables that we shall soon be all sellers with no one left to buy. However, the market still exists, not only for the commercial grower but also for the amateur, and many a dark industrial city welcomes the golden bunch as a reminder that the daffodil blows somewhere in the orchards of the south.

It is to 'the man with a small income and a small garden' that a new little book, *Amateur Gardening for Pleasure and Profit*, by C. C. Vyvyan (Museum Press, 6s.), is addressed. The writer supposes a garden owner, anxious to obtain some information about the most saleable crop of flowers, fruits, or vegetables; how to pick and pack them; what kind of string and boxes to use; what policy to pursue (honesty is recommended), and, most important, how to find a market. As a start Lady Vyvyan favours local shops, hotels, friends and neighbours. This saves much cost in transport and packing materials, more especially if you can induce the customer to come and collect the produce from your own door; it also cuts out the commission exacted by the middleman. Direct selling, then, is the thing, until you become so ambitious that you start dispatching weekly consignments to Covent Garden. I suspect also that Lady Vyvyan, although she does not explicitly say so, favours making use of friends and visitors who come in motor-cars. 'Oh, must you go? *Would* you mind dropping this bundle of holly for me? It isn't very prickly and it won't take you more than a mile out of your way.' Thus is a local business built up.

It is a really practical little book, written by someone with personal experience who knows the snags as well as the ropes. She is full of good hints. Did you realize, for instance, the marketable value of such 'common property' as ivy, ferns, or that weed the Winter Heliotrope, an invasive danger in the garden but a scented delight in January to those unfortunates who are condemned to live in towns? Or moss? Though, as Lady Vyvyan sagely says, moss-gathering is suitable only for a man with much leisure or for children and visitors who need to be given some harmless occupation. It takes too long for busy people. Rightly, she did not mention the rolling stone.

April 6, 1952

To the true plant-lover, there are few treasures greater than those he has collected for himself, preferably on a holiday abroad. I know myself how preciously I value those few precarious survivors I have managed to bring home in the form of cuttings damply wrapped in my sponge-bag, or in the form of bulbs stuffed into the toe-caps of a pair of shoes. The foreign soil I found lingering, when next I put the shoes on, was not the least part of my pleasure. It might be gritty, but it was a bit of Persia, France, Italy, or Spain. These survivors are dearer to me than anything I could have ordered or paid shillings for from a nurseryman. So, as Easter approaches and some people may be preparing to spend their £25 across the Channel, let me utter a word of warning.

I recently received a series of ecstatic letters from a traveller in Greece. 'I wish you could see', he wrote, 'the hillsides here covered with anemones, narcissus, iris, jonquil, cyclamen . . . I am digging a lot up, with the trowel I had the foresight to bring with me. Would you please ascertain from the Ministry of Agriculture what permit is necessary to import bulbs and corms into England? It would break my heart if, on arrival, I had to throw them all with a splash into the harbour at Dover.'

The Ministry of Agriculture was most courteously co-operative, granting the permit by return of post, on the understanding that the said bulbs or corms were for personal not commercial use; in other words, that the digger-up intended them only for his own garden. At the same time, it pointed out that a permit should, strictly speaking, have been obtained *before* the traveller left England. (Prospective plant-collectors, please note this important condition.)

The sad part of the story comes now. My traveller in Greece, who is no smuggler, had rightly foreseen the difficulty of getting his little parcels legitimately through the English Customs. What he had not foreseen was that they might be taken away from him by the Italian *Dogana* when he landed at Brindisi on his way home from Greece. Dozens of Greek bulbs therefore splashed, not into Dover harbour, but into the Adriatic Sea.

The moral of this article is: if you are going abroad, and want to bring plants home with you, make sure before you go what regulations apply in every country, not only in your own.

April 13, 1952

At this time of year, or even a month earlier, a few pans of small, brightly coloured flowers give vast pleasure. If you want to see what I mean, done on the grand scale, go to the Alpine House at Kew. No need to be so ambitious, for even half a dozen pans on the staging of a small greenhouse produce an effect of clean brilliance, which I suppose is enhanced by the light coming on all sides, and overhead, through glass; and also because each bloom is unsmirched by rain or soil-splash, unnibbled by slugs, and unpecked by birds. Furthermore, the greyness of the stone chippings with which you will, I hope, have sprinkled your pans, throws up the colours into strong relief. Ideally, the pans should be whitewashed, for no one can pretend that the red of a flower-pot is pleasing, or of an agreeable texture.

Some of the little primulas lend themselves very happily to this treatment, *P. marginata*, for instance, or the lovely pale lavender *Linda Pope*; or even a clump of the ordinary blue primrose which suffers so from the mischief of birds when growing out of doors in the garden. I would like also to see a pan of larger size, interplanted with some of the choicer varieties of common bulbs, coming up between the primulas: the intensely blue hanging bells of *Scilla Spring Beauty*, or the strange greenish-turquoise of the grape-hyacinth called *Tubergeniana* or the pale blue of *Chionodoxa gigantea*, which in spite of its adjectival name resembles a tiny lily. Endless variations could be played on different colour schemes; you could have a cool pan of yellow primroses interplanted with the white grape-hyacinth and the white chionodoxa; or, for something looking rich and ecclesiastical, a pan of that very ordinary magenta *Primula Wanda* with the inky blue *Muscari latifolium* amongst it. The grey cushions of saxifrage, with their miniature pink or rosy flowers, look charming in low pans with some stones to set them off, but these, I think, should be grown by themselves, not interplanted.

It is too late this year, of course, and is an idea to materialize twelve months hence. It may be a bit of a time-taker for busy people, but a welcome occupation for an invalid or a convalescent. Meanwhile, do visit the Alpine House at Kew.

April 20, 1952
Several times in this column I have written about growing grapes out of doors. There are several hardy kinds which will do perfectly well, and ripen, either in the open or allowed to ramble over a porch or trained against a wall. Now comes Mr Edward Hyams with a further suggestion: why not grow some under cloches? Many people use the big barn-type of cloche for tomatoes; why not spare a few for a row of vines?

All particulars about how this can be done will be found in his new book, *Grapes Under Cloches*, published by Faber and Faber, 12s. 6d., illustrated, with lists of suitable varieties and addresses where to obtain them. This interesting monograph also tells how to cope with diseases, how to make wine, how to turn grapes into raisins, and how to destroy wasps by a new method. Even if you do not wish to divert any cloches in order to become a vinearoon, which is Mr Hyams's adopted translation of *vigneron*, you may still find a great deal of fascinating and sometimes amusing information. Did you, for instance, know that in Greek vineyards the two most redoubtable enemies are, not wasps or blackbirds, but tortoises and porcupines?

But the idea I really wanted to pick out of Mr Hyams's book is the ancient idea of making a hedge of vines. To do this, you allow your young vine to develop only one single rod, which you train horizontally, along a wire or along bamboo canes if you prefer, nailed to pegs driven into the soil; and when this rod has reached a length of thirteen feet, you bend the end of it downwards and push it firmly to a depth of six inches or more into the ground. It will then take root (we hope), and will spring up quite soon in new growth for the next rod, when you repeat the process, over and over again until your original vine with its recurrent progeny has attained the length you require.

You see the advantages. First, you need only one root-stock to start the process; very economical. (Of course, if you like to plant two, one at either end, it would go quicker, and they would meet in the middle, like engineers working through an Alpine tunnel.) Secondly, you can control your rods into any shape to suit the layout of your garden; you could grow them in a straight line down a long path, for example, or you could make them turn sharp corners at right angles to form an enclosure, vines being very flexible and tractable. Thirdly, by the time the rods have made old wood they should need no propping or staking; they will have grown tough enough to support themselves. Fourthly, you can, if you wish, grow this serialized vine a mile long. What a thought! Fifthly, you can eat the grapes.

Finally, you can buy or borrow Mr Hyams's book, where you will find far more detailed instructions than I have space to reproduce here.

April 27, 1952

A public activity is afoot which is bound to have a very considerable effect upon the future appearance of our country. I refer to the schemes for tree and hedge planting both in urban areas and along roads and by-passes. It is satisfactory to reflect that while on the one hand we are busy destroying our woodlands and our hedgerow timber, on the other hand a watchful Ministry is issuing leaflets for the guidance of local authorities and committees; leaflets which, on the whole, are sensibly and even imaginatively composed, with an eye to what Government departments will insist upon calling amenity value, but which we in our simplicity still obstinately call beauty.

It is encouraging to find that, apart from such obvious recommendations as the plane, the birch, the lime, the ash, the sycamore, the horse-chestnut, the beech and the poplar, including the sweet-scented balsam poplar, due consideration has also been given to the wild cherry, or gean, that bride of spring; to the whitebeam, whose underleaf blows silver in the breeze; to the tulip tree, with its strange green-and-yellow flowers; to the catalpa, whose flowers seem a mixture between the spotted foxglove and a miniature orchid; to the ginkgo, or maidenhair tree; and to the robinias, or false acacias, with special mention for the pale pink variety, *Decaisneana*, so much less familiar than the white.

All these proposals show more appreciation and imagination than we are accustomed to associate with an office desk in Whitehall. Perusing Circular No. 24, we note also with delighted approval that autumn colouring has been remembered, and that the wild service tree finds a place with its bright gold, as well as the sweet gum, whose botanical name is for once far more descriptive: *Liquidambar*.

It is only when we come to what most people regard as the relatively small flowering trees, with that dangerous adjective *ornamental* attached to them, that our confidence begins to wobble. It is so easy, and so delusive, to become excited over a new introduction when first you see it. The sight of the golden rain of the laburnum must have been as intoxicating to our Victorian forebears as their glass of champagne poured out on rare occasions. Yet today, the laburnum suffers from 'cheap' associations. It retains its original beauty; but has become too common, too ubiquitous, to provide us with the pleasure of surprise.

We should not, I think, maintain too horticulturally snobbish an attitude towards such things. Ubiquity should not necessarily affect beauty, properly used. Yet at the same time I would like to suggest that what is commonly known as 'an eye-full' does not always survive the test of years. Popular taste, easily caught, quickly turns into bad taste; or, at any rate, into a taste rejected by the more fastidious. We do not want to see our new roads and council sites planted with the screaming pink that once caught our raw fancy.

I observe, for instance, with regret, that a variety of the Japanese flowering cherry known as *Hisakura* is given an 'esp.' mark of commendation. Why? If the Ministry means the true *Hisakura*, well and good, but I suspect that what the local authorities will in fact obtain is that wickedly vulgar *Kanzan*, so strong and crude that it will spread like measles in an infectious rash.

Let us drop from this high temperature to a cooler degree. Let us consider the less garish flowering trees, which should survive the test of taste and time better than the 'eye-fulls'. The Ministry rightly recommends the common almond, and some of the Japanese cherries such as *Yedoensis*, *Sargentii*, and *Lannesiana erecta*, which, with its fastigiate or poplar-like habit, seems particularly well adapted to roadside planting. But no mention is made of other even more subtly beautiful varieties such as *Tai-Haku*, the great white cherry; or the greenish *Ukon*; or the hill cherry, an object of inspiration in Japan; or of the snowy mespilus, *Amelanchier canadensis*.

It may be argued that the general public prefer the bright pinks – 'So cheerful' – and that the proof is to be found in a myriad suburban gardens; but this private planting should suffice without the encouragement of re-inforcements supplied from the municipal purse. It is, we submit, the duty of Governmental advisers gently to decoy the public taste (and the taste of local councils) into more desirable channels.

It is already apparent that somebody in Whitehall knows a great deal of what he is talking about: could he not go a step further and empanel some of our great gardeners, amateur and professional, in an extra-advisory capacity? In this country of gardens and garden-lovers the opportunity has never been greater; it would be a sad pity if our roads and open spaces, our new towns, our housing estates, were now to be filled officially with a type of planting analogous, in terms of trees, to the begonias and calceolarias of many a public garden.

May

May 6, 1951

There was once a man, it is said, who furnished his garden entirely with the wild flowers of Britain. He was not one of those well-intentioned vandals who dig up a plant with no knowledge of how or when to transplant it; who have no regard for the conditions in which it would wish to be replanted; and who then turn plaintively indignant when it dies. For such people there is no excuse save the excuse of ignorance, which is the worst of all. This man knew what he was about, and no doubt was responsible for saving many things that might otherwise have perished.

In these days there is ample justification for such judicious rescues. Our native flowers are threatened. Intensive agriculture has ploughed up many an acre of the Lent-lily, the cowslip, and the orchid. Tree-felling has trampled many a wood where the lily of the valley once flourished. Clearance of ditches has buried many a thriving violet under mounds of soggy earth. (I am happy to say that I retrieved masses of wild white violets when I noticed that this fate was about to overtake them; they are now safe in my garden.) All this effort towards better agriculture was, and is, of course, necessary, but other horrible ideas now menace our wild flowers. Report suggests that selective weed-killers are to be used, or perhaps are already being used, on the grass verges of our lanes. This will mean the disappearance of many graceful things such as the Meadow-sweet, the wild strawberry, the Lords-and-Ladies, the Lady's smock . . . all innocents, no match for the abominable ingenuity of man.

What can be done about it? How can we combat this chemical destruction? I wish that someone, perhaps a reader of this article, would write a practical pamphlet about the salvation of our wild flowers, advising us how to mark a plant for its seed at the ripening season; how to mark a bulb or a root for lifting at the right time; how to save, in fact, our native treasures which the selective weed-killer will, with its wicked efficiency, regard merely as weeds.

For those readers especially interested in the survival of our native orchids, I would like to recommend *Wild Orchids of Britain*, by V. S. Summerhayes (Collins, 21s., illustrated). Mr Summerhayes is the Kew Gardens authority on orchids, so you may take it that his word is to be believed. He gives some useful maps as an appendix to his book, showing where our native orchids are mostly to be found. It is exciting to see an outline map of Britain, blocked out in black, area by area, county by county, where these rarities occur. The maps alone should be enough to send orchid hunters out on the quest; and the text will certainly ensure a respectful care.

May 13, 1951

There is a race of little irises, flowering in April and May, too seldom grown. They do not aspire to make a great splash; their colours are frail; they grow only six to twelve inches high; they demand a small place to match their small size; they must be regarded as intimate flowers, to be peered into and protected from the vulgar slug. I am referring to miniature versions of the Bearded Iris, which is the sort most familiar to most people. These miniature versions are called *pumila* and *chamaeiris*.

I will not waste space quarrelling over botanical differences. I will say only that if you can buy what nurserymen usually term *Iris pumila* you will get a reward. There is *I. azurea*, and *I. coerulea*, and *I. lutea*, a yellow one. They cost about 1s. 6d. each. Having paid this price, where is it best to plant them?

The authorities seem to differ in their opinion. W. R. Dykes, who was the great authority on irises, says that *Iris pumila* ought to be divided and transplanted every second year. He says they exhaust the soil. Yet I have grown a patch of them in a stone sink for some ten years and they have never flowered better than this year. The behaviour of plants is indeed inexplicable. It breaks all the rules; and that is what makes gardening so endlessly various and interesting.

I have come to the conclusion, after many years of sometimes sad experience, that you cannot come to any conclusion at all. But one simple thing I have discovered in gardening; a simple thing one never sees mentioned in gardening books. It is the fact that many plants do better if they can get their roots under stones. This is a fact I would like to return to in a future article. In the meantime, since I set out to mention the little early irises, may I suggest that you might plant them into the cracks between paving or along the edges of a paved path, where they will not be walked on? I feel sure that this is the place to grow them, rather than down the front of a border, as is often recommended in books about gardening. They are not things for an herbaceous border: they are things for stone paths, surely; and the grey background of the paving enhances their delicacy of colouring. The worst that can be said against them is that they do not remain very long in flower, but they are so unobtrusive and take up so little room, that their few weeks of flowering life entitle them to a place where they can subsequently grow forgotten.

May 20, 1951

There is often a strip of ground in a garden which cannot be put to good purpose without more labour than we can devote to it. It may once have been a lawn, which means mowing; or a long border, which needs weeding and upkeep; or merely a strip along the boundary fence in the garden of a new house, hitherto uncultivated, which demands some treatment to turn it into something better than a rough waste. I had an idea for such a place, which should be both pretty and labour-saving.

The shape does not matter so very much; it could be rectangular, square, or even circular, though I fancy a long narrow rectangle would give the best effect. What is important is that it should be *flat*, and that the ground surface should be level. No bumps: no depressions. You then plant it at regular intervals (say fifteen feet apart either way) with young stripling sapling trees, straight of stem and twiggy of head; it will be important to keep the stems clean of growth so that you can always see through and between them. A thin little grove is what I have in mind. The silver birch with its pale bark would be ideal, especially in a light or sandy soil; the lime or linden, for any soil; the whitebeam, whose underside leaves show silver in the breeze; and even young oaks, round-topped and grown as standards.

The question will then arise of what you plant underneath. Since the heads of the little trees will be very green, the accent should be on emphasizing the greenness. Turf is probably impossible, because of the mowing, and anyway I think one should aim at a brighter green than that. I have a great weakness for Sweet Woodruff; it does not object to shade, it remains green from April until the autumn, it can be grown from seed, and it would make a dense cushion rather like those enormous eiderdowns (*duvets*) that one finds in old-fashioned French hotels. I would also plant some patches of greenish flowers; for instance, the green and silver Star-of-Bethlehem, *Ornithogalum nutans*; our native wood anemone; lily of the valley; and, for later in the year, some clumps of Solomon's Seal and the sweet-smelling *Smilacina racemosa*. I am not quite sure about these last two: they might be too tall, and might interrupt the vistas between the straight little trunks. Obviously such planting must depend upon individual taste, but of one thing I feel sure: that all colour must be excluded. It must all be green and white; cool, symmetrical, and severe.

May 27, 1951

May I go back to something I wrote a couple of weeks ago about many plants doing so well if they can get their roots under stones? I am not thinking specially of Alpines whose natural habit it is, but of casual strays, often self-sown, sometimes bulbous plants, sometimes merely annuals or biennials, which by a successful accident have pointed the way to this method of gardening. The narrowest crack in a path or paved terrace will surprisingly send up the finest seedling; I have known even such large unwanted subjects as delphiniums and hollyhocks to make the attempt. The reason, obviously, is that they never suffer from either excessive moisture or excessive drought; the stone preserves such moisture as is in the soil, but prevents the soggy puddling consequent on a heavy rainfall; furthermore, it protects from the scorching sun and conse-quent wilting which demands the watering-can.

If we are to take this hint from Nature it would be as well to dispose of the weeds first to save trouble later on. Weeds in paths are a constant worry to those who have not discovered the ghoulish pleasure of using weed-killer; and, even to the initiate, the cost of proprietary weed-killers is often a deter-rent, driving many a conscientious gardener back to the kneeling-pad and the broken knife-blade. It is now possible, however, to buy sodium chlorate by the pound; the price fluctuates so I had better not quote it, but as you must use only 1 lb. to 10 gallons of water you can see that it works out very cheaply. Sodium chlorate acts through the leaves, so should be applied when the weeds are green – the only drawback is that the ground is not safe to set other plants in for about six months.

I should then fill up the cracks with good soil or compost, and sow quite recklessly. I should not mind how ordinary my candidates were, Royal Blue forget-me-not, pansies, wallflowers, Indian pinks, alyssum Violet Queen, be-cause I should pull up ninety-five per cent later on, leaving only single specimens here and there. It is not, after all, a flower-bed that we are trying to create. If, however, you think it is a waste of opportunity to sow such ordinary things, there are plenty of low-growing plants of a choicer kind, especially those which dislike excessive damp at the root throughout the winter: this covering of stone would protect them from that. The old-fashioned pinks would make charming tufts: *Dad's Favourite*, or *Inchmery*, or *Little Jock*, or *Susan*, or *Thomas*. The Allwoodii, with their suggestion of chintz and of patchwork quilts, should also succeed under such conditions; I confess to repeated failures with them in open borders, but their neatness and variety encourage perseverance.

May 4, 1952
There must be some curious philological or Grimm's Law which makes English-speaking people call anemones anenomes, transferring the *m* into the place of the *n*. So perhaps it is better to adopt the pretty though unscientific

name of Wind-flower, as it is about the anemones or wind-flowers that I want to write on this day of spring.

How gay they are, how brilliantly gay, how shiny, how variegated in their colours, these wind-flowers that come to us from different parts of the world. The season starts for us from Greece, with the starry blue *Anemone blanda* flowering in March; succeeded by *A. apennina*, the equally starry and even more intensely blue Italian. Then there is the well-known double or semi-double *St Brigid*, on sale everywhere early in the year, but to my mind greatly excelled by the *de Caen*, or poppy-flowered single; and excelled above all by the single, starry, *St Bavo*. This is the one I ardently want to commend to your attention at the moment.

I cannot imagine why people don't grow *Anemone St Bavo* more generously. It is cheap to buy, 2s. 6d. a dozen of those little tubers which one doesn't know which way up to plant and it doesn't seem to matter anyhow – English as she is wrote. *St Bavo* is a hybrid of *Anemone coronaria*, and comes up in a range of colouring equalled by very few easy flowers. Any description of the various colours would sound, on paper, like an exaggeration: wine-velvet with an electric-blue centre; scarlet with a black centre, pink or lilac with a biscuit-coloured centre; or a particularly subtle named variety, more expensive at 6s. 6d. a dozen, called *Salmonea*, which is like a ripe apricot hanging in the sun. At least, I thought it was, but when with a conscientious qualm I went back to have another look at it, I found I had been quite wrong. It was more as though you had pounded some old Tudor bricks into a paste, varnished the paste, and then shredded it into pointed petals.

May 11, 1952

Often I receive plaintive appeals from gardeners who live in towns, or from gardeners whose site is heavily shaded, or from gardeners whose lot is cast in a combination of both. I never quite know what to reply, having no personal knowledge of such conditions, and being reluctant to proffer advice unsupported by practical experience. In common with everyone else, I know, roughly, that Morello cherries and the winter Jasmine will flourish on a North wall, and that periwinkles and foxgloves and ferns will tolerate a considerable amount of shade, but very soon after that I find myself coming to a full stop.

It was therefore with relief that I welcomed a little pamphlet called *Plants for the Shaded Garden*, by Barbara Acworth, published by the University of London Press at the modest price of 1s. 6d. Obviously, it would be unreasonable to demand a comprehensive treatise for eighteenpence, or to expect anything likely to tell the advanced, progressive gardener something he did not already know. I do feel, however, that I can confidently recommend this cheapest of all gardening books (most of them cost from 10s. 6d. to a guinea) to the amateur gardener struggling to make his patch of prettiness or beauty in unpropitious circumstances.

I noticed with particular pleasure that Miss Acworth hit on some favourites of mine: Sweet Woodruff, for example, *Asperula odorata*, which consents to make a broad green band of edging in deep shade, starred with tiny white flowers just now, in May. This is a native of Britain, much neglected; I have often tried to bring it into favour, and am glad to receive Miss Acworth's support. Altogether this is a most helpful and discriminating little book, with sensible notes of instruction to each plant mentioned. I cannot help suspecting, however, that something funny has happened on page 19 to the description of *Vitis heterophylla*, which is made to resemble what we usually call Virginia creeper. *Vitis heterophylla* is not self-clinging, as Miss Acworth states, nor does it turn crimson in autumn. Its claim to distinction lies in its china-blue berries. And if she wanted to call the Virginia creeper a vine at all, should she not have written *Vitis inconstans*?

May 18, 1952

The happy few who still maintain a greenhouse, however small, sufficiently warmed in winter to keep the frost out, will find themselves repaid if they can make room for a few pots of the unfamiliar, pretty, blue-flowered *Oxypetalum caeruleum*.* This, admittedly, is subtle rather than showy, but I notice that it always attracts attention when we stand the pots out of doors for the summer in the garden. It has downy-green leaves and flowers of a curious greyish-blue, with a bright blue button no bigger than a flattened seed-pearl in the middle. I like to associate it with some pots of *Plumbago capensis*, whose stronger blue marries into a mist of blues reinforcing one another. Both, of course, are cool greenhouse plants, but they will live very happily in the open from the end of May until October.

I like the habit of pot gardening. It reminds me of the South – Italy, Spain, Provence, where pots of carnations and zinnias are stood carelessly about, in a sunny courtyard or rising in tiers on the treads of an outside stair, dusty but oh how gay! I know it entails constant watering, but consider the convenience of being able to set down a smear of colour just where you need it, in some corner where an earlier flower has gone off. We should take this hint from other lands. We do not make nearly enough use of pots in our country, partly,

* *Oxypetalum caeruleum* is now known as *Tweedia caerulea*, or *Amblyopetalum caeruleum*. It is a native of Brazil.

I suspect, because we have no tradition of pot-making here, nothing to compare with the camellia-pot, a common thing in Italy, swagged with garlands looped from a lion's mouth. Several times have I tried to persuade brick-makers to reproduce this standardized Italian model. They look at it with suspicion and alarm. 'Oh, no, we couldn't do that. We have never done anything like that. Sorry, we can't oblige.'

Meanwhile we surround a huge black Chinese jar with the blue *Oxypetalum* and the blue plumbago all through the summer, and drop a potful of *Ipomea rubro-caerulea* (Morning Glory, Heavenly Blue) into the Chinese jar, to pour downwards into a symphony of different blues.

The Chinese jar is of romantic origin. It was made during the Ming dynasty, which might mean anything between 1368 and 1644 – and was used to transport porcelain from China to Egypt, packed in lard to keep it from rattling about. The very solid handles show where the ropes were passed through, to sling it on board ship. It is not really black, but a sort of aubergine colour.

May 25, 1952

The flowering shrubs and trees are full of especial richness this year, from the common hawthorn in the hedgerows to the treasured beauties in our gardens. They are over all too soon, and it is then, as they begin to fade, that we regret not having kept a record of them in their prime, with a view to possible rearrangements, alterations, eliminations or additions when planting time comes in the autumn. One thinks one will remember, but, in fact, the succession is so rapid and one picture is so quickly replaced by another picture, that our impressions become merged into a blur of colours, shapes, sizes, and seasons. Why, we cry too late, did we not take notes week by week at the time?

It is with a virtuous resolution that I have acquired a large note-book stamped GARDEN RECORDS and four bundles of inch-long labels, with gilt numerals incised on white, from 1 to 100. These, since they are each pierced with a little hole, can be tied to a branch and the corresponding description entered against the number in the note-book. Thus: 'No. 10. Shockingly poor washy lilac; destroy; and replace by No. 12.' A reference to No. 12 recalls that it is 'Fine double-red young lilac; deserves a better place.' There comes a moment in the history of every garden when the duds must be scrapped, and the ill-assorted companions separated. My little outfit, supplied by Messrs Woodman, High Street, Pinner, is by far the most convenient register of such ruthless intentions of future discipline.

A genus of small shrubs which I fancy would never require a removal ticket are the Deutzias. Graceful and arching, May–June flowerers, four to six feet, they are ideal for the small garden where space is a consideration. They are easy, not even resenting a little lime in the soil, but beware of pruning them if you do not wish to lose the next year's bloom. The most you should do is to cut off the faded sprays and, naturally, take out any dead wood. The only thing to be said against them is that a late frost will damage the flower, and that is a risk which can well be taken. *Deutzia gracilis rosea*, rosy as its name implies; *D. pulchra*, white; *D. scabra Pride of Rochester*, pinkish white, rather taller, should make a pretty group. They are not very expensive at 3s. 6d. to 4s. 6d.

June

June 3, 1951

'Doing the flowers.' This douce and dulcet though lengthy task has been facilitated for us by Constance Spry, whose ingenuity is boundless. Nothing comes amiss to her in the exercise of her art, whether it be a sheaf of purple roses, or a leaf of red cabbage, or a spray of ripe blackberries, cut from the hedgerow. Her latest book, *Summer and Autumn Flowers* (Dent, 21s.), is full of suggestions, and is to be followed by a second volume called *Winter and Spring Flowers*.

I have not the pleasure of knowing Mrs Spry personally,* but I can see that we would agree; we would click; we would say 'Oh, yes,' and 'Oh, no,' in the enthusiastic way that gardeners have of concurring over the things they value. Mrs Spry must have a large garden of her own, where she cultivates plants for her own pleasure as well as for her celebrated shop in London, but there is nothing necessarily extravagant about her methods; it is true that she can avail herself of an armful of lilies and mix them with *Humea elegans* in a golden urn, but she is equally happy with fir-cones or with some of the ordinary herbs such as fennel, whose lovely feathery foliage has not escaped her eye, or with the yellow heads of the Woad that once furnished our ancestors with a blue dye. The receptacles into which she puts her flowers are equally varied: a wooden bowl, a silver sauce-boat, a tin-lined Bible-box, and something which she calls a pancheon.

Not the least useful part of her book is the section which deals with the care of cut flowers. As most of us already know, flowers last very much longer if you have previously stamped on their stems, stripped them of their leaves, and plunged them into boiling water. Detailed instructions are given as to which flowers respond best to this medieval-sounding treatment.

June 10, 1951

Visitors to the Chelsea Show may have noticed a large platform or billiard-table entirely planted with *Gentiana acaulis*. Billiard-tables are usually green, but this one was blue. The deep yet brilliant colour of those trumpets, raised motionless in a fanfare of blue music, must have aroused envy in many hearts.

Perhaps one should hesitate to recommend so temperamental a plant. It is

* I had not then; I have now.

said, for instance, that *G. acaulis* will flower freely on one side of a path but not on the other, for no apparent reason; and certainly the advice given by successful growers is bewildering in its variety. Reginald Farrer believed in a rich diet; feed it, he said, on old boots, pig-trough garbage, and the blood of kings. Other people will tell you to stamp on it; others, again, that where a particular little cress-like weed flourishes, there also will the gentian thrive. Two things seem certain: that it dislikes drought at the roots, taking the usual revenge if you allow it to get parched; and that you must try it in different places until you find the right place. I have had three shots at it myself, and at last it seems pleased, though I cannot yet rival the gentleman who replied modestly to Farrer's inquiry by saying that he 'did not think he had much more than five miles of it'. A statement which, upon investigation, turned out to be true.

For the comfort of gardeners on an alkaline soil, it may be added that *G. acaulis* is a lime-lover, unlike the September-flowering gentian *sino-ornata*, which dies instantly at one distant sniff of lime. Mortar-rubble, with its natural content of a lot of lime, and a top-dressing of bone-meal are both gratefully received by *G. acaulis*. And for the further comfort of gardeners who want a patch of gentians, not necessarily five miles long, in their garden, and who want to depend on an August display, *Gentiana septemfida* is probably the best and easiest to grow. *Septemfida*, by the way, has nothing to do with September, although it sounds like it; 'septemfida' merely means 'cleaved into seven divisions'. This gentian wants a peaty, loamy, leaf-mouldy bed; and hates getting parched.

If you want to know more about this beautiful family, a work on gentians has recently been published: *Gentians*, by David Wilkie, Country Life, 25s., generously illustrated with photographs.

June 17, 1951

Mr William Robinson, in his classic work *The English Flower Garden*, was very scornful of the Alliums or ornamental garlics. He said that they were 'not of much value in the garden'; that they produced so many little bulblets as to make themselves too numerous; and that they smelt when crushed.

For once, I must disagree with that eminent authority. I think, on the contrary, that some of the Alliums have a high value in the June garden; far from objecting to a desirable plant making a spreading nuisance of itself, I am only too thankful that it should do so; and as for smelling nasty when crushed – well, who in his senses would wish wantonly to crush his own flowers?

Allium rosenbachianum is extremely handsome, four feet tall, with big, rounded lilac heads delicately touched with green. Its leaves, however, are far from handsome, so it should be planted behind something which will conceal them. If you are by nature a hoarder, you can cut down the long stems after the flowers have faded and keep them with their seed-pods for what is known to florists as 'interior decoration' throughout the winter. Like most of the garlics, they demand a sunny, well-drained situation. Not expensive at 5s. 6d. a dozen, for the effect they produce, they get better and better after the first year of planting.

Allium albo-pilosum, a Persian, my favourite, is lilac in colour, two feet high or so. (See also under June 29, 1952.) *Allium cyaneum* is a mite, four inches only, blue, suitable for sinks or troughs, or any place where it can be observed at eye-level. The white-headed garlic, *Allium neapolitanum*, is useful for cutting; is apparently indestructible; and is cheap at 2s. 6d. a dozen bulbs.

Allium giganteum, five feet tall, is generally agreed to be the grandest of all, but is also the most expensive at 6s. a bulb. I bought a single one last year, and am now watching it anxiously. It should flower in July.

Mr Ralph Cusack, whose address will be found on p. 271, is an Allium enthusiast and offers a grand list of varieties in his catalogue.

June 24, 1951

We all have associations with the familiar scents of our childhood, whether they be of Sweet-briar on a moist evening, or of a red rose warmed by the sun, or of our native honeysuckle threading its way through a hedge. It is thus rather a shock to find some honeysuckles which have no scent at all, but which have flowers of such surprising beauty that they are worth growing for their colour alone.

Some of these are now flowering in my garden. I like and admire them, though I cannot love them in the way one loves the old sentimental kinds which always smelt so good. The ones with the huge yellow scentless flowers are called *Lonicera tellmanniana* and *Lonicera tragophylla*. There is also a bright red-orange one, *Lonicera brownii Fuchsioides*. They seem to do well in sun or shade; trained against a wall, or scrambling over a fence. I never know whether I prefer them in sun or in shade. The sunshine paints a brilliance on them, with a varnishing brush of light; but in a shady corner they have the deep, secret glow of hidden things.

I have recently regretted that I did not plant more honeysuckles in my garden. I suppose that all gardeners are suddenly assailed by similar pangs of regret. Fortunately, in the case of the honeysuckles, which are fast-growing subjects, it is an omission which can be rectified this coming autumn. For the scented ones, I shall plant the Early Dutch, flowering in May and June: and the late Dutch, flowering from July to September or October. These are both related to our native honeysuckle. For winter flowering, I have already got *Lonicera fragrantissima* and its perhaps better fellow, *Lonicera standishii*. They do not flower very exuberantly, in my experience, but even a couple of sprays picked in January are welcome and will scent a whole room.

June 1, 1952

New York, so we are told, could not spread sideways beyond a certain area owing to the geological formations on which that astonishing city has arisen. It had to go vertically towards the sky because it could not spread horizontally across the land. This curious and interesting fact accounts for that most original form of architecture, the skyscraper. No one had even thought of building skyscrapers before, because there was no need to. There had always been plenty of ground-room.

Now in small gardens there is not always as much ground-room as the gardener greedily wants, and I saw recently in the relatively small garden of a friend a most ingenious idea for getting herself out of the cramped difficulty. She had been given a flat flower-bed to deal with, but instead of leaving it just flat and restricted in space, she had built it up into little terraces with rough stones; three storeys high, and into these little stone-walled terraces she had packed and crammed every kind of plant that enjoys good drainage conditions: pinks, thrift, campanulas, Lewisias, violas, all ordinary things, but so effective grown in tiers as she was growing them, in a foaming mass and fall of flower and colour. You see the idea? You get the benefit three ways. You get the stone-walling, you get the flat bits under the stone-walling, and then on the top you get a wide expanse of bed in which you can plant anything you like. You will, by this means, have increased your garden space threefold.

Apart from the gain in space, it is always amusing to try experiments with plants in a dry-wall, even though that wall may not be more than two stones high. Many plants will flourish which otherwise would perish from the damp of our climate. When they can get their roots back between stones they seem to tuck themselves in and preserve themselves from rot. We do not need to build a skyscraper: we need only two rows of stone to pack our native Cheddar Pink into, let us say, or some of the Allwoodii pinks which sometimes prove disappointing grown in an ordinary border.

June 8, 1952

There is a form of hypocrisy common to nearly all gardeners. It does not affect only the gentle amateur, but has been known to affect even the most hardened professional, who is not, generally speaking, a sentimental or squeamish man. It is the human weakness which, accompanying our determination to rid ourselves of our slugs and snails, makes us reluctant next morning to contemplate the result of our over-night efforts.

Having enjoyed our own good breakfast, we come out to behold the slimy greenish remains. Big black slugs, four inches long; little black slugs, one inch long; snails exuding their entrails from under their beautiful delicate shells . . . Meta-and-sawdust have done their work only too well. In what agony, during the dark hours, have these miserable members of God's Creation perished? We ordained it, knowing, nay, hoping for what would happen; but when we see it we do not like it. We remember the lyrical terms in which the poets have addressed our victims:

> To note on hedgerow baulks, in moisture sprent,
>   The jetty snail creep from the mossy thorn,
> With earnest heed, and tremulous intent,
>   Frail brother of the morn!

Shakespeare also had a flattering comparison for him:

> Love's feeling is more soft and sensible
> Than are the tender horns of cockled snails.

It is all very painful, unpleasant, and even nauseating. What is to be done about it? We must abolish our frail brother with his tender horns, or else sacrifice our seedlings: we have the choice. The seedlings, I think, will win; must win. We must kill their enemies, but, if we are humane in our hearts, we will commit this slaughter with the least distressing offence to our hypocritical selves.

I think I have found the answer in an anti-slug bait which causes slugs and snails to shrivel up, dryly. It really works: I have tried it. It is called Anti-slug, and it comes from Messrs Baker, Codsall, Wolverhampton. It is said to be harmless to plants, birds and animals. And all I hope is that it doesn't cause unnecessary suffering to those humble enemies who creep across our paths, and have to be destroyed.

June 15, 1952
Brave gardeners who have a sunny corner to spare, at the foot of a south wall for choice, and a poor sandy soil, should plant some bulbs of Ixia, the South African Corn-lily. It is a graceful thing, about eighteen inches high, with rush-

like leaves and a flower-spike in various colours: white, yellow, coral-pink, and sometimes striped like the boiled sweets of our childhood. These, in a mixture, cost about 2s. 6d. a dozen, or 17s. 6d. a hundred. There is also a particularly lovely and rather strange variety, green with a black centre, *Ixia viridiflora*, more expensive at 12s. 6d. a dozen.

Ixias are not entirely hardy, though hardier than the freesias which they somewhat resemble. Very sharp drainage, deep planting of about six inches, and a little cover throughout our damp winter, should, however, ensure their survival, and those which fail to reappear can be replaced annually for half a crown. Of course, the more you can plant, the better. They flower in June and take up very little room. They are ideal for picking, as they last a long time in water and arrange themselves with thin and slender elegance in a tall glass.

They do also very well as pot-plants in a cold greenhouse or a conservatory, not requiring any heat but only protection from frost. If you grow them this way, you must disregard the advice to plant them six inches deep, and cover them with only an inch or so of soil – sandy loam and a handful of leaf-mould mixed to each pot, and crocks for drainage at the bottom.

I do hope you will order some Ixias for planting next October or November. I admit that they are apt to die out after a year or so; but to those gardeners who have a poor, starved soil and a warm corner they are a God-given present in June.

June 22, 1952

Often one is asked for plants which will flourish in semi-shade, and in the month of June the noble peony comes to mind. (I mean the herbaceous sort, not the species or the Tree-peony.) It always seems to me that the herbaceous peony is the very epitome of June. Larger than any rose, it has something of the cabbage rose's voluminous quality; and when it finally drops from the vase, it sheds its vast petticoats with a bump on the table, all in an intact heap, much as a rose will suddenly fall, making us look up from our book or conversation, to notice for one moment the death of what had still appeared to be a living beauty.

To be practical, there is much to recommend the peony. I will make a list of its virtues. It is a very long-lived plant, increasing yearly in vigour if you will only leave it undisturbed. It likes to stay put. It will, as I said, flourish in half-shade, and indeed its brag of size and colour gains from the broken light of overhanging branches. It doesn't object to an alkaline soil, a great advantage to those who cannot grow lime-hating plants in their garden. Rabbits do not appear to care for its young shoots. Slugs don't care for it either; and the only disease it may seriously suffer from is *wilt*, a fungus, *Botrytis*. If this appears, you must cut out the diseased bits and burn them; but in the many years I have grown peonies in my garden I have, touch wood, never found any trace of disease amongst my gross Edwardian swagger ladies.

The secret of growing the herbaceous peonies is to plant them very shallow and give them a deep, rich root-run of manure for their roots to find as they go down in search of nourishment. Then they will go ahead, and probably outlive the person who planted them, so that his or her grandchild will be picking finer flowers fifty years hence.

June 29, 1952

I know a man who collects baths. He buys broken-down baths for a few shillings at local auction sales and buries them in his garden, with the waste-hole open and a thick layer of coke-clinker or some similar rough stuff underneath to ensure drainage. He then fills the bath up to the rim with whatever kind of soil he requires; covers the rim over to hide it; and there he is, with a securely insulated patch in which to grow his choosy plants.

I am not suggesting that our gardens should all become a submerged cemetery for obsolete baths, but it does seem to me a helpful idea for people who have a difficult soil to cope with – people who want to grow things that will not consent to flourish in the soil with which they have been blessed or cursed. The dwellers on chalk, for example, who wish to grow the lime-hating gentians, could overcome their difficulty. The dwellers on clay would find that the indestructible, uncontrollable clay could be eliminated in favour of a soft bed suitable to peat-loving subjects. Again, if you want a swampy bit of ground for moisture-loving primulas, you can create it, very suitably, in the buried bath. Again, if you have a flinty soil, which throws up flints over and over again from the bottom, however often you may think you have cleared them out, you can replace that spiteful bit of ground with a richer loam, controlled and contained within the rectangular shape of the sunken bath.

It is an idea lending itself to much expansion.

Meanwhile I have been deriving much pleasure from a June-flowering garlic called *Allium albo-pilosum*. A native of Turkestan, it comes up in a large mop-sized head of numerous perfectly star-shaped flowers of sheeny lilac, each with a little green button at the centre, on long thin stalks, so that the general effect is of a vast mauve-and-green cobweb, quivering with its own lightness and buoyancy. They can be bought for 5s. a dozen, but even a group of six makes a fine show. Quite easy to grow, they prefer a light soil and a sunny place, and may be increased to any extent by the little bulbils which

212

form round the parent bulb, a most economical way of multiplying your stock. They would mix very happily with the blue *Allium azureum*, sometimes called *A. caeruleum*, in front of them. These cost only 2s. 9d. a dozen, are not quite so tall, and overlap in their flowering season, thus prolonging the display.

July

July 1, 1951

I am astonished, and even alarmed, by the growth which certain roses will make in the course of a few years. There is one called *Madame Plantier*, which we planted at the foot of a worthless old apple tree, vaguely hoping that it might cover a few feet of the trunk. Now it is fifteen feet high with a girth of fifteen yards, tapering towards the top like the waist of a Victorian beauty and pouring down in a vast crinoline stitched all over with its white sweet-scented clusters of flower.

Madame Plantier dates back, in fact, to 1835, just two years before Queen Victoria came to the throne, so she and the Queen may be said to have grown up together towards the crinolines of their maturity. Queen Victoria is dead, but *Madame Plantier* still very much alive. I go out to look at her in the moonlight: she gleams, a pear-shaped ghost, contriving to look both matronly and virginal. She has to be tied up round her tree, in long strands, otherwise she would make only a big straggly bush; we have found that the best method is to fix a sort of tripod of bean-poles against the tree and tie the strands to that.

Another favourite white rose of mine is *Paul's Lemon Pillar*. It should not be called white. A painter might see it as greenish, suffused with sulphur-yellow, and its great merit lies not only in the vigour of its growth and wealth of flowering, but also in the perfection of its form. The shapeliness of each bud has a sculptural quality which suggests curled shavings of marble, if one may imagine marble made of the softest ivory suede. The full-grown flower is scarcely less beautiful; and when the first explosion of bloom is over, a carpet of thick white petals covers the ground, so dense as to look as though it had been deliberately laid.

The old *Madame Alfred Carrière* is likewise in full flower. Smaller than Paul's rose, and with no pretensions to a marmoreal shape, *Madame Alfred*, white, flushed with shell-pink, has the advantage of a sweet, true-rose scent, and will grow to the eaves of any reasonably proportioned house, even on a west or north wall. I should like to see every Airey house in this country rendered invisible behind this curtain of white and green.

July 8, 1951

One of these days I must cope with what once tried to be an herbaceous border, but which is now a mess and a compromise. Herbaceous borders, perhaps, have had their day. They require to be immaculately kept and elaborately planned if they are to give their best; no pleasure can be derived from a jumble of plants, stuck in irrespective of colour or character, flopping after rain, prostrate after a sudden gale, tousled, sodden, leaning sideways at all angles, delphiniums in the back row, lupins and phlox in the middle, catmint and pinks along the front . . . one is only too familiar with these survivals of Edwardian times.

The question of staking is always a difficult one. Twiggy pea-sticks, pushed in at an early stage of the growth, are preferable to a stockade of bamboos hastily added as an afterthought when heads become top-heavy: pea-sticks will be hidden and covered over, as bamboos never will. I was told recently of an ingenious method for supporting perennial subjects in the border. In the idle, indoor days of winter you employ your leisure making large circles of stout wire, criss-crossing them with thinner wire into, say, four sections, meeting in a sort of hub at the middle; you then supply a central pole, of metal if you can get it, say bits of an old area railing, more durable than wood. In the spring you start your wire circle a few inches from the ground, raising it gradually up the central pole as the height of the plant increases, and as the plant grows up through the sections. I thought to myself that one might improve on the idea by placing two or more of the wire circles round the pole, according to the eventual height expected of the plant; this would save keeping a constant watch to see if the circle needed raising, and would also afford a double support to brittle stems.

It would entail a good deal of winter work, neat fingers, a pair of wire-cutters, a pair of pincers, and a couple of rolls of wire, thick and thin; but you would then have a fixture to last without renewal for many years. Even if you have not got an herbaceous border properly speaking, it should be a useful hint applied to any special treasure of a plant, too snappy and too tall to carry its own weight in high summer. All the same, I foresee that my border will soon become a border of flowering shrubs and the shrubby types of rose, with a solitary delphinium, overlooked in the background, to remind me of what the unlamented herbaceous border once was.

July 15, 1951

The other day I encountered a gentleman wearing amber-coloured spectacles. He was kind enough to say that I had a well-chosen range of colour in my garden. I expressed some surprise at this, since it was obvious that he could not be seeing any colours in their true colour, but must be seeing them in some fantastic alteration of tincture. Yes, he said, of course I do; it amuses me; try my glasses on, he said; look at your roses; look also at your brown-tiled roofs; look at the clouds in the sky. Look, he said, handing them to me. I looked, and was instantly transferred into a different world. A volcanic eruption, or possibly an earthquake, seemed imminent. Alarming, perhaps, but how strange, how magical.

Everything had become intensified. All the greens of turf or trees had deepened. All the blues were cut out, or turned to a blackish-brown. The whites turned to a rich buttercup-yellow. The most extraordinary effect of all was when you switched over to the pink variations of colour. There has been some correspondence in the Press recently about that old favourite rose, *Zéphyrine Drouhin*. Dear though she was to me, perfect in scent, vigorous in growth, magnificent in *floraison* (a lovely and expressive word we might well import from French into English, since we seem to have no equivalent in our language), and so kindly and obliging in having no thorns, never a cross word or a scratch as one picked her – dear though she was, I say, I had always deplored the crude pink of her complexion. It was her only fault. Seen through the magic glasses, she turned into a copper-orange; burnished; incredible.

Zéphyrine Drouhin has a romantic history, worthy of her breeze-like name. She derives from a hybrid found growing in 1817 in a hedge of roses in the Ile de Bourbon, now called Réunion, off the east coast of Africa. This hybrid became the parent of the whole race of Bourbon roses, which in their turn have given rise to the modern roses we call Hybrid Perpetuals and Hybrid Teas. This is putting it very briefly, and seems to bear no relation to the great pink bush flowering in the summer garden under the name *Zéphyrine Drouhin*. Who was Zéphyrine? Who was Monsieur Drouhin? These are questions I cannot answer. They sound like characters in a novel by Flaubert. I know only that this gentle, thornless, full-bosomed, generous trollop of a rose turned into a fabulous flaming bush under the sorcery of the tinted glasses.

July 22, 1951

Visitors to June and July flower-shows may have been surprised, pleased, and puzzled by enormous spikes, six to eight feet in height, which looked something like a giant lupin, but which, on closer inspection, proved to be very different. They were to be seen in various colours: pale yellow, buttercup-yellow, greenish-yellow, white and greenish-white, pink, and a curious fawn-pink which is as hard to describe, because as subtle, as the colour of a chaffinch's breast.

216

These were *Eremuri*, sometimes called the fox-tail lily and sometimes the giant asphodel. They belong, in fact, to the botanical family of the lilies, but, unlike most lilies, they do not grow from a bulb. They grow from a starfish-like root, which is brittle and needs very careful handling when you transplant it. I think this is probably the reason why some people fail to establish the eremurus satisfactorily. It should be moved in the last weeks of September or the first weeks of October, and it should be moved with the least possible delay. The roots should never be allowed to wait, shrivelling, out of the ground. Plant them instantly, as soon as they arrive from the nursery. Spread out the roots, flat, in a rather rich loamy soil, and cover them over with some bracken to protect them from frost during their first winter. Plant them under the shelter of a hedge, if you can; they dislike a strong wind, and the magnificence of their spires will show up better for the backing of a dark hedge. They like lime and sunshine.

Thus established, the fox-tail lily should give increasing delight as the years go by. They get better and better as they grow older and older, throwing up more and more spires of flower from each crown of their starfish root. I must admit that they cost about 7s. 6d. each, but it is a good investment. There are several sorts obtainable: the giant *Eremurus robustus*, which flowers in June, and then the smaller ones, the Shelford hybrids and the Warei hybrids in their strange colours. Splendid things; torches of pale colour, towering, dwarfing the ordinary little annuals. Aristocrats of the garden, they are well worth the three half-crowns they cost.

July 29, 1951

July is the best month for dividing the coloured primroses and polyantha, but the first week of August is not too late, especially if the ground is moist. I suppose they are amongst the easiest plants to grow; one sees them everywhere, in sun, in shade, in borders, in odd corners, most accommodating and obliging, though they do best with a little shade either from light woodland or under a north wall. They seem to prefer a rather heavy soil; and every three years or so they should be increased by division, pulling the clump gently apart and replanting the rooted pieces, a very economical method of multiplying the supply.

All this is A B C to every gardener, and it is really of the more difficult sorts that I want to write. How many of us have been tempted by the old varieties, and how many of us have come to grief! One does see the old double purple, and double lilac, and the double white which is like a tiny centifolia rose; but how seldom one sees the dark red Madame Pompadour or the Cloth of Gold.

The old doubles are probably the easiest to keep going, a supposition confirmed by the fact that they are also the cheapest to buy. Jack-in-the-green, with his ruff, is reliable, but as for some of the others it must be admitted that they defy even the expert. I have been making inquiries from various growers, and find a remarkable unanimity of opinion. It seems to be generally agreed that they are gross feeders, needing a strong diet of rotted manure or compost at their roots, and a yearly change of situation because they so quickly exhaust the soil. You must either dig them up and remake their bed and replant them in it, or dig them up and replant them in a freshly prepared bed somewhere else. Feed, feed, feed, is their motto. Never allow them to become parched, and never allow the clumps to become overcrowded. The soil should be stiff, not light. Then you may hope for some success.

There are some newer varieties which have much of the charm of old primroses. *Garryard Guinevere*, with bronze leaves and pinkish-lilac flowers, is easy; so are *Betty Green*, red, and *Craddock's White*. *Marie Crousse*, pink edged with white, is not too difficult, nor are *E. R. Janes* and *Arthur Dumoulin*, which might easily be mistaken for a Parma violet. They are all worth trying, especially if you live in Scotland or Eire, where they seem best to thrive. There is something in that damp climate which suits them. If you live in England, you must try to make up to them in other ways for the softness and humidity they pine for, and lack. Homesickness overtakes them; they peter out; they die.

July 6, 1952

Most people are already familiar with the miniature roses *Roulettii* and *Oakington Ruby*, but perhaps not everyone realizes that these pretty dwarfs are now obtainable in other varieties. Seldom growing more than eight to twelve inches high, thus taking up the minimum of space, they are ideal for the very small garden, or for a child's garden, or for a rockery, or for a deep stone trough raised to eye-level where their midget blooms can be easily appreciated. I can also imagine them giving much interest and pleasure grown in the window-box of an invalid's room. They are not particular as to soil, though like all roses they enjoy full sun. They can all be obtained in pots and thus can be put out at any season of the year, even now at the height of summer. They are not impossibly expensive, averaging 10s. for three, or in collections of three, five and six, ranging respectively from 10s. to 17s. 6d. Nothing extra for postage or packing.*

Some of their names are rather coy, but perhaps that was only to be expected. *Sweet Fairy*, pale pink; *Little Princess*, double white; *Baby Crimson*; *Bo*

* From Thomas Robinson, Porchester Nurseries, Carlton, Nottingham.

Peep, a tiny polyantha, double rose-pink; *Maid Marion*, dark red; *Pam*, rose-pink; *Cinderella*, white flushed pink, a little more expensive at 12s. 6d. for three, the same price as *Red Elf*. *Pumila* is the giant of the group, attaining fifteen inches, crimson with a white eye. *Roulettii* is still the smallest, seldom exceeding six inches.

I don't as a rule care much for roses grown as standards; they look top-heavy with their great blooms on one thin leg like a crane; but it would be a sour heart that could resist the appeal of standards nine to twelve inches in height, with flowers to scale. One of the charms, to me, of the little roses is that they give no suggestion of a cramped deformity, such as one finds in dwarfed Japanese trees. They are just simply roses seen through the wrong end of opera-glasses.

The standards, by the way, are more expensive than the bushes; they cost 10s. each.

July 13, 1952

The bushes of Mezereon or *Daphne mezereum* should now be hung with their fruits, if the birds have not already pecked them off. It is well worth while to save and sow some of them, for they germinate very freely and a crop of young plants is the result. I am told on good authority that the Daphne is not very long-lived but has a better expectation of life when it is growing on its own roots, i.e. has not been grafted, so the moral of growing it from seed (or cuttings) is obvious.

The Mezereon seems to share with the Madonna lily a predilection for cottage gardens. Bushes five feet high and four feet wide carry their wine-coloured bloom on the naked stems year after year in February and March in a luxuriance unknown to grander gardens where far more trouble is taken about them. Cottagers apparently just stick it in everywhere, when, with the perversity of an inverted snobbishness, it grows. It is useless to try to explain this peculiar psychology of certain plants. One must accept it and do the best one can to reproduce the conditions they appear to enjoy.

After struggling for years to induce *Daphne mezereum* to thrive in my garden, I have at last achieved a miserable degree of success by planting it in a mixture of leaf-mould and sand, in the broken shade of some trees of Kentish cob-nuts. This is the treatment I would recommend: a spongy soil with overhead shade in summer. After all, the Mezereon is sometimes claimed as a native of Britain, growing in woods, so it seems reasonable to plant it in the sort of soil it would be likely to encounter in its natural habitat, full of decayed leaves and humus, rich with the fallen wealth of centuries.

On the other hand, some people will tell you that it never thrives better than in a hot, dry place, such as a gravelly path right up against the house. So what is one to believe?

There are two kinds of *Daphne mezereum*. One is the familiar claret-coloured one, pink as a *Vin Rosé* held up to the light in a *carafe*. The other is white, *Daphne mezereum alba*. They have different-coloured berries. The familiar one has bright red berries. The white form has bright yellow berries. I would strongly advise you to poke some seeds of both into small pots, instead of letting the birds have them. Daphnes do not transplant well, and should always be tipped straight out of a pot, like a broom or a clematis.

I have not observed seed on any of the other Daphnes, with the exception of the scentless *D. acutiloba*, but there is a prostrate one called *Blagayana*, ivory in colour and intensely sweet-scented in the early spring. This likes to be layered and weighted down with stones at every point where the layer has been inserted. It will then spread outwards into a mat of fresh growth, which may eventually attain a width of six feet or more. It is a delight to pick in the cold days of March, to bring into the warmth of a room when the honeyed smell floats round into stray corners with a suggestion of bees and summer airs. The same is true of *Daphne odora*, but that unfortunately is not quite hardy and needs the protection of glass throughout the frosty months, either in a greenhouse or under a cloche.

July 20, 1952

This week I should like to write on a subject of general gardening interest, as a change from merely recommending certain plants to grow. These remarks will inevitably apply to the larger type of garden where plants can be grown in generous masses, but I think and hope that they may also be applicable to the small garden as a matter of principle.

You see, I believe that one ought always to regard a garden in terms of architecture as well as of colour. One has huge lumps of, let us say, the shrub roses making large voluminous bushes like a Victorian crinoline, or flinging themselves about in wild sprays; or, putting it another way, some plants make round fat bushes, and seem to demand a contrast in a tall sharp plant, say delphiniums, sticking up in a cathedral spire of bright blue amongst the roses instead of in the orthodox way at the back of a herbaceous border. It is all a question of shape. Architectural shape, demanding the pointed thin ones amongst the fat rounds, as a minaret rises above the dome of a mosque.

Let me say here, for the small garden, that one might happily cause some spikes of the pink *Linaria Canon J. Went* to rise above a carpeting of low pansies or violas. This Linaria comes true from seed; sows itself everywhere like a welcome, not an unwelcome, weed; and is as pretty a thing as you could wish to have in quantities for picking for the house indoors.

Another fine thing to make great steeples is *Yucca gloriosa*. This will tower in a vast heavy ivory pyramid in July, of a powerful architectural value. It does not flower every year, so you must have at least three plants in order to get a yearly blooming, and for this you need a certain amount of space. I did begin by saying that this article would be addressed to people with the larger type of garden; but if the smaller garden can spare even three yards of room in a corner, *Yucca gloriosa* will come as a fine surprise on the grand scale in July, and will carry out my contention that you want variety of shape and height to make an aesthetic composition instead of just an amorphous muddle. The Yucca, being a child of the desert in Mexico and some of the hotter parts of the United States, such as California, likes the driest possible place and the sunniest, but on the whole accommodates itself very obligingly to our soil and climate.

July 27, 1952

Often I am asked to recommend hedging plants for small or brand-new gardens, sometimes in order to shut out the neighbour, sometimes in order to shut out livestock of any size from rabbits to cows. Usually, for the former, I fall back upon hornbeam, which is rapid of growth, inexpensive to buy, pleasant to look at, whether green in spring and summer or brown in autumn or winter, a grand nesting place for birds, and willing to grow to any height you want it, up to fifteen or twenty feet if necessary. For the latter, I think at once of those two great stand-bys, *Berberis darwinii* and *Berberis stenophylla*, so decorative in the early part of the year with their orange and yellow flowers, respectively; both evergreen, with dark blue berries in autumn. Rabbits are said to have a particular but understandable aversion to making their way through a hedge of prickly berberis.

I now realize, however, that there are a lot of hedging plants which I have never hitherto recommended in this column. *Pyracantha*, for example. We are all well accustomed to seeing *Pyracantha* growing up the wall of a house, smothered in red or yellow berries in autumn, but it is seldom recognized that it will make a fine thorny hedge, obedient to any amount of clipping, and angry enough with its thorns to keep out any invader. I would recommend *Pyracantha Lalandei* or *Pyracantha angustifolia* to make a tough hedge, disagreeable to intruders but agreeable to yourselves, looking out on to it from the windows of your house.

There are many other things that may be planted to form a break between your garden and the next. A hedge of lilac, for instance; or a hedge of *Cydonia*, the Japanese quince, which most people still call Japonica, now called *Chaenomeles*; or a hedge of the shrubby roses which need so little attention; or a hedge of *Osmanthus delavayi*, evergreen, with sweet-scented white flowers in April or May. There are endless variations possible. No need to stick to the old privet or laurel of our Victorian grandfathers, dark, dank, dusty, and dull – how deadly dull.

August

August 5, 1951

In the summer days before the war, the village flower-show, which would be better called a produce-show, was quite a grand affair. There were two marquees, large enough to dwarf the Miniature-Gardens-on-Plates and the Victorian-Posy-in-an-Egg-cup into looking even tinier. The Supper-dish for Five People at one and ninepence did not necessarily have to be meatless in 1939. The local nurserymen staged handsome exhibits *Not for competition*, raising the standard and causing the Amateurs-without-help (Class A), the Amateurs-with-help (Class B), and the cottagers (Class C), Each Entry 2d., to exclaim 'Coo, look at that!' determined that next year at the show they would try to emulate their professional neighbours.

Those good days disappeared for a time; the village could no longer afford marquees, and had to arrange its show, more modestly, in any shelter it could get: the corrugated-iron shelter of the Women's Institute, or the Parish Room, or a barn borrowed from a farmer. It had to be staged somehow or somewhere, to keep the show going and to prevent interest from dying out.

Now, better days are returning. Marquees have reappeared, and the big nurserymen of the county are again willing to show their wares. The sumptuous effect of the Best Box of Vegetables again graces the trestle tables and how magnificent they are in shape and colour, those mixed collections of red tomatoes, orange carrots, ivory parsnips, pale potatoes freshly washed in milk, jade-green lettuce, blood-red beetroot, emerald peas, with one pod split open, and marrows like stranded whales.

How fine, indeed, in their assembly are the fruits of the earth, simply, and by cottagers, displayed. Great hairy gooseberries set out on kitchen plates; blackcurrants the size of marbles; raspberries like pink thimbles made for a giantess; and some soft peaches and brown figs from the greenhouse of an Amateur-with-help. How rural are the eggs, the bunches of herbs, the home-made cakes, the coloured jars of jam, the golden honey. How pretty the baskets of mixed flowers, and how touching the jam-pots of wild flowers and grasses collected by the children.

Everyone comes in clothes that seem to match the exhibits, flowered frocks, bright scarves, and here and there a sunbonnet. The children have been scrubbed until their cheeks shine. One knows that they are little scamps really, but today you could not convince even a policeman that they had ever climbed the gate into an orchard. There are some speeches, and everybody says something amiable about everybody else; local feuds are forgotten for the day. There is no ill-feeling when the red, blue, and green tickets meaning 1st, 2nd, and 3rd prizes have been hopefully inspected on the cards, nor any grievance against the glum silence of no ticket at all, for it is recognized that the judges have been fair and impartial. Someone is in charge of a gramophone, and in the evening after the prizes have been distributed there may be some dancing in the field outside. The corn is ripening down in the valley; the young moon hangs over the church tower, and a little breeze springs up to ruffle the leaves of the poplars.

I love the village flower-show; I prefer it even to the village fête, or *feet* as they usually pronounce it. This has a Bank Holiday tang about it, with a loudspeaker van blaring away, and squalid litter left blowing about somebody's garden. What I like about the show is its complete lack of self-consciousness. Here is no organized entertainment: no folk-dancing at 5 p.m. which might once have been spontaneous but now certainly isn't, except in a few remote villages; no one selling raffle tickets for a bottle of whisky; no pot-shots taken with darts at the effigy of some unpopular foreign dictator. The village show is honest-to-God, whatever that may mean, and I think it does mean something. It means honest work and long experience, no nonsense about green fingers, which is one of the most slip-shod, easy-going, indulgent expressions ever invented. Ask any gardener or countryman what he thinks of it, and you will be rewarded as you deserve by a slow cynical grin and no verbal answer at all, except possibly 'Green fingers, my foot!'

He knows better. He knows that hard digging, rich feeding, deep knowledge, and constant care, are the only way to produce the prize-winning exhibits he puts on to the trestle tables at his annual local show, for the admiration and esteem of his neighbours in competition.

There is no short cut to success in prize-taking, or to the silver trophy which has to be won three years running for the best exhibit on points and which will eventually stand between the pair of Staffordshire china dogs on the mantelpiece in the front parlour, suitably inscribed with the name of the winner, a record of triumph, and (one hopes) an incentive to his children and grandchildren for many years to come.

August 5, 1951

A lot of people have a lot of trouble with lilies. I have myself. I try. I fail. I despair. Then I try again. Only last week did it occur to me to go and ask for advice from a famous grower of lilies in my neighbourhood, which was the obvious and sensible thing to do. I might have thought of it before. Surely he will not mind my passing on the hints he gave me, especially if it leads to an encouragement to grow some varieties of this supremely beautiful family.

There are four cardinal points, he said, like the compass. Point 1: good drainage is essential; no stagnant moisture, even if it means digging out a hole and putting a layer of crocks or coarse clinker at the bottom. Point 2: make up a suitable bed to receive your bulbs, a bed rich in humus, which means leaf-mould, peat, compost, chopped bracken, or whatever form of humus you can command. Point 3: never plant lily bulbs which have been out of the ground too long or have had their basal roots cut off. Reject these, even if you find them offered at cheap rates in the horticultural department of some chain stores. Lily bulbs should be lifted fresh and replanted quickly, with their basal roots intact; therefore it is advisable to obtain them from any reputable nurseryman, who will pack them in moist peat and will never allow them to dry out before dispatch. Point 4: divide when they become overcrowded.

To these hints I might add another. Most lilies dislike what professional gardeners call 'movement of air', which in plain English means wind or a draught. I have also discovered by experience that the Regal lily, *Lilium regale*, likes growing amongst some covering shelter such as Southernwood (Old Man) or one of the artemisias, I suppose because the foliage gives protection to the young lily-growth against late frosts, but also because some plants take kindly to one another in association. Certainly the long white trumpets of the lily look their majestic best emerging above the grey-green cloud of these fluffy, gentle, aromatic herbs.

These notes on lilies are absurdly incomplete. I thought I would amplify them next Sunday, especially because August is the month to plant the Madonna lily, the *L. candidum*, that virginal lily, the flower of the Annunciation, which flourishes for the cottager and often refuses to flourish in grander gardens.

August 12, 1951

Promises must be fulfilled. I said I would write something more about lilies, especially the Madonna lily, *Lilium candidum*, whose bulbs ought to be planted in this month of August. Never having grown it successfully, I am the last person to preach about it, and my remarks must be taken as theoretical.

> Where did Gabriel get a lily
> In the month of March?

I once read, and have never forgotten, those two lines in a poem I have never been able to trace.* Wherever that bright Archangel found his lily, it was certainly not in the more ambitious sort of garden. It prefers the humbler home. There is an old tradition that the Madonna lily throve best in cottage gardens because the housewife was in the habit of chucking out her pail of soap-suds all over the flower-bed. Curiously enough, this tradition is now confirmed by the advice that the young growth of these lilies should be sprayed with a lather of soft-soap and water, to prevent the disease called *Botrytis*. Thus do these old wives' tales sometimes justify themselves.

The Madonna lily should be planted now without delay. There is a variety called *Salonica*, because it grows there, which is said to be more resistant to *Botrytis*, but whichever variety you plant put in the bulbs so shallow as to rest almost on top of the soil, showing their noses. If you bury them too deep they will have to shove themselves up in that wise way that plants have, knowing what suits them even better than we know, but this is giving them a lot of trouble and struggle which you might have spared them. So plant them shallow, and plant them as soon as they arrive; don't leave the bulbs lying about to get dry. And once planted, leave them alone. Don't dig them up to move

* It so happened that the author of these lines read this article and sent me the full text of the poem, which had been 'written many years ago and appeared in *Country Life*'. She has now given me permission to reprint it here.

LADY DAY

Where did Gabriel get a lily,
In the month of March,
When the green
Is hardly seen
On the early larch?
  Though I know
  Just where they grow,
I have pulled no daffodilly.
Where did Gabriel get a lily
In the month of March?
  Could I bring
  The tardy Spring
  Under Her foot's arch,
  Near or far
  The primrose star
Should bloom with violets, – willy-nilly.
  Where did Gabriel get a lily
  In the month of March?

GRACE JAMES

them to another place. Let them stay put. They are not modern-minded, wanting to roam about; they are statically minded; they are fond of their home, once you have induced them to take to it.

The Madonna lily is an exception to the general rule that lilies demand plenty of humus. It likes lime, which may take the form of old mortar rubble, and it likes a scratchy soil. The scratchy soil idea confirms the old theory that part of their success in cottage gardens was due to the fact that the grit from the surface of the lanes blew over the hedge and worked its way into the ground. Even today, when few country lanes are tarred, this may still hold good, and I have known cottagers send out their little boys with a shovel and a box mounted on old pram wheels to collect grit for the garden. It is never wise to disregard the sagacity of those who do not learn their lore from books.

August 19, 1951
People often ask what plants are suitable for a shady situation, by which they mean either the north side of a wall or house, or in the shadow cast by trees. There are so many such plants that no one need despair. A number of shrubby things will do well, such as the azaleas, the Kalmias, the rhododendrons, and a pretty, seldom seen, low-growing shrub with waxy white pendent flowers called *Zenobia pulverulenta*, always provided that the soil is lime-free for all these subjects. The many cotoneasters and berberis have no objection to shade, and are less pernickety as to soil. *Daphne laureola* will thrive, and so will *Viburnum burkwoodii*, very easy and sweet-scented, making a big bush. The well-known Snowberry, *Symphoricarpos racemosus*, will grow anywhere and is attractive in autumn with its ivory berries and tangle of black twigs. And if you want something more choice than the Snowberry, there are many magnolias which enjoy the protection of a north wall: *M. Lennei*, wine-pink; *M. soulangeana*, white; and *M. liliiflora Nigra*, a deep claret colour, which has the advantage of a very long-flowering season, all through May and June, with a few odd flowers appearing even in July and August. The magnolias all appreciate some peat or leaf-mould to fill in the hole you dig out when you plant them, and it is important not to let them suffer from drought before they have had time to become established.

If, however, you have no space for these rather large shrubs, there are plenty of things other than shrubs to fill up an un-sunny border. There are the foxgloves, which can now be obtained in varieties far superior to the woodland foxglove, flowering all round the stem, and in colours preferable to the old magenta, lovely though that may look in the woods. The Excelsior strain flowers all round; you can get seed from Messrs Sutton, Reading. The columbines will also tolerate shade, and there is a blue one called *Hensol Harebell* which I think looks better in an out-of-the-way corner than the long-spurred garden varieties. There is also a charming old plant called *Astrantia*, the Masterwort, seldom seen now except in cottage gardens, which will ramp away in an unpromising shady place and increase itself by seed. The *Epimediums* should not be overlooked; they make clumps of pretty foliage and throw up delicate sprays of flower-like tiny orchids in May. The hellebores and the lily of the valley, the primroses and the polyanthus, the candelabra primulas, and, as you grow more ambitious, the blue poppy *Meconopsis baileyi*, which is the dream of every gardener, will all take happily to a shaded home, especially if some moisture keeps them fresh.

August 26, 1951

In the hope of picking up some new ideas, I have just spent ten days visiting gardens, either famous or modest, in the West of England. My interest was concentrated on the shrubs or trees or climbers that one might find flowering at this jejune time of year; something I didn't know, or else through ignorance or prejudice had never attempted to grow. I must say at once that I was converted to some of the hydrangeas, not the mop-headed sort called *hortensis*, but the sort with a flat centre ringed with open flowers. They are known as *Hydrangea aspera*, and there are some decorative forms called *Villosa* and *Sargentiana*. A well-grown bush, pouring over a paved path or covering the angle of a flight of steps, is a rich and rewarding sight in August, when everything becomes heavy and dark and lumpish.

I was also impressed by the sight of acanthus in flower. Not only has this plant very noble leaves, looking fine and classical at any time of year, but its mauve flower spike is of great value in the August border. I saw also an immense growth of *Cotoneaster rotundifolia*, sweeping its petticoats to the ground, as in an old-time curtsey, red-berried among its small, dark green leaves. I saw also a little tree which particularly took my fancy; this was the Bladder Senna, *Colutea arborescens*, with bronze, pea-like flowers and large seed-pods looking as though they would pop with a small bang, like a blown-up paper bag, if you burst them between your hands. This little tree amused me, because it carried its flowers and its seed-pods at the same time. In one garden where I saw it the pods were turning pink, very pretty amongst the bronzy flowers.

The indigoferas were much in evidence, making me wonder, as I had often wondered before, why these graceful shrubs were not more freely planted. They throw out long sprays, seven or eight feet in length, dangling with pinkish, vetch-like flowers in August and September. *Indigofera potaninii* is a pale, pretty pink;

I. gerardiana is deeper in colour, with more mauve in it, and is perhaps the more showy of the two. They should both, I think, be planted in conjunction, so that their sprays can mingle in a cloud of the two different colours. I should like to see them combined with a front planting of a lovely new scabious, called *Grey Lady*, which I also discovered on my travels, and backed by a grey-blue clematis called *Perle d'Azur*. Anyone fortunate enough to have a wall could train the clematis on that, otherwise a couple of tall poles would support it.

August 3, 1952

This is the moment to order and plant the bulbs of *Amaryllis belladonna*, commonly called the Belladonna lily. Unlike Milton's Amaryllis, she will not sport in the shade; in fact she demands the hottest and sunniest place to produce her flowers at all. Given such a place, however, at the foot of a south-facing wall, or, ideally, a greenhouse wall, she will produce sheaves of pinkish-mauve trumpets on a naked stem which is in itself of a beautiful bloomy plum colour, in late September and October, just at the time when flowers for the house are rare, apart from the dahlias and chrysanthemums and the Japanese anemone.

Amaryllis belladonna, who is threatened before long with a change of name to *Callicore rosea*, is a native of South Africa and is reasonably hardy in the southern half of England. I would not recommend her for northern gardens, unless she could command special care, by which I mean protection in winter and at that ticklish moment when the growth begins to appear above the ground. In spring, the bulbs throw up their leaf growth, and should then be kept well watered while the leaves are green. A mulch of rotted manure or compost or leaf-mould will help, spread over the ground in May. When the leaves turn yellow and die down the bulbs can be left to themselves, to get dry and sun-baked, waiting for the flower to appear in autumn. They cost about 2s. each; or for anyone who can afford to be more extravagant, the variety called *Rubra* can be obtained at 5s. a bulb, and will throw a flower of a deeper, richer pink. This all sounds extravagant, but you will be surprised to find how quickly the bulbs increase in quantity after a few years, when they can be lifted in July or August, and the new little bulbs replanted to extend the clump. They can be expected to come to flowering size within a year or two. You can, if you like, regard this as a hint to cadge within the next few weeks some thinnings of overcrowded bulbs from the garden of a fortunate friend. But do remember that sun is all-important. It is remarkable what a difference even a few hours of afternoon shade will make to the crop of flowers. I know, because I have tried it, some in sun all day, and some in partial shade. The ones in partial shade don't flower at all; the ones in full sun flower generously.

August 10, 1952

I have a myrtle growing on a wall. It is only the common myrtle, *Myrtus communis*, but I think you would have to travel far afield to find a lovelier shrub for July and August flowering. The small, pointed, dark green leaves are smothered at this time of year by a mass of white flowers with quivering centres of the palest green-yellow, so delicate in their white and gold that it appears as though a cloud of butterflies had alighted on the dark shrub.

The myrtle is a plant full of romantic associations in mythology and poetry, the sacred emblem of Venus and of love, though why Milton called it brown I never could understand, unless he was referring to the fact that the leaves, which are by way of being evergreen, do turn brown in frosty weather or under a cold wind. Even if it gets cut down in winter there is nothing to worry about, for it springs up again, at any rate in the South of England. In the north it might be grateful for a covering of ashes or fir branches over the roots. It strikes very easily from cuttings, and a plant in a pot is a pretty thing to possess, especially if it can be stood near the house door, where the aromatic leaves may be pinched as you go in and out. In very mild counties, such as Cornwall, it should not require the protection of a wall, but may be grown as a bush or small tree in the open, or even, which I think should be most charming of all, into a small grove suggestive of Greece and her nymphs.

The flowers are followed by little inky berries, which in their turn are quite decorative, and would probably grow if you sowed a handful of them.

In this connection, I might mention the Bog myrtle, though it is not really a myrtle except in common parlance. It is a native of Britain, and thus by some people might be regarded as a weed, but for its strong, resinous scent, which gives it its second lovely name, Sweet Gale; it is well worth bringing in from the moors if you come across it, and give it a place in a rough corner, where it will catch the prevailing wind. It does, however, exact a purely acid soil, as peaty as possible, so is of no use to the dwellers on chalk or lime. The more moisture it gets the better, when it will spread by means of its underground roots. Travellers across Dartmoor may remember getting unexpected whiffs, like passing through a pine forest on a warm day.

August 17, 1952

The bulb catalogues arrive by every post, leaving us in a state of confused temptation. It is suitable to remember that today, August 17th, is the feast of Saint Hyacinth, who lived in Poland during the thirteenth century, though Saint Hyacinth has nothing to do with the bulbs we are about to order for planting in fibre in bowls or outdoors in the garden. It would be far more appropriate to remember the pagan Hyacinthus, the beautiful youth beloved of Apollo, who changed the boy's murdered body into the flower we still call by his name.

In so short an article I can do no more than mention a few of the bulbs I cannot resist. This will just be a personal list representing a personal taste. Taking the tulips first, I like the great yellow *Mongolia*, and the great white *Carrara* and *Zwanenberg*. I like *The Bishop*, deep violet in colour, sturdy and reliable, on a strong stem, tall, coming up year after year. I like the little fringe-edged *Sundew*, of a deep rose colour, cheap at 5s. a dozen and seldom seen. I like all the fantastic Parrot tulips, wild in their colouring, floppy in their growth, not stiff as the Darwins, a tulip to pick for the house rather than to regard as a flower for the garden. Then I like the broken tulips, the Rembrandts, Bizarres, and the Bybloemens, all in their different feathery stripes and flakes; and I must not omit the early little *Couleur Cardinal*, which puts up as pretty and neat a chalice of plummy bloom as any ecclesiastic could wish to see. I always think of it as a young nephew of *The Bishop*, and should like to see them planted together. Nepotism, if you like to call it that. Only they would not flower at the same time.

Leaving the tulips, we come to the narcissi; and here again we find ourselves in a confusion. I cannot here cope with the innumerable sorts, but would like to draw your attention to some of the smaller ones, *Canaliculatus*, for instance, so sweet-scented, and *Triandrus albus*, called Angel's Tears; and also to the single jonquil, bright yellow and strong of scent. These are treasures for the appreciative grower.

Please do not forget the fritillaries. They cost so little, 3s. a dozen, and they increase so surprisingly in grass. They sow themselves, appearing in odd corners where they were never planted.

August 24, 1952
I know I have written before now about the advantages of raising lilies from seed, but that was several years ago, and I think I might return to the charge. This method of obtaining lilies for nothing requires a considerable amount of patience, three to four years before you get a bulb old enough to flower, but how rewarding is the result. It also ensures that your bulbs have not been left lying about to dry up, a fatal destiny for any lily. It means also that you are not getting a stock infected by any virus disease; the plants may develop it later on, since no one can guarantee against this, but at least you know that you have started clean.

I have found that seeds sown in fairly deep pans will make little bulbs ready to plant out in their second season. The seeds can also be sown in a prepared seed-bed in drills in the open, but pans are more easily controlled, especially in the matter of weeding. Stand them on a floor of ashes to prevent the incursion of undesirable insects.

Lilies, in my experience, are tricky and unpredictable. Some of them do not object to lime in the soil; others will have nothing to say to it. For this division of taste you must consult the catalogue of a good lily nurseryman,* which will give you detailed comments on each separate variety. I cannot generalize here; but as I recently had the benefit of a visit from a well-known lily grower, I might pass on some crumbs of his wisdom.

Good drainage, he said, is essential to all lilies; they like moisture, but they will not tolerate a wetly stagnant bed. Therefore, when you dig out the site in which you intend to plant them, filling it up with the kind of soil they require – leaf-mould and loam and sand as a general rule – make sure it has a layer of rough drainage placed at the bottom. Then, he said, lilies dislike being blown about by the wind, so give them an abode within the shelter of shrubs. Finally, he said, remember that nothing makes a finer mulch than bracken cut green, chopped up into short pieces, and allowed to rot. He deprecated the use of lawn-grass mowings; of artificial fertilizers; and of over-fresh organic manure. Manure, he said, should never be allowed to come into contact with the bulb itself: it should be placed well beneath it, or used as a top mulch. Bone-meal, he said, was always safe and useful.

August 31, 1952

A note on some roses not often seen. *Comtesse du Cayla*, a China rose, so red in the stem on young wood as to appear transparent in a bright light; very pointed in the coral-coloured bud; very early to flower, continuing to flower throughout the summer until the frosts come (I once picked a bunch on Christmas morning); somewhat romantic in her associations, for the lady in whose honour she is named was the mistress of Louis XVIII; altogether a desirable rose, not liable to black spot or mildew; needing little pruning apart from the removal of wood when it has become too old, say, every two or three years. *Mutabilis*, or *Rosa turkestanica*,† makes an amusing bush, five to six feet high and correspondingly wide, covered throughout the summer with single flowers in different colours, yellow, dusky red, and coppery, all out at the same time. It is perhaps a trifle tender, and thus a sheltered corner will suit this particular harlequin.

* For instance, Messrs Constable or Messrs Wallace, see p. 271 for addresses.

† *Comtesse du Cayla* and *R. turkestanica* from Messrs T. Hilling; address on p. 273.

If you want a very vigorous climber, making an incredible length of growth in one season, do try to obtain *Rosa filipes*.* It is ideal for growing into an old tree, which it will quickly drape with pale green dangling trails and clusters of small white yellow-centred flowers. I can only describe the general effect as lacy, with myriads of little golden eyes looking down at you from amongst the lace. This sounds like a fanciful description, of the kind I abhor in other writers on horticultural subjects, but really there are times when one is reduced to such low depths in the struggle to convey the impression one has oneself derived, on some perfect summer evening when everything is breathless, and one just sits, and gazes, and tries to sum up what one is seeing, mixed in with the sounds of a summer night – the young owls hissing in their nest over the cowshed, the bray of a donkey, the plop of an acorn into the pool.

Filipes means thread-like, or with thread-like stems, so perhaps my comparison to lace is not so fanciful, after all. Certainly the reticulation of the long strands overhead, clumped with the white clusters, faintly sweet-scented, always makes me think of some frock of faded green, trimmed with Point d'Alençon – or is it Point de Venise that I mean?

---

* *Rosa filipes* from J. Russell, Sunningdale Nurseries, Windlesham, Surrey.

September

It surprises me always when people fail to recognize the common rosemary. 'What is that?' they say, looking at the great dark green bushes that sprawl so generously over the paths at the entrance to the place where I live. I should have thought that rosemary was one of our most common plants, if only for the sake of its sentimental associations. It was said to have the peculiar property of strengthening the memory, and thus became a symbol of fidelity for lovers. 'A sprig of it hath a dumb language,' said Sir Thomas More; and another legend connects it with the age of Our Lord, thirty-three years, after which it stops growing in height but never in width. A romantic plant, yet so oddly, it seems, unknown.

There are several different forms of the rosemary. There is the ordinary bushy type, *Rosmarinus officinalis*, which can be grown either as a bush or clipped into shape as a hedge. I don't like it so well as a hedge, because the constant clipping means the loss of the flowers which are half its beauty, but all the same it makes a dense neat hedge if you want one. Do not cut back into the old wood. Then there is the Corsican rosemary, *R. Angustifolius Corsicus* with a more feathery growth of leaf and bright blue flowers, almost gentian blue; it is less tough-looking than the common rosemary, and perhaps not quite so hardy, but so lovely a thing that it well deserves a sheltered corner. It hates cold winds. The fastigiate or pyramidal rosemary, pleasingly called *Miss Jessup's Upright*, will make sentinels six feet high within a couple of years. (Who was Miss Jessup, I wonder?) There is also a creeping form, suitable for rock gardens, called *Prostratus*, but this is not very hardy and I would not recommend it to anybody not living in the warmer counties. If it can be persuaded to thrive, however, as it might be induced to do with its roots sheltering a long way back between stones, away from frost and damp, it makes a grateful mat of evergreen and a good covering plant for little early bulbs coming up through it, such as the Lady Tulip, *T. clusiana*, or the jonquils, or the miniature narcissi such as *N. juncifolius*, so sweet-scented.

It should not be forgotten, either, that a white-flowered form of the common rosemary is obtainable, making a change from the blue-flowered form more usually seen.

Most of the rosemaries will flourish anywhere in the sun, preferring a light soil, even a poor sandy stony soil, and will root very easily from cuttings taken off in September, stuck firmly into sand, and left to grow on until next spring when they can be planted out.

September 9, 1951

A most pleasing and original suggestion reaches me in a nurseryman's catalogue. It is the sort of suggestion which could provide extra colour and interest in a small garden, without taking up too much space and without involving too much labour. It is, simply, the idea of growing low Alpines in a narrow border on both sides of the path running from your gate to your door, or, of course, on both sides or even one side of any path you may find suitable.

By 'low' Alpines I do not mean those plants which occur only on the lower slopes of mountains, a technical term in horticulture, as opposed to the 'high' Alpines. I mean flat-growing; close to the ground; the sorts that make little tufts and squabs and cushions and pools of colour when in flower, and neat tight bumps of grey or green for the rest of the year when the flowers have gone over. The range of choice is wide. Saxifrages, Silene, stonecrops, thrift, Raoulia, Acaene, Androsace, aubrietia in moderation, thyme, *Achillea argentea*, *Erinus alpinus*, *Tunica saxifraga*, *Morisia hypogea*, *Bellis Dresden China*, sempervivum or houseleeks, some campanulas such as *C. garganica*, so easy and self-sowing – the list is endless, and gives scope for much variety.

I would not restrict it only to the rugs and mats and pillows, but would break its level with some inches of flower-stalks, such as the orange Alpine poppy, *Papaver alpinum*, and some violas such as *V. gracilis* or *V. bosniaca*, and some clumps of dianthus such as the Cheddar pink or the prettily named Dad's Favourite, and even some primroses specially chosen, such as *Rosea* or *Garryard*, *Ganymede* or *Betty Green*, and any other favourite which may occur to you. This list is not intended to dictate. It is intended only to suggest that a ribbon or band of colour, no more than twelve inches wide, might well wend its flat way beside a path in even the most conventional garden.

But if you had a garden on a slope, in a hilly district, what an opportunity would be yours! Then your flat ribbon would become a rill, a rivulet, a beck, a burn, a brook, pouring crookedly downhill between stones towards the trout-stream flowing along the valley at the bottom. I suppose some people do possess gardens like that, in Gloucestershire for instance, or in Cumberland, or in the Highlands. Let those fortunate ones take notice, and, dipping an enormous paint-brush into the wealth offered by the autumn catalogues, splash its rainbow result wherever their steps may lead them.

September 16, 1951

A correspondent wants me to write about gadgets. He points out, with commendable good sense, that one hesitates to spend money on such things unless one can be sure that they will justify their cost. Now this is just the difficulty. I have found by experience that gadgets, however ingenious and alluring, rarely replace with advantage the old and tried tools. One always goes back, in the end, to the simple designs that have proved themselves best adapted to their use throughout the centuries. It would be hard, indeed, to improve upon the spade, the fork, the shovel, the shears, the birch-broom, the rake, or even the little humble trowel.

Nevertheless there are certain things which one discovers during a lifetime of gardening, not gadgets exactly, but helpful hints. I see that I shall have to make two articles out of this subject, the first one to be concerned entirely with string. For example, I find it far more economical to buy a huge ball of hop-twine, such as we use in our Kentish hop-gardens, three times the size of any known football, instead of many balls of tarred twine. As hop-twine will last for two or three years without rotting, it is invaluable for securing big shrubs or shrub-roses to their stakes. It is also possible to buy old stock of telephone wire by the mile, the wire enclosed in some sort of rubber, at £2 15s. a mile, but who wants a mile? And anyway, I find that the rubber soon perishes. Far more generally useful are those spools of green twist, which, neatly rolled in a paper cylinder, mendaciously imply that they will remain tidily exuding their life down to its last inch. Surely I am not the only gardener to find that after the first fifty yards or so you come up against an impossible tangle, when, in desperation, you cut disorderly ends here and there.

A way out of this muddle is to put your spool into a tin, say an old slug-bait tin, piercing a hole in the top of the lid. You should pierce the hole *outwards*, otherwise the jagged points of the hole will catch the string, interrupting its free run.

Another brief hint. One can now buy packets of paper strips about four inches long and a quarter of an inch wide, reinforced by a thin wire up the middle, which makes them both flexible and tough. You twiddle them into any circlet you want and thus save all that business of tying knots – usually granny knots, I suspect. They save a lot of time, where a light, temporary tie is needed, for tall, brittle annuals such as Salpiglossis or even sweet peas, if you are growing them on the ambitious, single-stem system for exhibition.

236

September 23, 1951

More gadgets. The essence of a gadget is that it shall be (*a*) small and (*b*) unknown to other people. It must be one's own discovery; something that one has found out for oneself. The rubber-tyred wheelbarrow is thus too large and too well known to be called a gadget; but what a weight of wheeling, and what a sparing of turf, it saves! A little companion I would not be without is the fern-trowel; it is long and narrow, indispensable for weeding between small plants, such as you might find in a rockery or a stone-trough-garden. Like all the hand-tools, it should be of stainless steel, bright to look at and easy to clean. (A rag wrung out of paraffin should be mentioned here.) Pocket-sized secateurs may meet with contempt from the professional gardener, who is usually a scornful man, but should be constantly carried by the amateur. Speaking for myself, I am a miserable lost creature whenever I mislay my Wilkinson Sword secateurs. Less portable, but still very useful, are the soluble flower-pots obtainable in various sizes; they are for seedlings that do not enjoy being transplanted and prefer being dropped straight into the ground in their home-pot which will quickly dissolve in the damp earth.

Labels. I wish I had good advice to give about labels; they are always my worry. The strong metal label called Acme, which can be printed with any name or date you like, is completely satisfactory but much too expensive for anything except the permanent trees or shrubs. What I want is a nice neat label which I can write for myself, and set to mark, say, a dozen special daffodils or some chosen bulbs; but, as we all know, white paint is not what it once was, and indelible ink is now only too delible.*

This article seems to be deteriorating from a list into something more like a grumble. The time has come for me to lift it out of this rut, with a more constructive suggestion. I have one to make. It is about a belt, the sort of belt you wear round your waist. It could be made of strong buckram or of leather, and it should not be beyond the skill of any cobbler or harness-maker. From the belt would dangle every minor adjunct that the amateur gardener wandering round his garden could possibly wish to have ready to his hand: a roll of string, a knife, a tin of slug-bait, a pencil, a tin to collect seeds, a trowel, secateurs . . . Each to his choice and need. A belt that Alice's White Knight would have approved. I might take out a patent for it.†

---

* Messrs Woodman, High Street, Pinner, supply the best answer to my problem.
† May I here make a grateful acknowledgment to the kind and clever *Observer* reader who made and sent me one, exactly to this specification?

237

September 30, 1951

The more I see of other people's gardens the more convinced do I become of the value of good grouping and shapely training. These remarks must necessarily apply most forcibly to gardens of a certain size, where sufficient space is available for large clumps or for large specimens of individual plants, but even in a small garden the spotty effect can be avoided by massing instead of dotting plants here and there.

It is a truly satisfactory thing to see a garden well schemed and wisely planted. Well schemed are the operative words. Every garden, large or small, ought to be planned from the outset, getting its bones, its skeleton, into the shape that it will preserve all through the year even after the flowers have faded and died away. Then, when all colour has gone, is the moment to revise, to make notes for additions, and even to take the mattock for removals. This is gardening on the large scale, not in details. There can be no rules, in so fluid and personal a pursuit, but it is safe to say that a sense of substance and solidity can be achieved only by the presence of an occasional mass breaking the more airy companies of the little flowers.

What this mass shall consist of must depend upon many things: upon the soil, the aspect, the colour of neighbouring plants, and above all upon the taste of the owner. I can imagine, for example, a border arranged entirely in purple and mauve – phlox, stocks, pansies, *Clematis Jackmanii* trained over low hoops – all planted in bays between great promontories of the plum-coloured sumach, *Rhus cotinus foliis purpureis*, but many people, thinking this too mournful, might prefer a scheme in red and gold. It would be equally easy of accomplishment, with a planting of the feathery *Thalictrum glaucum, gaillardias, Achillea eupatorium* (the flat-headed yellow yarrow), *helenium, Lychnis chalcedonica*, and a host of other ordinary, willing, herbaceous things. In this case, I suppose, the mass would have to be provided by bushes of something like the golden privet or the golden yew, both of which I detest when planted as 'specimens' on a lawn, but which in so aureate a border would come into their own.

The possibilities of variation are manifold, but on the main point one must remain adamant; the alternation between colour and solidity, decoration and architecture, frivolity and seriousness. Every good garden, large or small, must have some architectural quality about it; and, apart from the all-important question of the general lay-out, including hedges, the best way to achieve this imperative effect is by massive lumps of planting such as I have suggested.

I wish only that I could practise in my own garden the principles which I so complacently preach, week after week, in this column.

September 7, 1952

Writing this article away from home, I make a few notes of things seen in the course of a fortnight's motoring, things which were either new to me, or else forgotten until the reminder came along. I had forgotten, for instance, the summer-flowering mauve *Solanum crispum* var. *autumnalis*, so useful in August, a trifle tender, perhaps, wanting a warm south wall; and the white *Solanum jasminoides*, another August flowerer, a most graceful climber, also a trifle tender, but well worth trying in southern counties. I had forgotten the white – or, rather, creamy – *Buddleia fallowiana alba*, with grey leaves, an uncommon thing and a pleasant change from the ordinary mauve. *Buddleia nivea* is even more grey-leaved and woolly, almost as woolly and felted as that old favourite cottage plant, *Stachys lanata*, commonly called Rabbit's Ears or Saviour's Flannel, or, in Scotland, Lamb's Lugs. I had forgotten *Itea ilicifolia*, a wall shrub with long, grey-white catkins of soft beauty, an evergreen, fragrant and, alas, tender; and *Berberis trifoliata*, expressly made to appeal to anyone with a liking for glaucous foliage.

Then I saw also a shrubby plant which I was later enabled to identify as *Abelia grandiflora*. This struck me as a surprisingly pretty shrub; it throws a wealth of pointed, bright pink buds, opening into pink-white flowers. It is quite hardy, and I would recommend it to anyone who wants some colour in the August–September garden.

Another shrub I saw was *Decaisnea fargesii*. This is called the bean-plant, because it develops bright blue seed-pods in autumn; very decorative. It is quite hardy and should be planted in any unwanted corner, just for the sake of its yellow-green flowers and its steel-blue pods in autumn.

These are all just notes; but I must end by urging you to grow *Indigofera pendula*. This is a surprisingly lovely thing. It arches in long sprays of pinkish-mauve pea-like flowers, growing ten feet high, dangling very gracefully from its delicate foliage. It combines very prettily with the mauve Solanum I mentioned above; or, I can imagine, with the August-flowering blue Ceanothus, *Gloire de Versailles*, or even mingling with the blue plumbago, *Ceratostigma willmottiana*.

If you have any difficulty in finding any of these shrubs, Messrs Hillier have them all. Address on p. 271.

September 14, 1952

I revert to some ideas I picked up while motoring away from home. One learns a lot from seeing other people's gardens. There were some roses I saw: *Independence*, for instance, of a colour difficult to describe. The nearest I can get to it is tomato lightly brushed with grey. It might associate well with the coppery polyantha *Fashion*, a very effective rose, lacking the subtlety of *Independence*, but a fine showy thing for a bed and for picking. There is a whole range now of these coppery-orange roses, *Catalonia*, *United Nations*, and *Opera* are all good; and for a fine rich yellow, with a particularly sweet scent, *Spun Gold* should come as the discovery it was to me. It was a discovery to the present grower, who found it accidentally.* By what I can only imagine to be a printer's error, it is accorded only one X for scent in the catalogue; in my opinion it deserves three XXX.

There are also the bi-coloured roses, yellow on one side of the petal, red-orange on the other, making an extraordinarily brilliant effect. They resemble the old briar *Austrian Copper*, well known to rose-lovers but often their despair, owing to its tendency to black-spot and die-back; and they resemble also that blazing shrub-cum-climber, *Réveil Dijonnais*, which a gardener-acquaintance of mine firmly calls Revil Die-Johnny. This should be more often planted, for it is extremely showy and goes on flowering at intervals throughout the summer; it suffers, however, from one terrible fault: it fades into a really dreadful sickly mauve, so if you have not the leisure to pick off the dying flowers every morning before breakfast you had better give it a miss.

If, however, you like the bi-coloured roses, as I do, and want something more reliable than *Austrian Copper* in the same colouring, please consider planting *Sultane* and *Madame Dieudonné*.

I see that this article has turned itself into a symphony of all the wild sunset colours, a sort of western sky after a stormy day. The sunset colours are not always very good mixers in a garden, happily though they may consort in the heavens. In a garden they should, I think, be kept apart from the pinks, and be given, if possible, a place to themselves. I know that few gardens nowadays can afford this extravagance of separate space, but I can still imagine a hedged-off enclosure where nothing but the glow of blood-orange-and-yellow roses should have its own way.

September 21, 1952

Readers of this column may have observed that I was away from home recently, getting ideas from other people's gardens. I did pick up one very good idea for a hedge. It is the Worcesterberry. This is a cross between the blackcurrant and the gooseberry. It has small black gooseberry-like fruits which are said to make excellent jam; and as it grows very vigorously and is

* Miss Hilda Murrell, address under Edwin Murrell, Ltd, on p. 273, from whom the other roses mentioned can also be obtained.

exceedingly thorny, it quickly provides the densest and most repellent protection against livestock, marauding children, and even rabbits. The hedge I saw was about seven feet high, but, of course, you could clip it if you wanted it lower, not to obscure a view. You would be wise to wear a complete suit of armour and steel gauntlets whilst thus engaged.

A correspondent kindly tells me of an attractive hedge she knows, made of Forsythia. I can imagine that this would look very gay in the spring, a barrier of thick gold, rather low, clipped square on top and sides, an operation which should take place annually immediately after the flowers have faded. *Forsythia intermedia Spectabilis* would be the best variety to get; portentous as this name may appear, it represents nothing more recondite than the ordinary Forsythia now to be seen in every other roadside garden. Using it as a hedging-plant would give it a twist of originality more interesting than the usual bush-form. It would have a special advantage, in so far as it may be obtained without cost if you take the trouble to insert some cuttings next month, October, in an outdoor six-inch-deep trench filled with sharp sand. Take twelve-inch-long cuttings; strip the leaves off them; then press them firmly in, with your foot or your hand; see to it that they don't get loosened by wind or frost during the winter, and then by the spring you may look forward to having a long row of rooted cuttings ready to set out wherever you want your hedge. In fact, I can see no reason why you should not start your cuttings in the first place where you intend the hedge to be. It would save a lot of transplanting, which always checks the young growth. I never believe in moving plants if one can possibly help it, unless, of course, they are becoming overcrowded and demanding division or a shift.

The Worcesterberry can be obtained from Messrs John Scott, address on p. 271. I know they disagree with me and maintain that it doesn't make a good hedge; but all I can say is that I have seen a hedge with my own eyes.

September 28, 1952
This must be a paragraph addressed to those fortunate dwellers in a kind climate: Cornwall, Devon, the west coast of Scotland, or some parts of Wales and Ireland, for the flowering tree which caught my fancy last week is marked by one of those ominous little asterisks in nurserymen's catalogues, meaning 'not quite hardy'. It is *Lagerstroemia indica*, sometimes known as the Crape Myrtle, though there is nothing crape-like about its fluffy pink, red, or white flowers. I cannot think how it came by so dismal a name. Pride of India is a much better one. It is a gay little tree, said to attain twenty to thirty feet in height, though the specimens I saw growing by the roadside in Italy were not

more than ten to twelve feet, just tall enough to enjoy comfortably with a slight raising of the eyes. I recommend it with some diffidence, since I suspect that only an exceptionally sunny summer would bring it to the perfection of its flowering in this country. It could, of course, be grown against a wall, which would give it protection and an extra allowance of sun-baking, instead of as a standard in the open ground. A loamy soil suits it, and it should be pruned during the winter.

Another thing I noted was the Mediterranean heath, *Erica mediterranea*, grown in the unusual form of a standard. This struck me as an amusing way to train a heath, into a neat tall standard instead of a straggly spreading bush. It was not in flower when I saw it, but I could well imagine what it would look like in March and April: a fuzz of pink on the top of a straight pole. Somewhat artificial, I admit, but the Italians are an inventive people and enjoy anything in the nature of a joke. I thought that four of these standards, one at each corner of a square flower-bed, might look decorative as little sentinels, not taking up much ground-space, and agreeably green all the year round, whether in flower or not; or placed at intervals to form a small avenue bordering a path. They would not grow more than four or five feet high.

Erica mediterranea, unlike most of the heaths, does not object to the presence of a little lime in the soil, though naturally its preference is for peat. People whose gardens are on that type of soil could treat the white-flowered Tree Heath, *Erica arborea*, in a similar way; this grows much taller, even to ten feet where it is happy, but unfortunately it is somewhat tender and should thus be reserved for the warmer counties.

The heaths cost from 2s. 6d. to 5s. 6d. according to size.

October

Plaintive letters reach me from time to time saying that if I do not like herbaceous borders what would I put in their place? It is quite true that I have no great love for herbaceous borders or for the plants that usually fill them – coarse things with no delicacy or quality about them. I think the only justification for such borders is that they shall be perfectly planned, both in regard to colour and to grouping; perfectly staked; and perfectly weeded. How many people have the time or the labour? The alternative is a border largely composed of flowering shrubs, including the big bush roses; but for those who still desire a mixed border it is possible to design one which will (more or less) look after itself once it has become established.

It could be carried out in various colour schemes. Here is an idea for one in red and purple and pink: Polyantha roses *Dusky Maiden, Frensham, Donald Prior*; musk roses *Wilhelm, Pink Prosperity, Cornelia, Felicia, Vanity*; the common old red herbaceous peonies, with Darwin tulips planted amongst them if you like; and a front edging of the dwarf asters and daisies such as *Dresden China* and *Rob Roy*, which make big mats and go on for ever, and even violets for early flowering, and some patches of *Fragaria indica*, the ornamental strawberry with bright red fruits all through the summer. Nor would I despise a counterpane, at intervals, of *Cotoneaster horizontalis*, crawling over the ground with its herring-bone spine, its small box-like leaves of darkest green and its brilliantly red berries in autumn.

Another idea, pale and rather ghostly, a twilight-moonlight border. *Forsythia* along the back; musk roses *Danae, Moonlight* and *Thisbe* in the middle; evening primroses, *Oenothera biennis*, self-sowing; *Iris ochroleuca*, tall and white and yellow; creamy peonies; and a front carpet of silver-foliaged artemisias and stachys.

Of course, these are only the roughest indications, outlines to be filled in. The main thing, it seems to me, is to have a foundation of large, tough, untroublesome plants with intervening spaces for the occupation of annuals, bulbs, or anything that takes your fancy. The initial outlay would seem extravagant, but at least it would not have to be repeated, and the effect would improve with every year.

May I thank all the kind people who have sent me helpful letters, pencils, and samples of labels? I now have a wonderful collection of every shape, size, colour, and substance. I am most grateful, and regret only that I have not been able to acknowledge each letter separately. Will those to whom I have not written, please accept my thanks in this way?

The most useful label comes from Messrs G. J. Woodman, High Street, Pinner; strips of white plastic which you cut into lengths and fit into a metal holder.

October 14, 1951

As this month and the next bring round the time for planting shrubs, the ornamental quinces should not be forgotten. They may take a little while to get going, but, once they have made a start, they are there for ever, increasing in size and luxuriance from year to year. They need little attention, and will grow almost anywhere, in sun or shade. Although they are usually seen trained against a wall, notably on old farm-houses and cottages, it is not necessary to give them this protection, for they will do equally well grown as loose bushes in the open or in a border, and, indeed, it seems to me that their beauty is enhanced by this liberty offered to their arching sprays. Their fruits, which in autumn are as handsome as their flowers, make excellent jelly; in fact, there is everything to be said in favour of this well-mannered, easy-going, obliging and pleasantly old-fashioned plant.

The only grievance that people hold against it, for which the poor thing itself is scarcely to be blamed, is its frequent change of name. It started its career as *Pyrus japonica*, and became familiarly known as Japonica, which simply means Japanese, and is thus as silly as calling a plant 'English' or 'French'. It then changed to Cydonia, meaning quince: *Cydonia japonica*, the Japanese quince. Now we are told to call it *Chaenomeles*, but as I don't know what that means, beyond a vague idea that *chae* means hairy and *meles* means sombre or black, and as, furthermore, I am not at all sure how to pronounce it, I think I shall stick to Cydonia, which is in itself a pretty word.*

There are many varieties. There is the old red one, *C. lagenaria*, hard to surpass in richness of colour, beautiful against a grey wall or a whitewashed wall, horrible against modern red brick. There is *C. nivalis*, pure white, safely lovely against any background. There is *C. Moerloesii*, or the Apple-blossom quince, whose name is enough to suggest its shell-pink colouring. There is *Knaphill Scarlet*, not scarlet at all but coral-red; it goes on flowering at odd moments throughout the summer long after its true flowering season is done. There is

* A correspondent rightly reproves me for ignorance and frivolity. *Chaenomeles*, he says, means 'Splitting Apple', from the Greek *chaineis*, and *melea*, apple. Obviously, he is right, but I still don't like it.

C. cathayensis, with small flowers succeeded by the biggest green fruits you ever saw – a sight in themselves. Finally, if you want a prostrate kind, there is *C. Simonii*, spreading horizontally, with dark red flowers, much to be recommended for a bank or a rock garden.

Would Mr J. Napier Proctor, who wrote to me asking for an address, please supply me with his own? Otherwise I shall be in his debt for life for 2½d., representing the stamp he so thoughtfully sent me.

October 21, 1951

The apples are ripening, and according to the old theory we shake them to hear if the pips rattle, or cut them in half to see if the pips have turned black. To how many of us has it occurred that those pips may be sown in a flower-pot, to be grown on into a little fruit-bearing tree for years to come? It might be a nice idea to sow some apple pips in commemoration of a birth or a christening, and to watch the growth of the infant tree keeping pace with the growth of the human infant. This is perhaps not a very serious form of gardening, but it is fun if you have the time to give to it. Nothing could be prettier than a small tree loaded with fruit. A correspondent tells me that after twelve years she picked a whole hundredweight of apples from a seedling she had raised herself; but then, admittedly, she had planted her seedling out: she had not kept it permanently in its pot.

All the same, it is possible to grow fruit trees in pots. Figs do very well. They fruit best when their roots are restricted, so the restriction of a pot is the very thing a fig needs, if it is not to run to leaf instead of to fruit. A pot-grown fig, heavily hung with its fruit among its beautifully shaped leaves, is a thing to stand on a paved path or beside a front door; it is decorative; and you can eat the figs. The hardy vines also make very good pot-plants. A fruiting vine, hung with bunches trained to arch round bamboo sticks stuck into a barrel sawn in half, is as pretty a sight as you could wish to see: it reminds one of some Italian paintings, and brings a suggestion of Mediterranean countries into our northern land. The hardy vines are not difficult to grow. I should plant the *Royal Muscadine*, with pale green-yellow grapes; or *Black Hamburgh*, which will do out of doors in our southern counties; or the Strawberry grape which I recommended in this column years ago, and which seems to have found favour with those enterprising gardeners who took my advice and acquired it. Its grey-pink bunches, hanging amongst the leaves, have a powdered look, as though they had been dusted over, delicately, with a puff.

Soft fruit can also be grown in pots. It is well known that strawberries can be made to pour out of a barrel pierced with holes all the way up; the small

Alpine strawberry looks charming grown in this way. I remember also seeing a redcurrant, taught to grow as a little standard, about four feet high, with an umbrella-shaped head dripping with the tassels of its bright red beads. I see no reason why this idea should not be extended to the black and the white currants, and to gooseberries, or indeed to anything that will make a woody stem. Wineberries, loganberries and raspberries would, of course, have to be trained round bamboo sticks, like the vines. There is great scope for inventiveness here; and the only recurrent care would be the renewal of the soil by an annual top-dressing, preferably of compost, to ensure that the plant with its limited root-run was not suffering from starvation. Also to see that it did not lack for water: plants in pots dry out very quickly.

October 28, 1951

If you are thinking of planting for autumn colouring, this is the time to look at the flaming shrubs and trees and to make your choice. In spring and summer one tends to forget the autumn days, but, when they arrive, with their melancholy and the spiders' webs so delicately and geometrically looped from the hedges, how grateful we are for the torch of a little tree or the low smoulder of leaves on azaleas and peonies. I feel sure that these effects should be concentrated into one area of the garden, preferably at a distance if space allows, so that they may be seen from the windows in a rabble incarnadine.

A visit to a local nursery will supply many suggestions. For my own part, I would plant a backing of the Cockspur thorn, *Crataegus crus-galli*, and of the Scarlet Oak, *Quercus coccinea*, slow in growth but magnificently red in its October–November colour. If I had enough room, I would plant *Koelreuteria paniculata* behind these; it makes a tall tree in time; is seldom seen in our gardens; and contributes an astonishing pyramid of pink, yellow, and green at this time of the year. Then in front of all these I would plant *Prunus sargentii*, a small tree pretty enough with its pink blossom in spring, but lovelier still in autumn when its leaves turn red, especially if you have planted it so that the early morning sun or the late afternoon sun can illuminate it and make the leaves transparent. This is a very important point, I think, which any gardener planting for autumn colour should observe: the transparency against the sun. I should then plant a whole host of autumn-colouring in front of these; little trees such as the peat-loving *Disanthus cercidifolius*, whose small round leaves dangle like golden coins; *Cornus kousa*; *Acer griseum*; *Nandina domestica*; *Euonymus alatus*, a most brilliant pink; *Rhus cotinoides*, the American sumach; and the low-growing, rounded bush of *Berberis thunbergii*. As a ground covering for the front, there is a charming little bristly rose called *R. nitida*, which creeps about and forms a mat of blackish-red leaf and stem, not very showy from afar off perhaps, but pretty and unusual close to.

These are only a very few of the suggestions that could be made. I have not even mentioned the ornamental vines, such as *Coignetiae*, or the larger trees such as *Cercidiphyllum* or *Parrotia persica*. I might, however, refer you to Mr Michael Haworth-Booth's new book, *Effective Flowering Shrubs* (Collins, 25s., with coloured photographs as illustrations), which is a reliable guide by that well-known authority.

I should like also to pay a tribute to Mr George Russell, who has just died at the age of ninety-four. Starting as a garden boy at ten years old, he devoted many years of his life to the production of the strain we now know as the Russell lupins, with their remarkable range of colour, so far removed from the old monotonous blue. He must have been a dear old man. I never met him, but he used to write to me and send me his poems. I wish I could say that his poems were as good as his lupins.

October 5, 1952

The leaves are turning, and if there has been frost by the time this article appears, many of them will have been brought off. Their beauty, in some years, is evanescent, but if they hang only for a week it is supremely worth while to plant those trees or shrubs which, in their sudden blaze, will so startlingly recall the first glories of summer.

Among our native trees, the wild cherry or Gean is one of the first to turn. (I should perhaps qualify the word 'native' by saying that it may possibly have been introduced by the Romans, but after two thousand years its naturalization papers may surely be regarded as obsolete.) There is no need to emphasize the loveliness of the wild cherry in the spring, its great puffs of white appearing like the smoke of a train inexplicably stationary in the middle of bare woods. Its autumn colouring is no less sensational, but somehow one does not notice it so readily, because the October leafage of the forest trees, oak, beech, and chestnut, still hangs so heavily green around it that it can be observed only close up or at a vista-cut of a distance.

Few people, alas, can afford to garden on so large a scale as to provide for long vista-cuts today. Those days of landscape gardening on the grand scale have gone, the days of Repton and Capability Brown, and the best hope now lies in the roadside planting carried out by local authorities. But we could still afford, modestly, to set our own wild cherry in a chosen place at the eastern or the western corner of the garden: I say eastern or western because the reddening leaves would then catch either the morning or the evening light, sunrise or sunset. Considering that it is a native, i.e. growing on its own roots without the labour of grafting, it is surprisingly expensive to buy from nurserymen, but energetic people living in the country can often find tall seedlings in the woods or hedgerows, or suckers springing up from the root in the neighbourhood of some mature specimen, and transplant them at no cost but an hour's labour. They can do so with the comforting reflection that their wildling has a life's anticipation of a century or more.

This is not written with any intention of encouraging people to despoil our countryside of its wild plants, but on the contrary with the intention of saving such wildlings as seem certain of an early doom at the hands of farmers or woodmen.

The Gean, or *Prunus avium*, is not to be confused with the Bird Cherry, in spite of its Latin name meaning 'of birds'. The Bird Cherry is *Prunus padus*, and is to be found growing wild in the north, rather than in the south, of Britain. There are also cultivated forms of the Bird Cherry: *P. padus Watereri* and *P. padus Albertii*. From personal acquaintance I can speak only of *P. padus Watereri*, which possesses what my nose tells me is a peculiarly honeyed scent.

October 12, 1952

A complaint commonly brought against many of the modern or 'improved' varieties of favourite old flowers is that they have lost their scent. In some cases this complaint is justified; in others not. The one which I want to consider in this article is the Sweet Pea, and it is quite an appropriate moment to do so, since this is the month when seeds may still be sown in pots for wintering in a frame and planting out next spring.

The true Sweet Pea, *Lathyrus odoratus*, small, hooded, and not remarkable for any beauty of colour, was originally sent from Italy in 1699 by a Father Cupani to Dr Robert Uvedale, headmaster of the Grammar School at Enfield, Middlesex. Of Father Cupani I know nothing, but Dr Uvedale, schoolmaster and horticulturist, seems to have been something of a character. He had a fine collection of foreign plants, which after his death in 1722 were sold to Sir Robert Walpole for his garden at Houghton in Norfolk. Of Dr Uvedale it was said that 'his flowers were choice, his stock numerous, and his culture of them very methodical and curious'. Amongst them was the Sweet Pea, native of southern Italy and Sicily, and it is this which I should like to see restored to favour in this country.

Undoubtedly the Grandiflora and Spencer hybrids offer a greater range of colour, a greater solidity and length of stalk, and more flower-heads to a stalk, nor can it be said that they lack the fragrance which gives them their popular name. But compared with the fragrance of the humble little wildling they have nothing to boast about in that respect. It must be realized that the wild pea is not showy, in fact its pink and purple are very washy and the individual flowers are small, but they have a certain wistful delicacy of appearance and the scent of even half a dozen in a bunch is astonishing.

Unfortunately I cannot find them listed in any catalogue. Even my favourite seedsman, who has over three thousand numbers to his credit and from whom one can buy the most improbable things, has failed me for once. This seems a depressingly negative conclusion to come to, after so warm a recommendation, and I can suggest only that people with friends in Italy (or Spain, where they also grow) should beg for a packet of seed to be sent by post. Of course it is no good attempting to grow them on the elaborate system of training one stem up a bean-pole and suppressing all side shoots; they must be left to scramble up twiggy pea-sticks in a tangle and kept entirely for picking, in an unwanted but sunny corner of the kitchen garden.

At the end of their season they can be left to set their own seed and a supply be thus ensured. I know for a fact that they do set and ripen their seed in this island, for I have seen them doing it in a private garden quite far north, and came away, I am glad to say, with a generous handful which I hope to have growing in my own garden next summer.

October 19, 1952
A word on the Burnet or Scots roses, so incredibly pretty, mottled and marbled, self-coloured and two-coloured, and moreover so easy to grow. As Mr Edward Bunyard did not fail to point out, there is no better covering for a dry bank, since they will not only bind it together with their dense root system, but will also run about underground and come up everywhere in a little thorny jungle or thicket, keeping the weeds away. They are also ideal plants for a poor starved soil or for a windy place where taller, less tough things might refuse to survive. Another of their virtues is that they will make a charming low hedge. Their one drawback, which one must admit to be serious, is that they flower only once a year; but their foliage is quite pleasant to the eye, and if they can be given a rough corner such as the dry bank suggested by Mr Bunyard, the brevity of their explosion in June may be forgiven them.

There is, however, an exception to this rule of short-lived flowering. *Stanwell perpetual* is its name. It is only half a Scot, being a hybrid between a Scot and a Damask, or possibly a Gallica; I like to think it has Gallica blood in it, since France and Scotland have always enjoyed a curious affinity as exemplified by their pepper-pot architecture and by certain phrases which have passed from one language into the other: *Ne vous fâchez pas*, dinna fash yoursel'; and as for barley-sugar, or *sucre d'orge*, I could expand into a whole article over that.

This is by the way. The rose *Stanwell perpetual* is what I was writing about. I have become very fond of this modest rose, who truly merits the description *perpetual*. One is apt to overlook her during the great foison of early summer; but now in October, when every chosen flower is precious, I feel grateful to her for offering me her shell-pink, highly scented, patiently produced flowers, delicately doing her job again for my delectation in a glass on my table, and filling my room with such a good smell that it puffs at me as I open the door.

Stanwell perpetual grows taller than the average Scots rose. It grows four to five feet high. It is, as I have said, a hybrid. It has another name, according to Miss Nancy Lindsay, who is an expert on these old roses, the *Victorian Valentine rose*. This evokes pictures of old Valentines – but, however that may be, I do urge you to plant *Stanwell perpetual* in your garden to give you a reward of picking in October. Edwin Murrell, Ltd, has it, see p. 273.

October 26, 1952

A spike of the brightest orange caught my eye, half hidden by a clump of *Berberis thunbergii* which had turned very much the same colour. They were both of an extraordinary brilliance in the low afternoon sunshine. I could not remember if I had planted them deliberately in juxtaposition, or if they had come together by a fortunate chance. Investigation revealed further spikes: three-sided seed-pods cracked wide open to expose the violent clusters of the berries within.

This was our native *Iris foetidissima* in its autumn dress, our only other native iris being the yellow waterside flag, *I. pseudo-acorus*. No one would plant *I. foetidissima* for the sake of its name, which in English is rendered the Stinking iris and derives from the unpleasant smell of the leaves if you bruise them. There is, however, no need to bruise leaves, a wanton pastime, and you can call it the Gladdon or Gladwyn iris if you prefer, or even the Roast-beef Plant. Some etymologists think that Gladdon or Gladwyn are corruptions of Gladiolus, owing to a similarity between the sword-like leaves; but I wish someone would tell me how it got its roast-beef name.

Its flowers, small, and of a dingy mauve, are of no value or charm, nor should we be wise to pick them, because it is for the seed-pods that we cherish it. Not that it needs much cherishing, and is even one of those amiable plants that will tolerate shade. Strugglers with shady gardens, or with difficult shaded areas, will doubtless note this point. The seed-pods are for late autumn and winter decoration indoors, for the seeds have the unusual property of not dropping out when the pod bursts open, and will last for a long time in a vase; they look fine, and warm, under a table-lamp on a bleak evening. Miss Gertrude Jekyll used to advise hanging the bunch upside down for a bit, to stiffen the stalks; I dare say she was right; she was usually right, and had an experimental mind.

Let me not claim for the Gladdon iris that its crop of orange berries makes a subtle bunch or one which would appeal to flower-lovers of very delicate taste; it is frankly as coarse as it is showy, and has all the appearance of having been brought in by a pleased child after an afternoon's ramble through the copse. Nevertheless, its brightness is welcome, and its coarseness can be lightened by a few sprays of its companion the berberis. It can be bought at the low price of 1s. 6d. from the Orpington iris nursery, see p. 272 for the address.

November

The Master of the Worshipful Company of Gardeners recently wrote a letter to *The Times* expressing the hope that the pleasant occupation of window-box gardening might become a habit with our town-dwellers and might extend far beyond the special effort made during the Festival year. Judging by the number of letters I intermittently receive, urging me to write an article about town gardening in general and window-boxes in particular, I should say that his plea was likely to meet with a good response. The Worshipful Company three years ago gave two cups for an annual competition for City window-boxes, one for amateurs and one for professionals. They hope the competition will continue to receive support. Provincial cities might well imitate this happy idea; perhaps some of them do.

To my own *Observer* correspondents I have always been obliged to return the regretful answer that I had no experience of town gardening. Now, however, I have found the solution in an excellent little book called *Window-box and Indoor Gardening*, by Xenia Field (Collins, 10s. 6d.). You will realize from the title that this does not include *outdoor* gardens in cities; perhaps Xenia Field's publishers may persuade her to write one as a sequel, for I cannot imagine a better guide. She is knowledgeable, clear, practical to the point of being fool-proof, and full of ideas. She tells us all about how to make the window-box or boxes; how to fill them with soil and drainage; what to plant in them; how to look after them; how to arrange for the seasonal flowers to succeed one another; giving admirably arranged lists of the take-it-or-leave-it type. 'These are my favourites,' she says in effect, 'but they may not be yours, so here I will give you an alternative choice.' Then, having finished with window-boxes filled with flowers, she comes on to window-boxes filled with herbs and salads; and then on to such varied things as Alpine gardens where 'Mountain peaks and ranges may be kept clean by wiping them over occasionally with soap and water, and if necessary a little Vim'; and then to gardens in miniature, and to plants to grow indoors, ending up with a chapter on nursery gardening, not the nursery of the nurseryman, but of the child, where bulbs may be grown in sponges, or grass in fir-cones, or acorns in eggshells, or a magic hyacinth may be created by splitting two bulbs in half, binding them together, and then growing the reconstructed bulb into a mongrel strange enough to stir the pride of any infant gardener exhibiting his trophy to his adult friends.

A nice, nice book; a useful book; a book to give for Christmas to all those flower-lovers who are condemned to live between bricks and stones; a book that will bring a touch of the country into the town.

November 11, 1951

A correspondent invites me to deal with a problem which he suggests must be confronting many people. He has, he says, a new house and a new garden in a new housing estate, and after three or four years his work will almost certainly compel him to move to another part of the country. What is he to do, (1) to secure privacy from his neighbours, and (2) to create some sort of a flower garden in the shortest possible time?

I am afraid the question does not offer much scope for original suggestions. Impatience and gardening do not go well together. Still, something must be done. Privacy is the first essential, and privacy means a hedge. I do not much care for *Lonicera nitida*, which achieved so violent a popularity when it was first introduced some years ago, but there is no doubt that it is quick-growing, dense, evergreen, and cheap at 90s. a hundred. The drawback is that it requires clipping so often if it is not to become straggly. Hornbeam is also quick-growing; a little more expensive at 120s. a hundred, it is not evergreen but does retain its crisp brown leaves throughout the winter so that it seldom looks quite bare. For a very rapid effect, *Polygonum baldschuanicum*, the Russian vine, with feathery white flowers in summer, is a good investment at 4s. 6d. each; not many plants would be needed to train along a fence, wires, or trellis. It is, however, deciduous, and would thus provide no true screen in winter. If this is not an absolute objection, a hedge made of fruiting brambles would be more unusual, also more remunerative; loganberries, wineberries, or the new Boysenberry, or the cultivated blackberry, especially the one called *Himalaya*, all of which can be bought for 4s. 6d. a plant. There would also be the rambler roses, so vigorous that within a year or two, given good feeding, the fence should be covered; there is no need to plant the old *Dorothy Perkins* or *American Pillar*, for far lovelier ones can be obtained at the same price, 4s. 6d. I should suggest *The New Dawn, Albertine, Félicité et Perpétue, Dr Van Fleet, Albéric Barbier, François Juranville.*

As for the flower garden I suppose quantities of hardy annuals must be the principal stand-by. This would involve making beds or borders with a reasonably good tilth of top-soil for seed-sowing. If my correspondent chooses beds, I trust he makes them sharply square or rectangular, and not in the shape of hearts, crescents, or lozenges. Of course, if he is prepared to go to the expense there is nothing to prevent him from filling them with some herbaceous perennials, flowering shrubs, or roses. Each man's problem must eventually be his own.

November 18, 1951

The family of the Sages is well known both in the kitchen garden and the flower garden. Some are aromatic herbs, scenting the hillsides in the sun of Mediterranean countries, and are associated in our minds with rough paths, goats, and olives. The sage is altogether an amiable plant; indeed, its Latin name, *Salvia*, comes from *salvere*, to save, or heal, and one of its nicknames is *S. salvatrix*, which sounds very reassuring. The common clary, or *S. sclarea*, is also known as Clear Eye and See Bright, not to be confused with Eyebright, that tiny annual whose proper name is Euphrasia. The French bestow a very genial personality on clary by calling it simply Toute Bonne, which to me at any rate suggests a rosy old countrywoman in a blue apron.

The kitchen sages make decorative clumps, for they can be had with reddish or variegated leaves as well as the ordinary grey-green. The garden sages are useful for the herbaceous border. I do not mean that half-hardy bedding-out plant beloved of the makers of public gardens, *S. splendens*, which should be forbidden by law to all but the most skilful handlers. I mean such old favourites as *S. virgata nemorosa*, a three-foot-high bushy grower whose blue-lipped flowers cluster amongst red-violet bracts and have the advantage of lasting a very long time in midsummer; or *S. grahamii*, equally familiar, with durable red flowers, a Mexican, reasonably but not absolutely hardy. A more recent introduction, not yet so well known as it should be, is *S. haematodes*, greatly to be recommended; it grows about five feet high in a cloud of pale blue rising very happily behind any grey-foliaged plant such as the old English lavender. This salvia grows readily from seed, especially if sown as soon as it ripens, and will in fact produce dozens of seedlings of its own accord. It is good for picking, if you bruise the stems or dip their tips for a few moments into boiling water.

Anybody with the time to spare should grow *S. patens*. It is a nuisance in the same way as a dahlia is a nuisance, because its tubers have to be lifted in autumn, stored in a frost-proof place, started into growth under glass in April, and planted out again at the end of May. The reason for this is not so much the tenderness of the tubers themselves as the risk that a late frost will destroy the young shoots; possibly the use of a cloche or hand-light might obviate this danger. The amazing azure of the flowers, however, compensates for any extra trouble. Like the gentians, they rival the luminosity of the blue bits in a stained-glass window.

November 25, 1951

Perhaps few people share my taste for tattered-bark trees. I must concede that it is a special taste. I must concede also that unless you have a fairly large garden you cannot afford the space even for one or two specimens set aside in a neglected corner, to grow taller and taller as the years go on. So this must be an article for the few, not for the many.

I like the tattery trees, whose bark curls off in strips like shavings. There is one called *Arbutus Menziesii*, with cinnamon-red bark which starts to peel of its own accord, and which you can then smooth away with your hand into something like the touch of sand-papered wood of a curious olive-green colour. It likes a sheltered corner, for it is not absolutely hardy. Then there is *Acer griseum*, the Paper-bark maple, with mahogany-coloured bark replaced by a brighter orange underneath, and brilliantly red leaves in autumn. It is, in fact, one of the best for October–November colour. *Betula albo-sinensis* var. *septentrionalis* is a birch with a beautiful white-and-grey trunk; unfortunately I cannot find any nurseryman who now lists it, though I dare say inquiry might produce it.* It is, I think, one of the loveliest, though *Betula japonica* drips with most attractive little catkins in spring. This also appears to be unobtainable.

Prunus serrula, sometimes sold as *serrula tibetica*, is a very striking tree with a shiny mahogany bark. This does not take on so shaggy an appearance as some, but sheds its outer covering in circular strips, leaving the trunk with annular ridges that make it look as though it were wearing bracelets. Reddish and glossy, the freshly revealed surface suggests the French polish sometimes used on fine old tables. It should be grown in very rich soil and planted where it can be seen, with the sun shining on it.

Now, having indulged myself by writing on a subject which I fear is not of very general interest, let me add a note on the Christmas roses or hellebores, which are just beginning to show their curly buds not unlike the first growth of young bracken. I have been told that the way to get long stems is to heap sand over the centre of the plant, when the flower-stalks, under the obligation of reaching for the light, will force their way upwards. I have never yet tried this method, but it seems common sense, and at the same time a glass cloche should be put right over the clump to prevent the flowers from getting splashed by rain and mud.

Everything is extraordinarily far forward this autumn; the winter jasmine is coming out rapidly, and the autumn-flowering cherry should be watched for its

* Messrs Hillier & Sons, Winchester, now list it at 15s. 6d.

fat buds, which will open within a few days in the warmth of a room. Even the slugs are beginning to think about some precocious buds of the Algerian iris.

November 2, 1952

I must depart for once from my usual practice of recommending plants to grow in anybody's garden. The fact is that I have got into trouble with my good friend Mr Jackman, of *Clematis Jackmanii* fame, and a very fine nursery-man of shrubs and flowering trees to boot. Mr Jackman is angry with me for having told readers of these articles to dig up wild cherries from the woods or hedgerows where you get them for nothing except the time and labour expended on finding them and digging them up.

I do see Mr Jackman's point of view. It must be infuriating for a nursery-man to read an article by an amateur gardener such as I am, when he knows the financial difficulties that he and his colleagues have to face. He points out that a specimen tree nine to ten feet high costs about 13s. 6d., and has taken fully five years to grow and to train, and has had to be transplanted at least twice to form a good root-system. You cannot just stick it in and leave it to its own devices. Further, the minimum horticultural wage for a 50-hour week in 1939 was 35s. It is now £5 12s. for 47 hours. There was then no statutory holiday with pay; two weeks are now given. Other costs beside wages have risen in proportion. Skilled work is still necessary and always will be, since mechanization can play but a relatively small part in the craft of gardening; yet the average price of nursery stock is only two and a half times the pre-war price.

So far, I must endorse every argument that Mr Jackman puts forward. The financial facts are indisputable. There is only one point in his letter which I would like to dispute, and dispute most vigorously. He says that I use my column to spread the idea that plants are surprisingly expensive to buy from nurserymen and that I recommend 'gardening on the cheap'. The very last purpose for which I should wish to use my column is to spread the idea that nurserymen overcharge. They don't. And as for recommending gardening on the cheap, I should like on the contrary to encourage the most lavish extravagant planting everywhere, bulbs by the thousand instead of the hundred, flowering trees and shrubs by the hundred instead of by the dozen.

If Mr Jackman were to read a cross-section of my correspondence, he would realize that, even as he is perfectly justified in stating the case for himself and his fellow-nurserymen, I, also, have a duty towards my more impecunious readers. Perhaps sixty per cent of my letters come from ardent gardeners whose desire for a bit of beauty is incommensurate with the dregs of their budget. Am I, therefore, to refrain from telling them to dig up a wild cherry, once in a way, when they can find one? And, in conclusion, if Mr Jackman could see the replies, running now into thousands, which I have dispatched giving addresses of appropriate nurserymen, he might realize that, far from wishing to do harm to his most honourable profession, I have done my utmost to increase their order lists.

November 9, 1952

Although I missed the talk myself, I was glad to hear from a friend that one of the BBC gardening experts, perhaps Mr Streeter or Mr Roy Hay, had spoken against the idea of red, white, and blue for Coronation-year planting. This combination of colour may be very much all right and heart-stirring for a flag, but it looks very discordant and unnatural in a garden. Patriotism, in this case, is not enough. We must look for something more permanent than the flag-like carpets of lobelia, alyssum, and scarlet salvia with which I fear our public and even our private gardens will be only too loyally patterned.

Not that I have anything against lobelia in itself. Properly used, in large pools, especially the sort called *Cambridge blue*, it can be regarded as a beautiful annual, rivalling my favourite *Phacelia campanularia*, blue as a gentian or the Mediterranean sea. Nor have I anything against Sweet Alyssum, smelling of honey in her lowly way. The thing I resent, on behalf of both these desirable plants, is that some bad godmother at their christening should have ordained a ribbon-development for them, an edging of bedding-out, where they have no space to expand into the big generous patches they deserve.

No. We must not be bound by thoughts of red, white, and blue in an effort to turn our gardens into temporary strips of bunting in 1953. We should concentrate rather on planting something more permanent: a young tree for a young Queen. A young tree that will grow with her reign until, as we hope, she attains the eventual age of her great-great-grandmother towards the year 2008; the sapling on which we expend half a guinea or as much more as we can afford today will by then have grown into a proud old tree, with a trunk and stout branches.

I might suggest planting a mulberry. It grows very quickly; it lives for hundreds of years; it produces fruit in a regular crop every summer; and it has a traditional historical character in this country. The fruit stains the hands, but Pliny tells us that the stain of the ripe berries can be cleaned off with the juice of unripe ones. I might also suggest planting a fig as a commemorative Coronation tree. Few people realize how well the fig will flourish in our southern counties, ripening its fruit as though in Italy. Naturally it does best against a wall, but there is at least one famous orchard, at Worthing, where it is grown as bushes in the open. A patriarchal bush in this orchard is said to date back to the days of Thomas à Becket, which speaks sufficiently well for its longevity.

November 16, 1952

In Tudor times, the Knot garden was fashionable. This meant a garden or parterre laid out on geometrical lines, with narrow paths between beds filled with flowers and outlined by little low hedges of some dwarf plant such as edging-box or cotton lavender, which would lend themselves to a neat clipping, or by certain clippable herbs such as the shrubby thymes, hyssop, and marjoram. An edging of thrift was also popular, and can be very pretty, both when it is in flower and when it is cushiony-green. The design of the knotted beds could be either simple or complicated; it could wriggle to any extent, as the word 'knot' clearly indicates; or it could be straight and severe, according to the taste of the owner. The flowers which filled the beds would necessarily be low-growing, not to over-top the little hedges; pansies and daisies come instantly to mind. If flowers were not wanted, the space could be filled in with tiny lawns of turf or camomile.

It occurred to me that the idea might well be adapted to present-day use. Even though we do not live in Tudor times, we do live in another Elizabethan age, and if we are thinking of Coronation planting we might well consecrate a separate area to the creation of such a garden. I think it should be flat, I mean level, though it need not be large; in fact the bit usually known as 'the front garden' would be eminently suitable and might be made to look very charming and unusual, as a change from the customary rose-beds or clumps of herbaceous plants. To vary the knots, it would be possible to plant the box or cotton lavender, or whatever you decide on, in the shape of initials, your own, your children's, or those of the Queen, an ER done in dwarf lavender for instance, closely trimmed, or in the dark green cushions of thrift which so soon join up and make a continuous line. There is scope for ingenuity.

To turn to a different subject, may I put in a plea for the Home for aged gardeners at Horton in Buckinghamshire? It will accommodate thirty-five old gardeners and their wives, and in some special cases, their widows, and it wants donations, annual subscriptions, gifts in kind, endowments, legacies, or anything that we can spare. The old gardener who is past his work and who probably lost his tied cottage when he had to give up his job is a very appealing character. Adam, after all, was not only our first father but also our first gardener, and his descendant now comes cap in hand saying, 'Madam, I'm Adam,' in the same words as he may have used to introduce himself to Eve. You can read those words either way, forwards or backwards. Try.

The Cottage Garden with the first rose planted by Vita Sackville-West, the white 'Madame Alfred Carrière', visible on the wall, Sissinghurst Castle Garden, Kent, 2005

Trilliums and euphorbia in the Nuttery, with Kentish cobnut trees framing a statue of Dionysus, Sissinghurst Castle Garden, Kent, April 2007

Above, view from the Old Garden at Hidcote Manor towards the pavilions, with tulips 'Negrita' and 'Pink Diamond' in the foreground, May 2003, and (*below*) the pond in the Pine Garden, with water lilies and 'Hidcote' lavender, in the background, Hidcote Manor, Gloucestershire, July 1994

The White Garden, Hidcote Manor, Gloucestershire, June 1994

A post-card to the Secretary, Gardeners' Royal Benevolent Institution, 92 Victoria Street, London, sw1, will bring all particulars of the appeal that Adam is making.

November 23, 1952

How often I regret, as surely many amateur gardeners must regret, that I did not know more about the elementary principles of gardening when I first embarked on this enticing but tricky pastime. How many mistakes I could have avoided, and how far smaller could have been the coffer which my gardener now calls the Morgue, and which contains a multitude of metal labels representing the plants that have died on us over two decades of years. I suppose, however, that these remarks might apply to the whole of life – *si jeunesse savait*, and so on – and that one must go forward in the spirit of 'It's never too late to learn'.

One lesson that I have learnt is to plant things well from the start. A good start in life is as important to plants as it is to children: they must develop strong roots in a congenial soil, otherwise they will never make the growth that will serve them richly according to their needs in their adult life. It is important, it is indeed vital, to give a good start to any plant that you are now adding to your garden in this great planting month.

You may be planting some extra roses in this month of November, when roses are usually planted. Let me urge you to plant them with some peat and a handful of bone-meal mixed in with the peat. I did this last autumn on the recommendation of some rose-grower, I think it may have been Mr Wheatcroft, and the effect on the root-growth of my experimental rose-bushes was truly surprising to me when I dug them up this autumn to move them to another place. They had made a system of fibrous root such as I had never seen in so short a time. The reason is probably that peat retains moisture at the same time as giving good drainage, and that the bone-meal supplies nourishment.

It is usually supposed that roses enjoy a clay soil, and this I do believe to be true, having gardened in my early years on the stickiest clay to be found in the Weald of Kent. But what I now also believe to be true, is that although some plants such as roses will put up with a most disagreeable soil, they prefer to be treated in a more kindly fashion, having their bed prepared for them, dug out, and filled in with the type of soil they particularly favour. It is no use trying to grow the peat-lovers in an alkaline or chalky soil, everybody knows that, but what everybody does not realize is the enormous advantage to be gained from a thorough initial preparation. There should be no difficulty about that, in these days when nearly every gardener is his own compost-maker.

November 30, 1952

The Arbutus or Strawberry tree is not very often seen in these islands, except in south-west Eire, where it grows wild, but is an attractive evergreen of manageable size and accommodating disposition. True, most varieties object to lime, belonging as they do to the family of *Ericaceae*, like the heaths and the rhododendrons, but the one called *Arbutus unedo* can safely be planted in any reasonable soil.

To enumerate its virtues. It is, as I have said, evergreen. It will withstand sea-gales, being tough and woody. It has an amusing, shaggy, reddish bark. It can be grown in the open as a shrub, or trained against a wall, which perhaps shows off the bark to its fullest advantage, especially if you can place it where the setting sun will strike on it, as on the trunk of a Scots pine. Its waxy, pinkish-white flowers, hanging like clusters of tiny bells among the dark green foliage, are useful for picking until the first frost of November browns them; a drawback which can be obviated by a hurried picking when frost threatens. And, to my mind, its greatest charm is that it bears flower and fruit at the same time, so that you get the strawberry-like berries dangling red beneath the pale flowers. These berries are edible, but I do not recommend them. According to Pliny, who confused it with the real strawberry, the word *unedo*, from *unum edo*, means 'I eat one', thus indicating that you don't come back for more.

After its virtues, its only fault: it is not quite hardy enough for very cold districts, or for the North.

There is another arbutus called *Menziesii*, which is the noble Madrona tree of California, reaching a height of a hundred feet and more in its native home. I doubt if it would ever reach that height in England, though I must admit that the one I planted here in Kent some fifteen years ago is growing with alarming rapidity and has already obscured a ground-floor window; soon it will have attained the next floor, and what do I do then? Let it grow as high as the roof, I suppose, and beyond. Its lovely bark – mahogany colour until it starts to peel, revealing an equally lovely olive-green underneath – gives me such pleasure that I could never bear to cut it down. Perhaps an exceptionally severe winter will deal with the problem, for it is marked with the dagger of warning, meaning 'tender' in the catalogues.

There is also *Arbutus andrachne*, with the characteristic red bark, but this, again, is suitable only for favoured regions such as south and south-west England, parts of Wales, Northern Ireland, and south-west Eire. On the whole it is safer to stick to *Arbutus unedo*, so rewarding with its green leaves throughout the winter, and so pretty with its waxy racemes and scarlet fruits in autumn. It costs anything from 5s. 6d. to 10s. 6d., according to size, and is readily obtainable from most good nurserymen.

December

I have often thought, and indeed have some recollection of having alluded to it in this column, that it would be amusing to devote a garden entirely to the native flora of the British Isles. Discrimination would be essential, and an avoidance of the stragglers and invaders, also some knowledge of the soil conditions necessary; for example, it would be absurd to plant heaths or other ericaceous subjects next to the chalk-lovers, or the inhabitants of marshy ground in the same patch as those tufts of thrift and sea-pink that blow so gaily and dryly from the crevices of our cliffs. But only an elementary recognition would be needed.

Let no impassioned preserver of our wild flowers imagine that I advocate a mischievous uprooting of rarities already threatened by the increase of arable land or by the depredations of well-meaning but ignorant amateur botanists. Over my dead body . . . It is, however, possible (1) to collect seeds, (2) to buy specimens from a nurseryman, and furthermore some species might usefully be rescued from the danger of extermination. They might even benefit by being transplanted into better soil, and grow into finer plants, as the sky-blue chicory will.

It is impossible in so short an article to do more than indicate some kinds of wild flowers suitable for garden cultivation. Probably the first reaction of some people will be to exclaim 'Wild flowers? Do you mean weeds?' Think again. There are many which could not possibly be regarded as weeds. The fritillary, the small daffodil or Lent-lily, the lily of the valley, the yellow tulip *Sylvestris*, the autumn crocus, the claret-coloured *Daphne mezereum*, the several kinds of violet, purple or white, the green hellebore, the Gladwyn iris, the golden trollius, the marsh marigold, the Cheddar pink, Sweet Cicely, various campanulas, the water forget-me-not, the Burnet rose, some spurges, the snowdrop and the snowflake. This is leaving out of account the entire primrose family, also the orchids, which are most unlikely to survive transplantation. Buy them from a nursery if you must have them, but on no account dig them up.

We can produce only a humble little selection compared with the splendours of the Alps, the Dolomites, the Pyrenees, or Lebanon, but perhaps enough has been said to show that a botanical holiday might furnish at least a patch, hidden away from more sophisticated floral neighbours. It would have a reminiscent charm: 'Do you remember the day we came on the Welsh poppy?' 'I saw the Pasque-flower before you did.' It so happens that Mr Walter Ingwersen has just brought out a book, *Wildflowers in the Garden* (Geoffrey Bles, 16s.), which is the ideal guide for anyone interested in this form of gardening; a book I had often wished for, and here it is.

December 9, 1951

It is pleasant to see the garden laid to bed for the winter. Brown blankets of earth cover the secret roots. Nothing is seen overground, but a lot is going on underneath in preparation for the spring. It is a good plan, I think, to leave a heavy mulch of fallen leaves over the flowering shrubs instead of sweeping them all away. They serve the double purpose of providing protection against frost, and of eventually rotting down into the valuable humus that all plants need. There are leaves and leaves, of course, and not all of them will rot as quickly as others. Oak and beech are the best, to compose into leaf-mould in a large square pile; but any leaves will serve as a mulch over beds and borders throughout the hard months to come.

The professional gardener will raise objections. He will tell you that the leaves will 'blow all over the place' as soon as a wind gets up. This is true up to a point, but can be prevented by a light scattering of soil or sand over the leaves to hold them down. This sort of objection may often be overcome by the application of some common sense. There are few people more obstinate than the professional or jobbing gardener. Stuck in his ideas, he won't budge.

November and December make a difficult blank time for the gardener. One has to fall back on the berrying plants; and amongst these I would like to recommend the seldom-grown *Celastrus orbiculatus*. This is a rampant climber, which will writhe itself up into any old valueless fruit tree, apple or pear, or over the roof of a shed, or over any space not wanted for anything more choice. It is rather a dull green plant during the summer months; you would not notice it then at all; but in the autumn months of October and November it produces its butter-yellow berries which presently break open to show the orange seeds, garish as heraldry, *gules* and *or*, startling to pick for indoors when set in trails against dark wood panelling, but equally lovely against a white-painted wall.

It is a twisting thing. It wriggles itself into corkscrews, not to be disentangled, but this does not matter because it never needs pruning unless you want to keep it under control. My only need has been to haul it down from a tree into which it was growing too vigorously; a young prunus, which would soon have been smothered. Planted at the foot of an old dead or dying tree, it can be left to find its way upwards and hang down in beaded swags, rich for indoor picking, like thousands of tiny Hunter's moons coming up over the eastern horizon on a frosty night.

December 16, 1951

An article I wrote some weeks ago about growing strawberries in tubs or barrels seems to have aroused interest in readers of *The Observer*. I did think it was a good idea for people who have a limited area of garden. You waste no ground space, and you set your tubs anywhere you want them, either side of the front door or sideways along the garden path. It now occurs to me that the idea could be extended to alpines or other small plants, grown in the same way in barrels sawn in half round their equator.

Why not? It is an easy idea to carry out. You buy your barrel from a local sale; put a thick layer of crocks all over the bottom, not forgetting to pierce a hole or holes for drainage first; you then fill it with soil and plant your treasures. The kind of soil you fill it with will depend upon what kind of treasures you wish to grow. Alpines, generally speaking, like a somewhat gritty soil which will afford them the good, open drainage that prevents them from rotting off. Stagnant damp is a far greater enemy than frost or drought in this country. A gritty soil may be achieved by mixing a barrow-full of fibrous loam, taken from the top-spit of an old meadow, with some sharp sand and a generous helping of stone chippings such as one sees piled in such enticing heaps by the roadside. It is unfortunate that these should be the property of the county council. Were I not inherently honest (or, perhaps, cowardly), I should be sorely tempted to go out with a shovel and barrow at dead of night.

Flat-growing subjects such as saxifrages would probably be best for a groundwork on top, making squabs of silvery grey, something like a round Victorian pincushion, breaking out into their tiny rosy flowers in the spring. The sorts called *Irvingii, Cranbourne, Jenkinsonii*, are all very small, tight, and pretty. But you can be more ambitious with your barrel if you want to plant other things half-way up it. You can plant things which like pouring out sideways, making miniature waterfalls of flower, little Niagaras of foam in the saxifrage called *Tumbling Waters* – twelve inches long in its flower-tassel, hanging down, very handsome and yet very delicate. Another plant I would like to set into the sideway holes of the sawn barrel is *Lewisia*. The *Lewisias* are not too easy-going, which is perhaps the reason they are so seldom seen; but they are certainly plants for any gardener prepared to accept a challenge. They make rosettes of leaf, and throw out sprays of chintz-like flowers, pink or creamy, very elegant and old-fashioned-looking. They should do well planted sideways in the barrel, on the principle that they are very happy growing out of a dry wall; it should be remembered, however, that they dislike lime. They also dislike disturbance, and the best way to propagate them is by seed.

December 23, 1951

As this article will appear two days before Christmas, I thought I would write on the most unsuitable unseasonable subject I could think of: roses. We may be under snow by then, and the very thought of a rose will be warming. Besides, roses can still be planted any time between December and March, so it is not too late to order extravagantly on any plant-token you may receive as a Christmas present.

There are roses and roses. My own taste in roses is perhaps not everybody's taste, and I am afraid that I may too often have tried to force it upon readers of *The Observer*. I know that I tend always towards the species roses, and the great wild shrubby roses flinging themselves about, instead of those neat little, hard little, tight little scrimpy dwarfs we call the hybrid teas.

On the subject of hybrid teas I have never quite made up my mind. I am torn. I see their beauty. I see their usefulness. I see that you can pick them all through the summer right up into the late autumn. You can fill a bowl with them even into December when, strangely enough, they sometimes throw a more richly coloured and more richly scented bloom. Yet for some reason they do not catch my heart. I have, however, succumbed at last and planted a dozen, purely for picking, in a corner of the kitchen garden. The chosen ones were *Ena Harkness, Ophelia, Etoile de Hollande, Charles Mallerin, Christopher Stone, Lady Sylvia, Mrs Van Rossem, Emma Wright, Crimson Glory, Mrs Sam McGredy, The Doctor, McGredy's Sunset*. I hope they will not all develop black spot, but I expect they will.

There are several schools of thought on the control of this worry, which causes complete defoliation in bad cases and must end in destroying the constitution of the plant, thus deprived of its natural means of breathing through the leaves. The orthodox method is spraying with Bordeaux mixture in January and February. TMT, or Thiram, sometimes supplied under the name *Tulisan*, is also recommended for fortnightly use from the end of May onwards. Some rose-growers also advise a thick mulch of lawn-clippings, peat-moss litter, or even sawdust. Others put their faith (such as it is) in rich feeding, on the principle that a healthy, well-nourished plant is more resistant to infection. I must say that I found this works well. It may sound unscientific, since black spot is a fungus, and you might imagine that a fungus would establish itself on weak or strong plants equally once it had made up its mind to do so; but I am not a scientific gardener and can judge only by results. The result of some barrow-loads of compost was: no black spot on some particularly vulnerable roses two summers running, including the damp summer we have recently disenjoyed.

I would like to mention here a useful new book called *The Rose in Britain*, by N. P. Harvey, published by Plant Protection, Ltd, 17s. 6d., with many illustrations in colour.

December 30, 1951

Nearly the New Year. I know someone who averts his eyes from all young growth, such as narcissus leaves pushing through, prior to January 1st, but who, after that date, peers eagerly in the hope of even a rathe snowdrop. We know full well that January and February can be the most unpleasant months in the calendar, but they do bring some consolation in the beginnings of re-vival. Crocuses and other small bulbs appear, miraculous and welcome; they are apt, however, to leave a blank after they have died down, and it is for that reason that I suggest overplanting them with some little shrubs which will flower in February or March.

I visualize a low bank or slope of ground, not necessarily more than two or three feet high, perhaps bordering some rough steps on a curve. You stuff and cram the bank with early-flowering bulbs, making a gay chintz-like or porcelain effect with their bright colours in yellow, blue, white, orange, red. Amongst these, you plant the little shrubs I want to recommend, *Corylopsis spicata* and *Corylopsis paucifolia* are two of the prettiest and softest, hung with yellow moths of flowers all along their twiggy branches. They are natives of Japan, and are related to the Witch-hazels. They seldom grow more than four feet high and about as much through; they need no pruning, and are graceful in their growth, pale as a prim-rose, and as early. Another little companion shrub on the bank would be *Forsythia ovata*. The big bushy forsythia is well known, but this small relation from Korea is not so often seen. It is perfectly hardy, and makes a tiny tree three to four feet high, flowering into the familiar golden blossoms, a golden rain pouring down in companionship with the *Corylopsis*, after the bulbs have died away.

There is also a dwarf variety of the favourite *Viburnum fragrans*, called *compactum*, which would associate happily.

If you have room in your garden at the top of the bank or slope, I would urge you to plant *Cornus mas*, the Cornelian cherry. This cornel or dog-wood produces its yellow flowers in February, and is one of the best winter flowerers for picking for indoors. A big full-grown tree of *Cornus mas* is a sight to be seen, as I once saw one growing in a wood in Kent. It towered up fifteen feet and more, smothered in its myriads of tiny clusters, each individual flower-head like a bunch of snipped ribbons. If at first it seems a little disappointing and makes only a thin show, do not be discouraged, for it improves yearly with age and size, and one year will suddenly surprise you by the wealth of its blossom. It also produces long scarlet berries which you can, if you wish, eat.

December 7, 1952

Christmas presents for gardening friends? People living in towns will presumably be reduced to visiting the nearest florist and will come away with a pot of Persian cyclamen, confident that, if properly treated, it will continue to give pleasure for years. May I point out to them that very occasionally you find a *scented* cyclamen? It is worth sniffing round the array in the hope of coming across one with this additional charm.

If, however, you want to give something rather less obvious than a ready-made plant in a pot, why not compose a miniature garden in what is known to horticultural sundriesmen as an Alpine pan? You can furnish this for yourself with suitable small subjects which can be ordered for about 1s. 6d. each from any appropriate nurseryman, and can safely be planted now or at any time, since they are supplied ex-pots. The *Sedums* or stone-crops, and the *Sempervivums* or house-leeks, are all useful for this purpose, being to all intents and purposes indestructible; but there are lovelier things such as the Saxifrages, and the little pink daisies, *Bellis Dresden China*, and the minute blue forget-me-not, *Myosotis rupicola*, which make a pretty group, not flowering in time for Christmas, but a delight to watch for, long after most Christmas presents have been absorbed into daily life.

Ingenuity and imagination can make a very pretty thing out of an Alpine pan. For instance, a few flat stones laid between the plants to divide them, stones an inch or so in width or length; or bulkier stones stuck upright like tiny Dolomites.

Other suggestions. For the country friend: plant-tokens, now available from most nurserymen and seedsmen as book-tokens are available from booksellers, enabling him or her to choose what he or she wants, instead of ordering something which may turn out to be more of a white elephant than a pleasure. Fertilizers such as bone-meal or hop-manure. Or a bale of Somerset or Cumberland peat. Tools: these are always useful, because tools wear out and have to be replaced. John Innes compost, for seed-boxes and many other uses. String, in tarred balls or in spools of green twist. Secateurs, to carry in the pocket. Knives, pruning, budding, or just a big sharp knife. And finally, for your own children or for your nephews and nieces, a cactus – because they couldn't kill it even if they tried.

December 14, 1952

May I remind readers about the winter-flowering cherry, *Prunus subhirtella Autumnalis*? I know I have mentioned it before, but that was a long time ago, and as the seasons come round one remembers the things one tends in one's ingratitude to forget during the rich months of spring and summer; besides, there are the Christmas plant-tokens to think of. This cherry was in full flower in the open during the first fortnight of November; I picked bucketfuls of the long, white sprays; then came two nights of frost on November 15th and 16th; the remaining blossom was very literally browned-off; I despaired of getting any more for weeks to come. But ten days later, when the weather had more or less recovered itself, a whole new batch of buds was ready to come out, and I got another bucketful as fresh and white and virgin as anything in May.

There is a variety of this cherry called *Rosea*, slightly tinged with pink; I prefer the pure white myself, but that is a matter of taste. There is also another winter-flowering cherry, *Prunus serrulata Fudanzakura*, which I confess I neither grow nor know, and I don't like recommending plants of which I have no personal experience, but the advice of Captain Collingwood Ingram, the 'Cherry' Ingram of Japanese cherry fame, is good enough for me and should be good enough for anybody. This, again, is a white single-flowered blossom with a pink bud, and may be admired out of doors or picked for indoors any time between November and April. So obliging a visitor from the Far East is surely to be welcomed to our gardens.

By the way, I suppose all those who like to have some flowers in their rooms even during the bleakest months are familiar with the hint of putting the cut branches, such as the winter-flowering cherry, into almost boiling hot water? It makes them, in the common phrase, 'jump to it'.

Have I ever mentioned, amongst early flowering shrubs, *Corylopsis pauci-folia*? I believe I have, but it will do no harm to put in a reminder. The Cory-lopsis is a little shrub, not more than four or five feet high and about the same in width, gracefully hung with pale yellow flowers along the leafless twigs, March to April, a darling of prettiness. *Corylopsis spicata* is much the same, but grows rather taller, up to six feet, and is, if anything, more frost-resistant. They are not particular as to soil, but they do like a sheltered position, if you can give it them, say with a backing of other wind-breaking shrubs against the prevailing wind.

Sparrows . . . They peck the buds off, so put a bit of old fruit-netting over the plant in October or November when the buds are forming. Sparrows are doing the same to my Winter-sweet this year, as never before; sheer mischief;

an avian form of juvenile delinquency; so take the hint and protect the buds with netting before it is too late.

December 21, 1952

Christmas approaches, and perhaps I ought to be writing about mistletoe and holly, but I would rather go back to summer and try to revive some of its warm pleasures. We had the nastiest month of November, when the weather did everything it could think of: frost, snow, rain, floods, gales; but, even through that disagreeable span, one little climber persisted in flowering and I would like to record my gratitude. It had started flowering from early May onwards, and by December 1st it was still in flower.

This was *Abutilon megapotamicum*. Its apparently alarming name means merely an Arabic word associated with the Mallows, a botanical family to which our familiar garden hollyhocks belong; and *megapotamicum*, the great river, meaning the Amazon in Brazil.

Abutilon megapotamicum bears no resemblance at all to the hollyhocks as we know them in cottage gardens. It is a thing to train up against a sunny south wall, and if you should happen to have a whitewashed wall or even a wall of grey stone, it will show up to special advantage against it. It has long pointed leaves and a curiously shaped flower, dark red and yellow, somewhat like a fuchsia, hanging from flexible, limp, graceful sprays. It is on the tender side, not liking too many degrees of frost, so should be covered over in winter. But perhaps you know all this already.

The idea I wanted to put forward is something that occurred to me accidentally, as gardening ideas do sometimes occur to one. I thought how pretty it might be to train an Abutilon as a standard. You see, it could be persuaded to weep downwards, like a weeping willow or a weeping cherry, if you grew it up on a short stem and constantly trimmed off all the side shoots it tried to make, till you got a big rounded head pouring downwards like a fountain dripping with the red and yellow flowers for months and months and months throughout the summer.

Is that a good idea? I have not tried it yet, but I intend to. Of course, for anyone who has the advantage of a greenhouse, however small and unheated, a little standard of an Abutilon in a big flower-pot might remain in flower well into the winter, and could be carried indoors for Christmas.

December 28, 1952

This seems a good occasion to mention the Christmas rose, *Helleborus niger*, in high Dutch called Christ's herb, 'because it flowereth about the birth of our

Lord'. Its white flowers are, or should be, already on our tables. There is a variety called *altifolius*, which is considered superior, owing to its longer stalks; but it is often stained with a somewhat dirty pink, and I think the pure white is far lovelier. Christmas roses like a rather moist, semi-shady place in rich soil, though they have no objection to lime; they do not relish disturbance, but if you decide to plant some clumps you should do so as soon as they have finished flowering, which is another good reason for mentioning them now. If you already have old-established clumps, feed them well in February with a top dressing of compost or rotted manure, or even a watering of liquid manure, and never let them get too dry in summer. It is perhaps superfluous to say that they should be protected by a cloche when the buds begin to open, not because they are not hardy but because the low-growing flowers get splashed and spoilt by rain and bouncing mud.

The Christmas rose, although not a native of Britain, has been for centuries in our gardens. Spenser refers to it in the *Faerie Queene*, and it is described as early as 1597 in his *Herball* by John Gerard, who considered that a purgation of hellebore was 'good for mad and furious men'. Such a decoction might still come in useful today. Perhaps Gerard was quoting Epictetus, who, writing in the first century AD, remarks that the more firmly deluded is a madman, the more hellebore he needs. Unfortunately, this serviceable plant is not very cheap to buy, costing anything from 5s. 6d. to 7s. 6d., but on the other hand it is a very good investment because, to my positive knowledge, it will endure and even increase in strength for fifty years and more. It is also possible, and not difficult, to grow it from seed, but if you want to do that you should make sure of getting freshly ripened seed, otherwise you may despair of germination after twelve months have gone by and will crossly throw away a pan of perfectly viable seeds which only demanded a little more patience.

I have a great affection for all the hellebores, and would like to return to the subject, with especial reference to our own two native kinds, *H. viridis* and *H. foetidus*. (See p. 165.)

APPENDIX

For Shrubs, Trees, Flowering Trees, Climbing Plants, etc.

George Jackman & Sons,
   Woking Nurseries,
     Woking, Surrey.

John Scott & Co.,
   The Royal Nurseries,
     Merriott, Somerset.

Hillier & Sons,
   Winchester.

Arthur Charlton,
   Tunbridge Wells.

R. C. Notcutt,
   The Nursery,
     Woodbridge, Suffolk.

Donard Nursery Co.,
   Newcastle,
     Co. Down,
       Northern Ireland.

Burkwood & Skipwith,
   Park Road,
     Kingston, Surrey.

John Waterer Sons & Crisp, Ltd,
   The Floral Mile,
     Twyford, Berkshire.

Winkfield Manor Nurseries,
   Ascot,
     Berkshire.

Robert Veitch,
   Exeter, Devon.

W. J. Marchant,
   Keeper's Hill,
     Stapehill,
       Wimborne, Dorset.

Treseder's Nurseries,
   Truro, Cornwall.

Bulbs, Corms, Tubers, Rhizomes, etc.

W. A. Constable,
   The Lily Gardens,
     Southborough,
       Tunbridge Wells.
   (Lilies a speciality.)

R. Wallace & Co.,
   The Old Gardens,
     Tunbridge Wells,
       Kent.
   (Lilies and irises a speciality.)

Barr & Sons,
   King Street,
     Covent Garden,
       London, WC2.

Ralph Cusack,
   Uplands, Roundwood,
     County Wicklow.
   (Uncommon things a speciality.)

P. de Jager & Sons,
  Regis House,
    43–46, King William Street,
      London, EC4.

Walter Blom & Son, Ltd,
  Coombelands Nurseries,
    Leavesden,
      Watford, Hertfordshire.

The Orpington Nurseries,
  Crofton Lane,
    Orpington, Kent.
  (For irises.)

Alec Gray,
  Treswithian Daffodil Farm,
    Camborne, Cornwall.
  (Miniature narcissi a speciality.)

Seeds

Thompson & Morgan,
  Ipswich, Suffolk.
  (A very long list, including
    many varieties not obtainable
    elsewhere.)

Sutton & Sons,
  Reading, Berkshire.

Thomas Butcher,
  Shirley,
    Croydon, Surrey.

Carter's, Ltd,
  Raynes Park,
    London, SW20.

Ryder & Sons,
  St Albans, Hertfordshire.

R. Bolton,
  Birdbrook,
    Near Halstead, Essex.
  (Sweet Pea specialists.)

Dobbie & Co.,
  Edinburgh, 7.

W. J. Unwin, Ltd,
  Histon, near Cambridge.

Alexander & Brown,
  Perth.

Alpines

W. E. Th. Ingwersen,
  Birch Farm Nurseries,
    Gravetye,
      East Grinstead, Sussex.

H. G. & P. M. Lyall,
  Mount Pleasant Lane,
    Bricket Wood,
      Watford, Hertfordshire.

Jack Drake,
  Inshriach Alpine Plant Nursery,
    Aviemore, Inverness-shire.

Fruit Trees – and Fruit in General

Rivers,
  Sawbridgeworth,
    Hertfordshire.

Laxton Bros,
  63, High Street,
    Bedford.

General Garden Stock – Herbaceous Plants

It is not possible to give an exhaustive list, as most nurserymen who specialize in something or other usually carry a general list as well, but here are a few:

Baker,
    Codsall, Wolverhampton.
    (Russell lupins a speciality.)

R. H. Bath,
    The Floral Farms,
        Wisbech, Cambridgeshire.

Robinson's Gardens, Ltd,
    Eltham, Kent.

Blackmore & Langdon,
    Bath, Somerset.
    (Delphiniums a speciality.)

Wm. Wood & Son,
    Taplow, Buckinghamshire.

Kelway & Son,
    Langport, Somerset.
    (Peonies a speciality.)

Maurice Prichard & Sons,
    Christchurch, Hampshire.

Perry's Plant Farm,
    Enfield, Middlesex.
    (Water plants a speciality.)

Bees, Ltd,
    Sealand Nurseries,
        Chester.

Roses

Archer & Daughter,
    Monk's Horton,
        Sellindge, Near Ashford,
            Kent.

Edwin Murrell,
    Portland Nurseries,
        Shrewsbury.
    (Old-fashioned and specie.)

T. Hilling & Co.,
    The Nurseries,
        Chobham,
            Woking, Surrey.
    (Old-fashioned and specie roses.)

The Sunningdale Nurseries,
    Windlesham, Surrey.
    (Old-fashioned and specie roses.)

F. Ley,
    Windlesham, Surrey.

Wheatcroft Bros,
    Ruddington, Nottingham.

H. Merryweather & Sons,
    Southwell,
        Nottinghamshire.

Daisy Hill Nurseries,
    (Successors to T. Smith),
        Newry,
            Northern Ireland.

McGredy & Son,
    Royal Nurseries,
        Portadown,
            Northern Ireland.

Benjamin Cant & Sons,
    Old Rose Gardens,
        Colchester.

Herbs

The Herb Farm,
  Seal,
    Sevenoaks, Kent.

Heath and Heather,
  Lullingstone,
    Eynsford, Kent.

Uncommon Vegetables

Miss Kathleen Hunter,
  Wheal Frances,
    Callestick, Truro, Cornwall.

Oddments of Useful Addresses

The Royal Horticultural Society –
  Vincent Square,
    London, SW1.
and
  Wisley Gardens, Ripley,
    Near Woking, Surrey.

Selective Weed-killers, etc.
  Plant Protection,
    Yalding, Kent.

Hop-Manure
  Wakeley Bros & Co.,
    235, Blackfriars Road,
    London, SE1.

Cloches
  Chase Protected Cultivation, Ltd,
    38, Cloche House,
    Shepperton,
      Middlesex.

Labels
  John Pinches,
    3, Crown Buildings,
    Crown Street,
    Camberwell,
      London, SE5.
    (Acme labels, metal.)

INDEX OF PLANT NAMES

Many of the plants in this index may not be currently available. Some have changed names and where possible this is indicated. Some Latin names have been corrected where they were spelled wrongly, or possibly have changed in spelling over the years. The abbreviation 'form.' means 'formerly', where a plant's classification has changed.

275

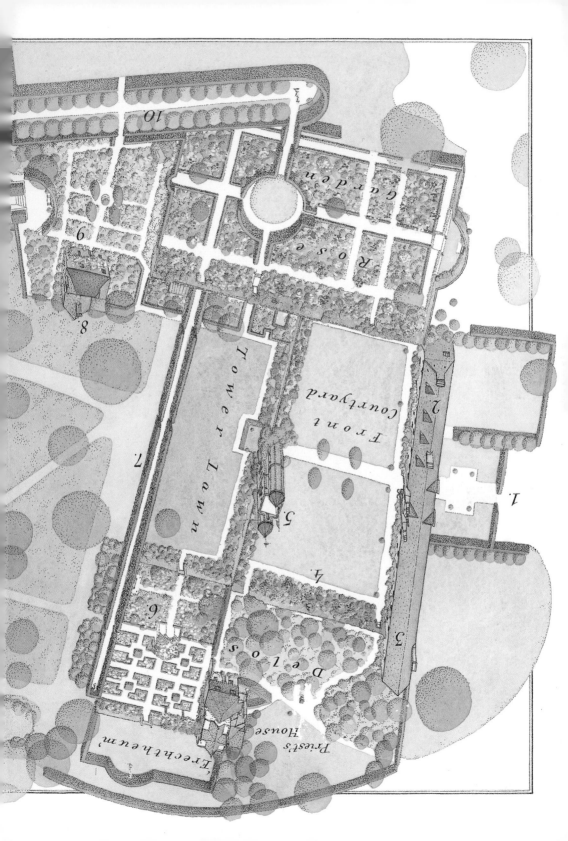